FATHER, SON AND HOLY SPIRIT

FATHER, SON AND HOLY SPIRIT

Essays Toward a Fully Trinitarian Theology

COLIN E. GUNTON

T & T CLARK
A Continuum imprint
LONDON • NEW YORK

T&T CLARK LTD

A Continuum imprint

The Tower Building	15 East 26th Street
11 York Road	New York, NY 10010
London SE1 7NX, UK	USA

www.continuumbooks.com

British Library Cataloguing-in-Publication Data
A catalogue record for this book is available from the British Library

ISBN 0 567 08971 1 (Hardback)
ISBN 0 567 08982 7 (Paperback)

Typeset by RefineCatch Limited, Bungay, Suffolk
Printed and bound in Great Britain by The
Cromwell Press, Trowbridge, Wiltshire

To welcome Nicholas

Contents

Foreword

This volume is the third set of Colin Gunton's collected papers to be published (following *Theology through the Theologians: Selected Papers 1975–1995* (T&T Clark, 1996) and *Intellect and Action: Elucidations on Christian Theology and the Life of Faith* (T&T Clark, 2000); it is also the last writing he prepared for press before his sudden and untimely death on 6 May 2003. Those to whom he entrusted the task are looking to see if anything of the work he had underway when he died was sufficiently complete to be placed before a wider readership; in the meantime, this is his last book.

It is tempting to look for a fitting finale to a lifetime of faithful, dedicated and profound theological thinking, weaving together the themes which had been deployed and developed in a profound mature statement of Colin's theological vision. This book was never intended to be that, of course; indeed, that role was consciously reserved for another work. Mentioned herein (p. xiv) is a multi-volume *Dogmatics*, which Colin had begun to work on (and indeed to read in draft to a group of colleagues and students) before he died, and which would, had it been completed, have been the proper and intended summit and summary of his work. Here, instead, are a set of essays and lectures which at times consciously represent work in progress (see the 'retraction' concerning Chapter 4 in the Preface, p. xiv), but which together contribute to 'a continuing project of trinitarian theology' (p. xiii). This book, then, was to be the next step, and tragically has become the last step, in Colin's central intellectual endeavour of articulating and applying a doctrine of the Trinity.

Many characteristic themes that have informed his work do re-appear here, therefore, and some newer notes emerge into prominence. Among the former is of course the overall subject matter – the central importance of Trinitarian theology – and some of the themes of individual chapters: for example, christology and metaphors of atonement and sacrifice. Readers of Gunton's works will also recognize features of the method adopted in these papers: the careful listening to the Scriptures and the Christian tradition (Irenaeus, Basil, Calvin, Irving and Barth make repeated appearances once again, as does a fascination with the christological implications of the Letter to the Hebrews); the patient explication and, where necessary, modification (or at least amplification) of classical orthodoxy; and the always respectful, if sometimes sharp, dialogue with those contemporaries who are or were attempting a similar task (T. F. Torrance, Robert Jenson, John Zizioulas and Wolfhart Pannenberg are to the fore in this title). The 'tone' of the book will also be familiar: the sense of joy in the possibilities of theology, and in the final triumph of the gospel; the awareness that theology, pursued in the academy, is nonetheless of the Church and for the Church; the generous references to friends, colleagues and students, to whom he gave far more than he ever received, although he refused to see it like that; the constant context, marked once again through the dedication, of his family that was so important to his theology, as to every other area of his life – all is here.

Less familiar, perhaps, is the focus on ecclesiology and sacrament in the last two chapters; although one of these chapters is quite old, together they reflect an area of theology that was becoming more important to Colin in his latter years. Two tasks sparked this interest: a lecture series on ecclesiology and eschatology at Fuller Seminary, and a midweek Bible study on I Corinthians in Brentwood United Reformed Church, where Colin had been associate pastor for about thirty years. I suppose that those who requested the former lecture series saw the two subjects as separate courses, but being asked to think about them at the same time enabled Colin to see a significant and distinctive way of approaching ecclesiology as a thoroughly eschatological topic. This was reinforced by studying I Corinthians with his church – only another example of how being embedded in that local Christian community shaped his theological thinking.

Colin would reflect regularly in conversation, and occasionally in print, on the incompleteness of Barth's *Church Dogmatics*; amongst those reflections was the awareness that no theological project can ever be finished, this side of the End: only when we 'see face to face' can we hope to 'know fully, even as we are known.' Had he lived to complete the projected four volumes of his *Dogmatics*, he would still have begun writing again the morning after publication, to correct an inbalance, clear up a mis-understanding, explain a consequence, or perhaps admit a mistake. Quite apart from such intellectual reflections, his mind was far too fertile and restless, and his love of theology far too deep, for him to stop writing! That this book, so clearly merely a step on the way, has become his last word, is perhaps oddly fitting.

There is a definition of the work of theology in this book: 'Theology's task is to essay a rational account of the creed of the Church whilst remaining deeply entrenched in the gospel' (p. 34). Colin gave himself unstintingly to this task. He did so with vigour and enthusiasm and transparent enjoyment. He cared about the Church, and about the gospel that forms the Church. He instructed and inspired many by his writing, his teaching and his example. Reading through these papers I could remember hearing several of them in the weekly seminars of the Research Institute in Systematic Theology, recalling Colin's passion as he paused mid-reading to develop this point or that; and his pleasure as students who he had taught to be confident in their own theological ability offered counter-arguments, and defended them stoutly, forcing him to refine or justify his own position. Many readers of this book will have occasion to mourn his passing once again.

But if theology is only true to itself if it 'remains deeply entrenched in the gospel', that cannot be the final word. Had Colin known this was to be his last book, I am sure it would have been very different in many ways. I suspect, however, that the thought of the last paragraph, and the very words of the last clause, might have remained. Colin was indeed deeply entrenched in the gospel, and profoundly faithful to Christ. So it perhaps seems appropriate that his last published words speak (with Isaac Watts) of the Triune God's delight in his saints, look to the promise of the coming Kingdom, and, right at the end, confess once more the 'sure hope of the resurrection of the dead' (p. 234).

Stephen R. Holmes
King's College, London
July 2003

Preface

This set of papers, which forms part of a continuing project of trinitarian theology, might well be entitled 'Father, Son *and* Holy Spirit', for it contains an account of the work of the triune God in which a more secure place is sought for the doctrine of the Holy Spirit than has often been the case in theology, especially the theology of the West. Almost all of the papers seek to show that a theology of divine action that does not incorporate the distinctive work of the Spirit as well as that of the Son fails in some way to encompass the breadth of the biblical economy. For it is primarily that with which we are concerned in Christian theology: to show that God the Father creates, acts to provide for and redeem, and will finally complete the world which he has called into being through his two hands, his Son and his Spirit.

The book falls into two parts. The first, 'The Triune God of Christian Confession', explores various aspects of what it means to confess God as one being in three persons. The five papers it contains can also be divided into two. Chapters 1 to 3, all of them seeking to say something about what is the theology of the Trinity, are in ascending technicality and difficulty. The first was a lecture designed – as requested by those who commissioned it – to commend the Trinity to an audience mostly from the Churches. It is a fairly straightforward summary of what it seems to me that the doctrine means and, more broadly, signifies for the life of the Christian in the Church. The second chapter was also commissioned, this time to introduce readers of a journal to the recent growth of interest in the doctrine. It reviews some of the immense variety of approaches to the doctrine available at present, with a view to indicating which of them best accord with the faith of the Church once for all given to the saints. There is a defence of the necessity of the doctrine of the immanent Trinity, and warnings against the use of the doctrine for whatever worthy purposes an author wishes to justify. Arguments from analogy here tread a slippery slope towards mere projection. To avoid the various pitfalls, Christology is necessary, and, indeed, one which develops two senses of the expression, 'The God of Jesus Christ'. Trinitarian theology is not theory; it is an account of God's being which is tied to his action, and that action centres on a gospel rooted in the life, suffering and resurrection of Jesus. The account of God's action in the Son and the Spirit indicates the need for a doctrine of the immanent Trinity, but does not supply one.

To explore the outlines of such a doctrine is the function of the next, and more technical essay, which was commissioned for a book devoted to the theology of one of the major trinitarian theologians of our era, Thomas F. Torrance. The chapter enables an opening up of the question of the relation between the persons of the Trinity and the being of the one God. It is a central question for all theology, especially since East and West are effectively divided by their different answers to it. Torrance's enterprise focuses on what is perhaps the dominating concept of his thought, the *homoousion*, derived from the incarnation of the eternal Son in Jesus of Nazareth. Where is the unitary rule of God, his monarchy, centred? Is it in the Father, or in the whole Trinity? In opting for the latter, Torrance shows himself to be essentially a Western theologian; in drawing on Athanasius of Alexandria, however, he becomes an ecumenical bridge-figure between the two traditions.

The next two chapters deal, respectively, with the identity of the so-called second and third persons of the Trinity: what we mean when we speak of the Son and the Holy Spirit. In both cases, attempts are made to tie the answer closely to the economy, to Jesus and the Spirit made known in historical action. Chapter 4 was originally a paper written in defence of the credal affirmation that the Son is 'Begotten not made', and enquires about the meaning of eternal begottenness. Some criticism is offered of Pannenberg's attempt to widen the definition to include a more directly historical reference, and I have let the paper stand although I would now wish to modify that criticism. There is indeed, as Pannenberg claims, a need for us to tie what we say about the eternal Son more rigorously to the life, death, resurrection and ascension of Jesus of Nazareth, though I would still not do it quite in the way that he does, as readers of my projected dogmatics will be able to see. The paper (forming Chapter 5) on the Spirit, again attending to a credal confession – 'who with the Father and the Son together is worshipped and glorified' – is more satisfactory as it stands, seeking as it does to find a more concrete *persona* for the Spirit than the Western tradition often does, and at the same time showing how the completed doctrine of the Trinity (completed by the Spirit, not by us!) enables us truly to worship God.

Part two, 'Triune Divine Action' and containing the remaining eight chapters, consists of papers, all of them originally commissioned for conferences or public lectures. All are devoted to showing the difference the doctrine makes: how it enables us to understand the Father at work in the world through his 'two hands'. There are two occupied with aspects of the doctrine of creation, and then follows Christology, in three phases, and after that atonement, baptism and the Church. The first of the two chapters on creation is part of a continuing conversation with Robert Jenson, and was indeed written for a collection of papers devoted to the exposition and assessment of his theology. There is, at present and especially in America, something of a vogue for speaking of things – and the Christian life – as taking place 'within' God. Can sense be made of this without falling in, or near, to the pantheism which it is precisely the merit of trinitarian thinking to avoid? Do we not need to understand the act of creation as God's enabling things to be themselves externally to, albeit in continuing relation to, himself? The second chapter oriented to creation explicates some of the consequences of saying that God creates a world with a relative independence of himself: with its own proper being, which it is the office of the Holy Spirit to conserve and perfect. It is a complicated matter, for we cannot understand the created order apart from the human calling within it to represent its maker to it, so that the topic of the Spirit and the created order, raised in the very first few verses of the canon, cannot be approached without considering also the part played by men and women in responding – or failing to respond – to that work by the human creation.

Chapter 8 – the first christological paper – is directly relevant to such a theme, for, in addressing itself to Christ, the wisdom of God, it also necessarily raises questions about both divine and human involvement in the created world. The quality of our human createdness determines, or should determine, how we understand the source and content of our wisdom, so that there are considerable differences to be discerned between those teachings which see it as deriving from our kinship with the divine and those according to which it depends upon the gift of God, which can be occluded or even lost by human sin. Crucial here is to begin our quest for wisdom with an exposition of what it means to say that Jesus Christ is the wisdom of God. When Paul speaks of this, he is directing our attention to the crucified Christ as the divine wisdom in action, and the implication of this – expanded with the assistance other biblical passages concerned with divine wisdom – is important for our understanding of God's action in creation and redemption. God creates a world which needs time to become what it is created to be, and all his action is accommodated to this end. Only by attention to the wisdom of the cross can we integrate theologically what God does in creation and redemption.

That Jesus, the fully human Lord, is, as such, identified as the wisdom of God in action calls attention to two features of a trinitarian theology: the necessity of affirming his true humanity and of doing so by careful attention to pneumatology, to the centrality of the action of God the Holy Spirit in the constitution of his human being. The next two chapters address themselves to this question. The first attends to his humanity as the topic is raised by the 'Quest of the Historical Jesus' and the assault on its assumptions by Martin Kähler. The latter, it is argued, is misunderstood if he is interpreted in the light of his more radical disciples as denying all knowledge of the historical Jesus. However, there is a real flaw in his Christology, and it is, again, one which can be mended only with a pneumatology which enables a broader conspectus of his humanity than Kähler's rather limited conception allows. The possibilities for a theology of Jesus' human priesthood are spelled out in the other christological chapter, whose chief authorities are the Letter to the Hebrews and one of its greatest exponents, John Calvin. It returns to the question of mediation which was raised in Chapter 8, and shows something of how Calvin developed a doctrine of Christ's mediation of the creation as well as of salvation.

The transition from Chapter 10 to Chapter 11 introduces a change of focus: from Christology to soteriology. Despite the facts that this paper was written rather earlier than most of the others and that its introductory sections indicate rather different interests from those at the centre so far – that is, it develops the interest in metaphor introduced in an earlier book on the

atonement – there are real continuities. The most prominent is
the focus on sacrifice, which both takes us to the heart of the
doctrine of the Trinity and its persons-in-relation and provides
an adumbration of the theme that was the topic of the preceding chapter. Similarly, it could be seen to adumbrate themes
taken up in the chapters on creation, and especially that of the
latter's God-given destiny to be taken up for the praise of the
God who made it.

The final two chapters take us to the life of the Church and
the two gospel sacraments, baptism and the Lord's Supper. The
paper on baptism continues the theme of the universal work of
the Spirit realized as it is in the material world. Definitions of
sacrament as outward signs of something inward tend to
obscure their material content: the fact that they use material
things for 'material' as well as narrowly 'spiritual' purposes.
Baptism, it is argued, is a churchly and public rite before it is an
individual or inner experience, because it derives from Jesus'
death on the cross, foreshadowed as that was in his own
baptism. In this chapter, an attempt is made to argue for the
rightness of the baptism of – some – infants in the light of a
particular doctrine of the Church as communal and catholic.
Baptism is accordingly a public rite in which we are brought
into living relation through Christ and the Spirit with God the
Father and consequently with other human beings in the community of faith. This, too, requires a treatment of how the Spirit
might be conceived to shape the life of the people of God.
Similarly, the Lord's Supper ought to be understood in its
communal and, indeed, ethical dimensions before its 'ritual'
significance can be adequately construed. Once again in this
chapter an effort is made to relate what is said about the Supper
to eschatology and the life of the community. At issue here is
the sense in which the Church is an eschatological community.
Light in this often dark place is sought from a not entirely clear
passage, 1 Corinthians 11, from which it becomes manifest that
the ritual, the churchly and the ethical are in such close interconnection that the Church's foundation in the Word, her worship in the truth and her life both as a communion of God's
people and in the social order in which she is set are inextricable. The final consideration of the Church's eschatological
being returns us to the topic of sacrifice, and so to trinitarian
themes which have run throughout the course of the book.

I am, as always in these matters, grateful for the love and friendship without which these developments would not have been anywhere near as rich as I hope that they are. Especially important for me are two features of my life: the continuing theological life of the Research Institute in Systematic Theology, many of whose members are mentioned in the footnotes, along with others who have helped along the way; and my wife and family, through whose support so much is made possible. The final preparations for publication coincide with the arrival and early months of our grandson, Nicholas, for whom this book can serve as an additional welcome. Appropriately, both of his parents have assisted in the process. I am most grateful to Peter, whose computing skills made the recovery of the two oldest papers possible without retyping; and to Carolyn, who has demonstrated yet again her skills at proof-reading and indexing, removing from me a considerable burden. The final editing of the book took place at the wonderful institution whose address appears below. It was especially good to spend a term there with Robert Jenson, under whose supervision my postgraduate work began, and with the director, Wallace Alston. To the other members in residence, drawn from six different nations, I am also grateful for their friendship and theological fellowship.

Colin Gunton
Center of Theological Inquiry
Princeton
November 2002

PART 1

The Triune God of Christian Confession

1

The Forgotten Trinity[1]

Remembering and Forgetting

'If I forget thee, O Jerusalem, let my right arm forget her cunning.' The psalmist was making a fairly extreme promise or request, for, disabling injury and great age apart, right hands do not forget their cunning. A musical skill once mastered is never forgotten, even though practice may be needed to restore it after periods of neglect. Something truly learned becomes part of us, and never, in one respect, forgotten. But it can be forgotten in other respects, in the sense that it can be crowded out of our conscious minds by other preoccupations and concerns. The title, *The Forgotten Trinity*, was chosen by the British Council of Churches' Study Commission largely for reasons of what now, and probably then, would be called marketing: a way of attracting public attention so that the reports were read – or at least, bought.[2] But, unlike many marketing ploys, it contained a good deal of truth. In what way?

My allusion to the impossibility of forgetting a skill was designed to make the point that there are different ways of forgetting. We may never forget the skill of choosing, writing and posting greeting cards, but may need to enter little Mary's birthday on a calendar if we are to remember to employ that

---

[1] The William Hodgkins Lecture, Cardiff Adult Christian Education Centre, 5 June 1998.

[2] British Council of Churches, *The Forgotten Trinity, Volume 1, The Report of the BCC Study Commission on Trinitarian Doctrine Today* (London: British Council of Churches, 1989).

skill when it is needed. So it is that the Western Church has each year a Sunday devoted to the Trinity, lest we forget. The Eastern Orthodox Churches do not, because their worship and thought is so steeped in trinitarian categories that they do not need to be reminded. Have we in the West of Christendom effectively forgotten the Trinity, so that we need to be reminded? Or is the trinitarian teaching like a skill, which is there but needs to be revived from time to time? Or – worse – does the difference between East and West suggest that we never really acquired it, and put the thing on a calendar once a year to awaken otherwise forgetful preachers into the realization that on this one Sunday in the year at least they must try to make sense of a sleeping dog they would rather leave alone? For Eastern Orthodoxy, I think it is true to say that their trinitarian belief is like the skill of a musician. It so permeates their being that they worship and think trinitarianly without, so to speak, having to think about it – rather in the way that musicians don't think about what their hands are doing; their skills are so written into their bodies that they need only concentrate on the music and what it means. The point underlying the illustration is this. Theological teaching is not an end in itself, but a means of ensuring that it is the real God we worship, the real God before whom we live. That is the point of the doctrine of the Trinity above all, as we shall see.

What of the West? Here the story becomes complicated. On the face of it, we once had the same way of living in the Trinity, but have lost it, through a number of influences. Our hymns and blessings are steeped in trinitarian imagery: 'Glory be to the Father, and to the Son, and to the Holy Spirit . . .' – that ascription of glory to God wonderfully described by Nathaniel Micklem as the triumph song of the redeemed. Go to the National Gallery in London, or to places like Florence, and you will see that once upon a time we were a deeply trinitarian culture: a long tradition of representations of the triune God shows at least that. But partly as the result of rationalist criticism, that has come under attack. When the doctrines of the Church came under fire in the seventeenth and eighteenth centuries, it was the Trinity that was most savagely attacked as the most absurd and pointless of the many apparently untenable beliefs of the Christian tradition. Reason, so it was claimed, taught that there was only one God; any elaboration on that was simply priestcraft and superstition. That is surely one reason why we have tended to forget, or have become rather embarrassed by the whole thing. Something of those attacks has entered the bloodstream of even the orthodox believer, so that we feel that there must be something in the critiques.

Yet there is a case to be made that things have never been as they ought, that the West never had its piety and worship deeply enough embedded in trinitarian categories. The Study Commission was often given reason to wonder whether, although trinitarian confession has always been a yardstick of authentic Christian belief, the Church had ever really attained the crucial grade 5 at which things are supposed to stick. A number of theologians have commented on various aspects of the problem. Karl Rahner asserted that in Roman Catholic manuals of dogmatics interest was effectively so concentrated on the one God that everything we need to know about God seems to have been decided before the reader comes to the Son and the Spirit. For practical piety, he said, the Trinity had become irrelevant. One test is this: Do you think that you know to all intents and purposes who and what kind of being God is, quite independently of what you learn in trinitarian teaching? In many cases, that seems to be the case, particularly in the deeply entrenched tendency to begin with philosophical definitions of God. The threeness seems somehow additional, merely a Christian addition to a generally accepted doctrine of God.[3]

But this is not simply a matter of theological teaching, important though that is. The worship of the Church is first of all praise of the God who has created and redeems us; but it is also the way we learn a kind of skill, the art of living. And the same question can be asked again. Is the worship of the Church truly informed by trinitarian categories? Do we think it matters? The Study Commission was taught some interesting truths here, particularly by the inestimable privilege of having some fine Eastern Orthodox theologians sharing in our thinking. They enabled us to notice that the *Alternative Service Book* rarely finds a place for the Holy Spirit in the wording of its prayers, while in the collects of its great predecessor, the *Book of*

---

[3] Karl Rahner, *The Trinity*, tr. Joseph Donceel (London: Burns & Oates, 1970).

Common Prayer, that handbook of so much English piety, the Holy Spirit scarcely makes an appearance. Similarly, Western orders for the Lord's Supper have usually omitted the epiclesis, the prayer to the Spirit asking him to bless the bread and wine and the people. If the Spirit is absent from the structuring of the worship, can a rite be truly trinitarian? Is the reason that the Trinity has been effectively forgotten that it has never really entered the bloodstream of the Church, so that there is *too little* to remember? And does this make a difference to that most important of all human skills, the art of living before God, with our neighbour and in the created world?

The suggestion behind all this is that a truly trinitarian framework for our worship and life has rarely been found in the life of the Western Christian Church; that we have forgotten because we never really remembered. The result is that on the face if it – and it is the suspicion of so many Christians, professional and lay alike – the doctrine of the Trinity is a piece of abstract theorizing, perhaps necessary as a test of Christian belief, but of little further interest. All that stuff about three in one and one in three tends to leave us cold. Does it not turn God into a mathematical conundrum? All those dreary attempts to show that three can really be one, all those unconvincing illustrations from the natural world or the workings of the mind: do they really contribute to the learning of that skill in living that is promised for those who follow the crucified Lord? Can we not get on quite adequately without this piece of theoretical baggage? That defines our problem: the relation between theology and life.

Thinking Trinitarianly

That this is not a matter of mathematics is shown by the way the doctrine of the Trinity developed. The New Testament shows quite clearly that the first Christians, who were almost universally Jews also, had no difficulty in believing that the God they worshipped through Jesus was the same as the one they had always known. They did not find a new God, but a new and living way of knowing him. The God of Abraham, Isaac and Jacob was the God and Father of the Lord Jesus Christ. Indeed, for those who had been given eyes to see, their Christ was everywhere present in the pages of what we now call the Old Testament, as was the Spirit of God who brought them to the Father through Jesus. The threefold patterning of their relation to God was nowhere more clearly explained than in the Fourth Gospel, though it is to be found elsewhere also. For this writer, as for others, a renewed relationship to God is given to sinful men and women through the action – mediation – of Jesus, the eternal creating Word of God become flesh. After the end of his earthly career, this redeemed relationship is realized by the Spirit, who relates people to the Father through Jesus, now ascended to be eternally with the Father. New Testament trinitarianism is about life; that is to say, about access to God through Jesus Christ and in the Spirit. Through Christ, 'we both' – Jew and Gentile – 'have access to the Father by one Spirit' (Eph. 2.18). One of the things I want to suggest in this lecture is that the crucial missing link in so much of the trinitarianism which has bored us off the doctrine is a demonstration that worshipping and thinking in a trinitarian way makes all the difference to our finding our place in the world. Developing doctrines of the Trinity, though that has its proper place, can only come in the light of what can be called concrete trinitarian thinking.

Let me give three examples of what I mean, the first two fairly brief, the third at greater length. When I was first taught the theology of the Reformers, it was by an Anglican, the late G. V. Bennett. He said something that has never left me: that Calvin is the greatest theologian of the West, Augustine not excepted, by virtue of the thoroughly trinitarian structure of his thinking. What is interesting here is that Calvin's explicit treatment of the Trinity is confined to one chapter of his great work. But, almost everywhere, his thought is structured by it, and nowhere more effectively than in his definition of faith: 'a firm and certain knowledge of God's benevolence toward us, founded upon the truth of the freely given promise in Christ, both revealed to our minds and sealed upon our hearts through the Holy Spirit'.[4] That tells us on whom faith rests – God the Father – how he

---

[4] John Calvin, *Institutes of the Christian Religion*, ed. J. T. McNeill, tr. and index F. L. Battles (Philadelphia: Westminster Press, 1960), Library of Christian Classics vols 20 and 21, III. ii. 7.

mediates it to us – through Christ – and how it is impressed upon our hearts. The trinitarian structure enables Calvin to explore something of the richness of our relation to God, not only in this context, but throughout his work. Indeed, it is when he forgets to think in that way that the notorious flaws in his work begin to show themselves – but that is another question we unfortunately cannot pursue here.

The second example comes from Basil, Bishop of Caesarea in the fourth century AD, and was given me in a recent book by Ellen Charry, called *By the Renewing of your Minds*, and, more importantly, perhaps, subtitled *The Pastoral Function of Christian Doctrine*.[5] Basil wrote a quite technical book on the Holy Spirit and his place within the Trinity. And why? It was partly, and only partly, to contribute to the intellectual debates about the being of God that were raging at the time. This author points out that there was a major pastoral problem as well. Despite Basil's careful preaching, the lives of the people in his churches were not being renewed in the gospel. He was particularly concerned that after feast days his flock was indulging in drunkenness and the resulting licentiousness and debauched behaviour. To put it simply, Basil wanted to develop the whole worship of the Church to embody the reality of the Trinity, so that the people would not just be preached at, but trained in holiness. To this effect he was concerned to show his readers something of the depth, range and richness of God's gracious involvement in the world, and so to incorporate it in their worship that it shaped them in holiness of life. It is that 'range and richness of God's gracious involvement in the world' of which Professor Charry speaks that is the demonstration of the fruitfulness of trinitarian ways of thinking.

That is nowhere better demonstrated than in our third example, Irenaeus, Bishop of Lyons towards the end of the second century AD. Irenaeus, too, was involved in a struggle that was both theological and pastoral. At stake theologically was the doctrine of creation – something with which we are ourselves concerned in these days of ecological anxiety. Irenaeus was opposing the views of those who claimed that this material

[5] Ellen T. Charry, *By the Renewing of your Minds. The Pastoral Function of Christian Doctrine* (New York and Oxford: Oxford University Press, 1997).

world of our daily experience was not the creation of, or the concern of, the high god, but at best the bungling effort of an inferior deity, mediated through a world of intermediate and inferior angelic beings. Irenaeus' denial of this is absolute. God cares enough for this material world to become part of it through his Son and to continue to work in it through his Spirit. God does not keep the world at arm's length, for he created it himself: not through intermediaries, but through the Son and the Spirit, who are God himself in action.

Why did all this matter pastorally and morally? Irenaeus was the proponent of a biblical view that we are created to glorify God with our whole persons, body and soul alike. The Christian life was not an escape from the material world, but a calling to live in and through it redemptively. He was in this doing no more than following Paul's urging on the Roman Christians to present their bodies as a living sacrifice, holy and acceptable to God (Rom. 12.2). His opponents believed that what they did in their bodies was an irrelevance, so that, as he pointed out, they were led to contradictory practices, some of them indulging in licence, others in extreme asceticism – and for the same reasons. If our bodies are not really ourselves, it matters not whether we crush them under a weight of harsh discipline or abuse them in self-indulgence. Are things any different today? The British Methodist theologian, Geoffrey Wainwright, has written as follows:

> We live in a very sensate and sensualist society. We are in some ways absorbed in our senses, a people defined by materialism and sexuality. Yet in other ways we are curiously detached from our bodies, as though we are not really affected by what happens to us in our bodies or what we do in them.

He proceeds to draw the conclusion that this is essentially the same as it was for Irenaeus:

> If our bodies are not us, then we are not responsible in and for them; and that irresponsibility may assume the character of either license or, indeed, of withdrawal.[6]

---

[6] Geoffrey Wainwright, *For Our Salvation: Two Approaches to the Work of Christ* (Grand Rapids, Eerdmans, 1997), pp. 16f.

Wainwright has put his finger on the root cause of much of the modern world's sheer incapacity to live in the body, with all the human damage which results. Let me suggest another symptom of the same modern disease. We are in our world subordinating the life of persons to the impersonal demands of market forces. Our world is materialistic, indeed, and yet in a way that completely misunderstands the true being of the material. Instead of living in it as God's gift, we use it in a way that subverts rather than enhances the way in which personal beings are created to live with one another and in God's good creation. I shall return to the theme of the personal later.

What has all this to do with the Trinity? Let us follow through this great theologian's logic. If you were to ask him how God works in the world, what are the means by which he creates and redeems it, Irenaeus would answer: God the Father achieves his creating and redeeming work through his two hands, the Son and the Holy Spirit. Now this is an apparently crude image, but actually is extremely subtle. Our hands are ourselves in action; so that when we paint a picture or extend the hand of friendship to another, it is we who are doing it. According to this image, the Son and the Spirit are God in action, his personal way of being and acting in his world – God, we might say, extending the hand of salvation, of his love to his lost and perishing creation, to the extent of his only Son's dying on the cross. Notice how close this is to the way in which we noticed John speaking of Jesus in his Gospel. The Son of God, who is one with God the Father, becomes flesh and lives among us. This movement of God into the world he loves but has made itself his enemy is the way by which we may return to him. The result of Jesus' lifting up – his movement to cross, resurrection and ascension – is the sending of the Holy Spirit, – 'another paraclete', or second hand of God the Father. The Spirit is the one sent by the Father at Jesus' request to relate us to the Father through him. Irenaeus takes this understanding of God's working and uses it to engage with one of the first great challenges to the Christian world view, a challenge that is with us still. He is important because his trinitarian vision of God's creation and redemption of the whole world, both spiritual and material, has much to teach us both about sexual ethics, and personal relations more generally, and about ecological ethics: what we do with our bodies in relation to one another and in relation to our world.

In sum, the lesson we can learn from our three examples is this: if you want to understand how God works in our world, then you must go through the route God himself has given us – the incarnation of the eternal Son and the life-giving action of the Spirit. Let me repeat: the Trinity is about life. Irenaeus is the writer of that great sentence, often heard from him: the glory of God is a human being truly alive. The Trinity is about life, life before God, with one another and in the world. If we forget that God's life is mediated to us trinitarianly, through his two hands, the Son and the Spirit, we forget the root of our lives, of what makes for life and what makes for death. In my third section, I want to take this further, and ask whether we need to do any more than this. Do we need also to go into the complications of whether, and in what sense, God is Trinity, in his eternal being, so to speak?

A Doctrine of the Trinity?

Irenaeus thought trinitarianly, but did not yet have a developed doctrine of the Trinity. That is to say, he did not spend time discussing in what sense Father, Son and Spirit are all God, yet together are one God. Do we need that? In particular, are all the convolutions into which later theologians were and are led necessary? Perhaps not all of them, but a number of questions remained unanswered. Irenaeus understands clearly that God the Father achieves his purposes in the world through his Son and Spirit. But he has not concerned himself with *the* question which became unavoidable. Who is the God who identified himself in such a distinctive and personal way? It was in approaching questions like this that later theologians developed what we call the doctrine of the Trinity. What is its point? The best way to answer this question is to attempt to outline what the doctrine of the Trinity says. By means of summaries, I shall try to identify the heart of the matter.

1. God the Son – the one made flesh in Jesus of Nazareth – and God the Spirit are as truly God as God the Father who sends his Son into the world and pours out his Spirit on all flesh. That, of course, is a taking of Irenaeus' point one stage further. If God

is like this in his action and presence with us; if it is through
Jesus and the Spirit that he makes himself known; if they truly
are his hands, God in personal action; then that is what he is
always like. God does not tell lies. What you see is what you get.
If God works among us through his two hands, it is argued, then
the Son and the Spirit belong intrinsically to his eternal being.
In some way, therefore, God must be Father, Son and Spirit
always, to the heart of his being. The doctrine of the Trinity is
the doctrine that attempts to do just that: to identify the God
who comes among us in the way that he does; to enable us to see
as much as we need of the nature of our God.

2. All this is done without in the least wanting to suggest that
the unity of God is in any way impugned. All the arguments
were, and still are, about how to avoid slipping into two equal
and opposite errors: of making God so blankly singular that he
loses the richness and plurality of his being – and, so, that
'range and richness of God's gracious involvement in the world'
– or of so stressing the threeness that there seem to be three
gods. There is not, that is to say, some divine stuff that is made
known sometimes as Father, sometimes as Son and sometimes
as Spirit, or in some way lies behind them; rather, together they
are so bound up with one another's being that they are the one
God. God the Father, God the Son and God the Holy Spirit
together make up all that there is of the being of God. That is
another implication of the fact that God's presence among us is
real. What you see is what you get. 'Everything is what it is and
not another thing,' as Bishop Butler famously remarked. God is
this particular kind of being, and not the gods of the heathen or
of our human projections about what we think God ought to be
like. He is one God only in this way, to be loved, worshipped and
praised in the unutterable richness of his being; and it is no
accident that so many of our confessions of worship have taken
trinitarian form.

3. The relation of plurality and oneness is expressed with the
help of one of the most central concepts, and indeed, one
invented by trinitarian theologians, that of the person. Each of
the three, Father, Son and Spirit, is so described, that, to use the
traditional language, God is one being in three persons. That is
where our real difficulties, but also our opportunities begin. In
our everyday language, three persons seem to mean three separate beings. If this is the case with God, does it mean that there

are three gods, linked together as a kind of family? Here we must take a detour to look more carefully at this central notion, which is the unique and indispensable contribution made to the world by the early trinitarian thinkers. I shall look at the matter through a discussion of what we mean when we speak of a human person.

What is a human being? We have already met one answer in the theories of those whom Irenaeus opposed. For them, human beings were bits of soul-stuff imprisoned in a gross material body, which was so unimportant that it did not really matter what they did with it. This is a variation on a very common ancient view. The body is a tomb, said the Pythagoreans, and Socrates appears to have agreed with them. Salvation, true life, therefore, is about escaping from the world of matter into the higher world of spirit. But is that only an ancient view? Is our culture so different? We have already heard Geoffrey Wainwright's observation on this, and there are two ways in which our continuity with that ancient view can be illustrated. Suppose, it is often asked, that a computer could think. Would it be a person? The assumption in that question is that to be a person is to be a mind: thought is what makes us human. It is an assumption that is almost universally made in our world. But are we not hearts as well as heads, bodies as well as minds? Could even a thinking machine be said to love? Can we truly relate to other human beings without a body – without eyes, vocal chords, hands and arms? Our civilization continues to be deeply confused about the nature of life, especially human life, because we are confused about what personal being truly is.

And the second example is this. We live in a deeply individualist culture, marked by the fact that the market likes to think of us as units of consumption rather than as persons who belong together. Think of the everyday use of the word 'relationship'. Is it not generally assumed that human beings are individuals who go around seeking relationships; and if one seems not to work very well, giving it up and trying another? Lesslie Newbigin used to say that the idea of self-fulfilment is the myth of the modern world. That, of course, is why children are often the last to be thought of when marriages break up. We are not here to be for others; rather, we use the world and others as the route to our individual self-fulfilment. In our world, it is not much of an exaggeration to say that we have lost the sense that we belong with one another: that we are the people we are because we are the children of particular parents, the wives and husbands of particular people – and, just as important in another way, fellow members of the people of God. We have our being not as individuals but because of what we give to and receive from God and from one another. We are only what God and other people enable us to become, or, indeed, prevent us from becoming. 'No man is an island, entire of itself . . .' To be a person is something more than being a mind encased in flesh or an individual seeking our own self-fulfilment. It is to be one whose being is bound up with other persons. But how do we know and, more important, *practise* this?

Among the great achievements of those who have thought trinitarianly is the concept of the person as a living whole rather than as a mind encased in matter. How it came about is a complicated and difficult matter to describe, but it is one of the fruits of the trinitarian teaching that God is three persons in one being. By thinking about the Trinity, the early theologians came to realize that they had come across an entirely new conception of what it is to be personally. To be is not to be an individual; it is not to be isolated from others, cut off from them by the body that is a tomb, but in some way to be bound up with one another in relationship. Being a person is about being from and for and with the other. I need you – and particularly those of you who are nearest to me – in order to be myself. That is the first thing to say: persons are beings who exist only in relation – in relation to God, to others and to the world from which they come.

And there is a second thing to say, a pitfall to be avoided on the other side, also. If our relations with each other are to be truly personal, they cannot take the form of coercion either. Being a person is not simply being part of a greater whole, of simply existing for the collective, for the nation or for the market. We are not simply 'a piece of the continent, a part of the main . . .'. Our otherness and particularity are important, too. To be a person is not only to live from and for others; it is also to be uniquely what we are – ourselves and not identical with others. The two aspects are not contradictories that have to be somehow reconciled, as if everything done for another person has to be in some way thought of as contradictory of our own self-fulfilment. That is, of course, the case in our fallen condition. As sinful human beings, we don't want to bother with the other, except as the object of our needs, someone to be exploited. But the order of creation, our personal being, is that we cannot be ourselves without others. Breaches of this order are what we call sin because they arise from a distorted relation to our creator, and so a false relation to one another. The triune God's gracious dispensation is that we need each other if we are to be truly and particularly ourselves.

One of the things of which much has been made in recent writing about the Trinity is that this view of persons as being from and for and with one another in their very otherness contrasts with both of the dominant theories of social order in the modern world: the individualist, that we are like atoms which are only accidentally related to other human beings; and the collectivist, which makes us simply exist for the sake of the whole. It may appear, with the collapse of much of the communist world, that the latter danger has disappeared. But that is far from being the case. For all its apparent pluralism, the world of the market that so dominates our lives is actually working to make us all identical: all to drink coca cola and to eat at McDonald's, those symbols of the homogenizing forces of modernity, all to wear the same only superficially different designer clothes. That is simply another way of swallowing us up into a whole, of effectively depriving us of our individuality. Personal being is precisely what is at stake in this modern world. Wherever we look, the many – particular people with all their differences – are depersonalized by being swallowed up into the one, the mass, where individuality is suppressed in the interests of efficiency, economics and homogeneity: where babies with a risk of handicap are killed in the womb because we don't want to bother with those who are different, and where all have cosmetic surgery so that we all look alike. (I exaggerate, but only for the sake of allowing certain trends to come into view.)

Over against this, the triune God is a God in whom the one is not played against the many, nor the many against the one. In the words of John Zizioulas – though he is only interpreting the fourth century Greek theologians – God is one who has his being in communion.[7] Now, the word communion, and more

---

[7] John D. Zizioulas, *Being as Communion. Studies in Personhood and the Church* (London: Darton, Longman & Todd, 1985).

especially its associated word, community, is on many a lip these days, and therefore has to be interpreted very carefully. Certainly there are supposed 'communities' many of whose members do not know each other from Adam, the very opposite of what is intended here. (I recently saw an advertisement referring to 'the academic community', to take an example at random.) The point about the communion that is the Trinity is that in God the three persons are such that they receive from and give to each other their unique particularity. They have their being in relation to one another. The Son is not the Father, but receives his being from him; the Father cannot be the Father without the Son; and so on. Being in communion is being that belongs together, but not at the expense of the particular existence of the members. The Father, Son and Spirit are *persons* because they enable each other to be truly what the other is: they neither assert at the expense of, nor lose themselves in the being of, the others. Being in communion is being that realizes the reality of the particular person within a structure of being together. There are not three gods, but one, because in the divine being a person is one whose being is so bound up with the being of the other two, that together they make up the one God.

There are, to be sure, differences between divine and human persons, and we need to spend some time looking at this also. It is one thing to be the creator, quite another to be beings created in the image of God. This means that the differences between divine and human persons are as important as the similarities. First, we are created persons, and created out of the material world – out of the dust of the earth, to which we return. As we have seen, this is not something to be regarded negatively. The Son of God became one of us, thus marking and restoring our proper place in God's purposes. We are therefore made for particular kinds of relationships, those especially that respect the kinds of beings that we are. We are not God, and so not bound up together in the same way, only in a way appropriate to our createdness. The point of the notion of created persons is the immense range and variety of human beings, and the immense range of relationships in which we stand. It is easy to illustrate. Our relationships with our immediate family are different from those with whom we worship, and different again from our relationship with the social worker or the builder.

Particularity means precisely that: a vast range of ways of being and of being in relationship, all of which are in different ways personal – or should be. As we have seen, so many of the ways of being in our modern world deny our personal being in ways which distort our relation to each other and the world. Here, God's triune personal being stands as a model for ours: a being in which all accept their need of one another, while enabling all to be truly themselves.

And that takes us to a second point. How that is realized through the saving work of Christ and its embodiment in the Church would take (more than) another lecture: but the point must be made. We need not only a model of personhood, but the means for its redemption and realization. As things are, we fail in our relationships, not only with people but with the world in general. Because it is through the eternal Son of God that the world was created and is upheld, it is through his incarnation and reign with God the Father that personal being is redeemed and reshaped. The Church as the body of Christ is the human community called so to order its life with and before the triune God that it becomes a school of personal being – a place where, among other things, we learn to be with, from and for one another. Life in communion is one of the gifts of God the Spirit, as again and again is made clear in Scripture.[8]

4. And that brings me to the fourth and final thing I want to say about the doctrine of the Trinity. The three persons who make up the being of God; who, together, *are* the one God, are bound up together in such a way that only one word can be used to describe their relation: love. God is love says 1 John chapter 4, and the doctrine of the Trinity is that teaching which shows something of what that means. Notice that this chapter is already implicitly trinitarian. 'This is how God showed his love among us: He sent his one and only Son into the world that we might live through him . . . We know that we live in him and he in us, because he has given us of his Spirit' (vv. 9, 13). In the end the doctrine of the Trinity is only worth remembering if it

---

[8] The person, as John Zizioulas has also pointed out, is an eschatological conception, in the sense that it is something held out in promise, only more or less successfully realized this side of eternity, and only through the mediating work of the Son and the Spirit.

enables us to know – both theoretically and practically – something of the truth of the Bible's God: of who the God is who meets us in Jesus Christ and his Spirit.

Much is made of the fact that many moderns have rejected God because the God of the Church seemed the source of unfreedom and oppression rather than of love. We know, of course, that the God rejected by many an atheist is not the one we know and worship. Yet there is something in the charges, in the fact that our civilization stands so uneasily towards its religious past. The Church has failed to practise the Trinity. There are many ways of forgetting who is the true source of our life, and we are guilty of some of them. Without the doctrine of the Trinity we might have a God of power, or a God in some way identical with the world, but not the God of the Bible, who is a God of love, and whose love takes shape in the story of creation and redemption.

I began the lecture by alluding to skills and the practice of art. Craftsmen and artists live by their skills, which they have learned so thoroughly that they have become part of their very bodies, their tools and musical instruments extensions of their very persons. The Church lives by a kind of skill, if it can be metaphorically so described, or, better, by a way of being towards God and in the world. It is called love, and is founded above all in worship, the worship of the Father through the Son that is enabled only by the gift of the Spirit. The point of all this theology is not that it is the whole of what we need, but that it is an indispensable part. If we do not know who our God is, then we shall not know how we are to grow like him. That was Basil's point in his discourse on the Spirit. Without the Trinity, we cannot know that God is love, but we do know it, for the doctrine of the Trinity is the teaching that God is love, not only towards us, but in his deepest and eternal being.

2

The God of Jesus Christ[1]

Recent Theologies: Promise and Danger

One of the most remarkable and unpredicted developments in recent theology has been the renaissance of trinitarian theology. It has its less recent forerunners, especially perhaps in Barth's hermeneutical and structural use of the doctrine in the introductory volume of his *Church Dogmatics*, but also in the writings of younger contemporaries like Rahner and Lossky. Reference to the latter calls attention to the fact that among the influences generating the revival of interest are the increasing bearing of the thought of Eastern Orthodox theology on Western theology, as well as the continuing growth of Pentecostalism and the consequent attention given to the doctrine of the Spirit. Additionally, the continuing anxiety about the decline of civility in the Western world and its increasing depersonalization have called attention to the importance of personal being. It is often suggested that concepts of social and communal relations are encouraged by trinitarian thinking, particularly in view of the latter's part in the development of the concept of the person.

Two features mark the present expansion of writing on the topic. The first is its immense variety, and, indeed, it is a variety whose extreme forms are incompatible. On the one hand there is a series of approaches which maintains continuity with the

---

[1] With acknowledgement to Walter Kasper, *The God of Jesus Christ*, tr. M. J. O'Donnell (London: SCM Press, 1984).

revival of trinitarianism in the nineteenth century as that was inaugurated by Hegel. This great philosopher employed a form of the doctrine of the Trinity as the basis for a proposed Christianizing of modern culture. His Trinity served as the clue to the meaning of history, but it was a Trinity marked by the abandonment of the classical distinction, based on the doctrine of creation, between God and the world. Instead of a God who creates the world that is essentially other, we have one who *comes to be* through the processes of historical and cultural development. Kierkegaard, rightly I believe, saw this to represent the abandonment of Christianity's integrity, centred as that is on the particular and offensive form of the crucified Jesus. Hegel's view appears finally to abolish the distinction between Jesus and the rest of the human race by making him little more than an instance of a generally accessible human divinity. Any survey of recent trinitarian theology, however, must include some reference to this still strongly influential Hegelian tradition, as it is represented, for example, in recent work by the systematic theology of Peter Hodgson.

In this work, the writer does seek to overcome the Hegelian tendency that was criticized by Kierkegaard, and remain Christian by careful ambiguity, but comes near – at least – to turning Jesus of Nazareth from a historical figure into a historical principle. Hodgson loses at the outset the definitive place given to Jesus of Nazareth: 'Christ is not contained in a single historical individual.'[2] The result is a deep ambiguity about the significance of the cross, which is neither the unique act of God 'reconciling the world to himself' (2 Cor. 5.19) nor simply one focus in a market of religious possibilities, but tries to be both. 'The significance of the crucifixion of Jesus for God' is that it 'means the death of God, and that in turn means that suffering and tragedy are incorporated into the divine life'.[3] One objection to this is clear. To incorporate something into the divine life is to affirm it, and so to deny the essential character of Christianity

---

[2] Peter C. Hodgson, *Winds of the Spirit. A Constructive Christian Theology* (Louisville: Westminster John Knox Press, 1994), p. 49.

[3] Hodgson, *Winds of the Spirit*, p. 263.

as a religion of redemption, in which evil is not affirmed but conquered, eschatologically and by anticipation, in the cross and resurrection of Jesus of Nazareth.[4]

A treatment of the other end of the spectrum, which would stress the centrality of Jesus for the understanding of the triune God, indeed the Jesus who died and was raised, will follow below. But first something must be said about a second general feature of recent trinitarian writing. This is that from once sometimes appearing to be a largely technical discussion of a topic of theology of little relevance to others aspects, the doctrine of the Trinity has become a way of seeing all the topics of theology in a new light. Some of the detail of this development is to be found in Christoph Schwoebel's introduction to the collection he edited, *Trinitarian Theology Today*. I simply cite two statements:

> Trinitarian theology appears to be a summary label for doing theology that affects all aspects of the enterprise of doing theology in its various disciplines . . . This concerns not only major doctrinal topics such as the doctrine of creation, the destiny of humankind, the person and work of Christ, the church, its ministries and sacraments, and eschatology, but also those areas where doctrinal reflection and non-theological modes of enquiry overlap, such as the conversation with the natural sciences, anthropological enquiries, historical investigation and social theory.
>
> . . . the doctrine of the Trinity matters. It is not a topic reserved for austere theological speculation or the language and practice of worship. The conceptual form in which the doctrine of the Trinity is expressed will affect not only the content and emphases of the doctrinal scheme of theology

---

[4] Another ambiguity to be found in this book is between pantheism and a Christian doctrine of creation. What are we to make of this: 'God goes out from godself, creates a world seemingly infinite in extension but strictly nondivine in its perishability and contingency, yet enters into relationship with the world, makes it God's own "body" . . .'? Hodgson, *Winds of the Spirit*, pp. 163f. The ambiguity is revealed by the quotation marks, but a choice cannot be evaded. If the world is God's body, it is not finite and contingent, for it participates in divinity rather than being truly the creation. The alternatives are mutually exclusive.

but also the forms of community organisation in the church and its life of worship.[5]

As Professor Schwoebel remarks, other matters such as the relation of the Christian doctrine of God to the tradition of philosophical theism are also being rethought in the light of the revival,[6] and the list could be extended. We might add that he has himself contributed to consideration of the relation of trinitarian thinking to inter-religious dialogue,[7] while the matter of feminism has come within the purview of trinitarian theologians,[8] as has an argument that neglect of the Trinity has been instrumental in generating modern atheism.[9] Everything looks different when it is theologized with and through the doctrine of the Trinity.

However, with revival come also the dangers of oversimplification and the superficiality so often attendant on being fashionable. They lie to the right and to the left of the narrow path which all theology must tread, though it is important to remember that that metaphor is not intended to be a political one. The first set of dangers derives from a mistaken attempt to remain concretely relevant by casting doubt on the necessity of an immanent, or, better, ontological Trinity – of any doctrine, that is, of who and what kind of being God is essentially, in the eternal *taxis* or order of persons in relation. Two recent and influential American books on the doctrine of the Trinity have in different ways advocated the limitation of enquiry to the historical or economic Trinity – the Trinity made known in action and revelation in the world. In this respect Lutheran theology's tendency to restrict what we may say of the being of God to his being for and in relation to us contrasts with a concern more

[5] Christoph Schwoebel, ed., *Trinitarian Theology Today. Essays in Divine Being and Act* (Edinburgh: T&T Clark, 1995), pp. 1–30 (pp. 1f., 4).

[6] Schwoebel, *Trinitarian Theology Today*, p. 8.

[7] Christoph Schwoebel, 'Particularity, Universality and the Religions. Towards a Christian Theology of Religions', in Gavin D'Costa, ed., *Christian Uniqueness Reconsidered. The Myth of a Pluralistic Theology of Religions* (New York: Orbis Books, 1990), pp. 30–46.

[8] Alvin Kimel, ed., *Speaking the Christian God. The Holy Trinity and the Challenge of Feminism* (Leominster: Gracewing, 1992).

[9] Michael Buckley, *At the Origins of Modern Atheism* (New Haven and London: Yale University Press, 1987).

characteristic of the Reformed tradition, especially as that is represented by Calvin and Barth, to draw conclusions about the eternal being of God.

Thus it is that Ted Peters, in *God as Trinity*, takes to task even Robert Jenson's justification of a doctrine of the immanent Trinity in the interest of the freedom of God. Against this, Peters concludes that all we need to affirm is that 'God is in the process of self-relating through relating to the world he loves and redeems. God is in the process of constituting himself as a God who is in relationship with what is other than God.'[10] No more than that, it seems, is needed. A second book, with a similar tendency, is by a Roman Catholic, Catherine Mowry LaCugna, who contends, in a thesis similar to Harnack's famous judgement about the contamination of early theology by Greek philosophy, that the move into ontology – to an account of God's eternal being – in the early centuries was mistaken.[11] She claims that any doctrine of an immanent Trinity, even one derived from an understanding of the economy, is to be rejected. For her, even Rahner, in retaining vestiges of *theologia*, does not go far enough. From the outset it is made clear that we must not 'reify the idea of communion by positing an intra-divine "community" or society of persons that exists alongside, or above, the human community'.[12] All talk of the Trinity must therefore be in some way a function of the economy of salvation, so that we cannot, for example, develop a concept of *perichoresis* and use it to throw light from God's reality to ours. *Perichoresis* is not an analogy drawn between divine and worldly being, but a way of showing how God and the world are related. 'The starting point . . . locates *perichoresis* not in God's inner life, but in the mystery of the one communion of all persons, divine as well as human.' 'There are not two sets of communion – one among the divine persons, the other among human persons, with the latter supposed to replicate the former.'[13]

In face of both of these polemics against the doctrine of the

---

[10] Ted Peters, *God as Trinity. Relationality and Temporality in Divine Life* (Louisville: Westminster/John Knox Press, 1993), p. 145.

[11] Catherine Mowry LaCugna, *God for Us. The Trinity and Christian Life* (New York: HarperCollins, 1991).

[12] LaCugna, *God for Us*, p. 15.

[13] LaCugna, *God for Us*, p. 274.

ontological Trinity, and against any suggestion that it is *only* the freedom of God that is at stake here, a number of points can be made. The first derives from Barth's argument that if God is truly revealed in Jesus Christ, then that is what he is like eternally. God does not lie or play us false. Another point is that a distinction between God's reality and that of the world serves the world's interest. The doctrine of the eternal Trinity serves as a foundation for the relative independence and so integrity of worldly reality also, and thus for human freedom. It is because God is a communion of love prior to and in independence of the creation that he can enable the creation to be itself. The question that must be asked therefore is whether Peters's and LaCugna's approaches finally escape the pantheism which results from any attempt to bring God and the world too close. From the logic of their position, it is difficult not to conclude that there is ultimately only one reality, the divine-worldly emanation, which constitutes the world and then swallows it up. Against this it must be contended that far from ensuring the relevance of trinitarian categories, the outcome of such a process is to destroy it. God's personal otherness from the world is needed if there is to be a true establishing of the world in its own right, as truly worldly creation.

The second set of perils derives from the opposite tendency, which is using the doctrine to validate, on the basis of a doctrine of the immanent or ontological Trinity, causes which the theologian believes, for whatever reasons, to be worthy ones. That is to say, the doctrine of the Trinity is used as a kind of principle of explanation and ethics. Because God is like this, it is argued, then the world is, or ought to be, like that. Like almost all arguments, it is one from analogy, and none the worse for that. Much has rightly been made, for example, of the way in which the relational being of the immanent Trinity can provide a model for personal relations in human social order. Just as in God neither the one nor the three is any less real than the other, so in modern society, it is argued, we should stress neither the individual (the many) at the expense of the community (the one), nor the reverse.

For all the value of such arguments from analogy, they tread a slippery slope. The danger is to be seen in premature appeals to something called the social analogy, as if it is easily distinguishable from what is opposed to it as the psychological analogy, to support a vision of society without first passing through a difficult and complex process of intermediate argumentation. The assumption often seems to be that these are both fixed and intelligible quantities which can be 'applied' to society or the world, when they are neither. It may be true that the Trinity encourages neither an individualist nor a collectivist form of social order, as I have elsewhere argued to be the case.[14] Yet it remains true that moves from the immanent Trinity to the created world are not obvious, and are fraught with dangers of idealizing and projection. This is especially the case with those books in the Hegelian tradition to which reference has already been made. In it, trinitarian categories are used in order to discern the work of the divine Spirit largely or chiefly from immanent patterns of modern history and social development. Their chief defect is that they turn Christ into a world principle at the expense of Jesus of Nazareth, and often construe his cross as a focus for the suffering of God rather than as the centre of that history in which God overcomes sin and evil. That is to say, the doctrine of the Trinity must not be abstracted from the doctrine of the atonement. The point of this is that, if the atonement is maintained in the field of vision, history cannot be believed simply to develop, dialectically or otherwise, but is shown to be disrupted and redirected to its proper direction by the unique incarnation, ministry, death, resurrection and ascension of Jesus of Nazareth. Without that focus, the Trinity is no longer the Christian Trinity but, as Kierkegaard rightly claimed to be the case with Hegel, simply an uncritical validation of modern culture – or whatever – and so effectively Christianity's opposite.

The Centrality of Christology

This brings us, then, to the other pole of the tendencies to which I referred near the beginning of the chapter. It is represented by those theologians of the Trinity who give a central

[14] Colin E. Gunton, *The One, the Three and the Many. God, Creation and the Culture of Modernity. The 1992 Bampton Lectures* (Cambridge: Cambridge University Press, 1993).

place in their doctrine of God to the historical Jesus of Nazareth. I use that expression not to deny the divinity of Christ – for there is no Jesus who is not also the incarnate Lord – but to suggest that any doctrine of the Trinity which loses its hold on that particular historical human being no longer represents the historic faith of the Church. The key to Jesus' place in the construction of a doctrine of God is to be found in the possible ambiguity in the title of a book on the Trinity written some time ago by the Roman Catholic dogmatician, Walter Kasper: *The God of Jesus Christ*.[15] While there is no ambiguity in this theologian's account of the matter, his title enables us to realize that the expression, 'the God of Jesus Christ' can mean one of two things. It can refer to the God to whom Jesus is in some form of relation or to the God that Jesus in some sense is. An adequate theology of the Trinity will take account of both of these meanings.

First, it remains the case that any identification of God apart from Jesus of Nazareth is in danger of becoming an abstraction. The strength of Robert Jenson's theology of the Trinity is that Jesus of Nazareth serves in it as the means of God's self-identification. 'God is what he does among us. All the complicated subtleties of Barth's . . . doctrine of the Trinity say this one things at all the different places where it might be forgotten.'[16] The point, ultimately dependent on Barth's Trinity of revelation, is amplified in Eberhard Jüngel's view that Christian theology is our interpretation of the triune God's self-interpretation.[17] Some such view of the matter lies also behind both Calvin's trinitarianism and Barth's polemics against natural theology. We must place ourselves theologically where the action is, because if we turn away from God's actual historical self-identification in Jesus, we simply manufacture an idol, or a series of idols. One central value of the doctrine of the Trinity, therefore, is that it ties our speech of God to Jesus, and thus helps to prevent the creation of idols or of any God projected

---

[15] See note 1.

[16] Robert W. Jenson, *God After God. The God of the Past and the God of the Future, Seen in the Work of Karl Barth* (Indianapolis and New York: Bobbs Merrill, 1969), p. 113.

[17] Eberhard Jüngel, *Gottes Sein ist im Werden*; ET *God's Being is in Becoming*, tr. Horton Harris (Edinburgh: Scottish Academic Press, 1976).

conveniently to confirm our wishes or prejudices. That is why Barth could accept without feeling under threat many of Feuerbach's contentions that God is simply the projection on to eternity of human beliefs and wishes. The God revealed as Jesus Christ resists such dismissal, because this is simply too offensive and unlikely a doctrine to be dismissed as mere projection.[18]

Second, and in qualification of the first point, it must be argued that any absolute identification of Jesus with God detracts from his proper humanity. The New Testament makes it quite clear that Jesus is not simply God, but also who he is in relation to God – God the Father. His Father is not only the one to whom he prayed, but the one to whom he was, by the Holy Spirit, related in such a way that he became, humanly, that which he was called to be. To understand the human meaning of Jesus we need a trinitarian construal of his relations with God and the world. Here, the Christology of the Letter to the Hebrews is particularly helpful. Jesus is one who, having learned obedience through what he suffered – and that seems to refer not only to what we call the passion, but to the whole human life and experience of Jesus – offered to God the Father that perfected human life without which no other human life can be perfect. When this author speaks of 'Christ who, through the eternal Spirit offered himself without blemish to God' (Heb. 9. 14) we must remember that the human being of whom he speaks is none other than the 'Son ... through whom he created the world' (Heb. 1.2). There is a difference within identity.

Of many recent doctrines that have made much of the notion of the suffering God it must be asked whether they can do justice to this side of the atonement. The point they are seeking to make is clear. Too many past accounts of the cross have been so dominated by the doctrine of the impassibility of God that they appear to introduce a division between God and Jesus, so that, in extreme forms of the teaching, it appears that God the

---

[18] This is not to deny that Feuerbach did attempt to argue that this, too, is a projection: Feuerbach's view that the doctrine of the Trinity really means that 'participated life is alone true, self-satisfying divine life' begs the question of the origin of our belief in the importance of participated life. Ludwig Feuerbach, *The Essence of Christianity*, tr. George Eliot (New York: Harper and Bros., 1957 edn), p. 67.

Father visits upon his Son that punishment which human sin has earned. Moreover, such doctrines appear to make God indifferent to suffering, a problem of which Moltmann has made much, particularly in his response to Auschwitz, which was the occasion for his well-known treatment of *The Crucified God*.[19] However, caution is here in order. Just as it is sometimes said of Barth that he is occasionally so insistent on the humanity of God that the humanity of Jesus Christ is cast into the shade, so we must remember that one point of the doctrine of the Trinity is that it should enable us to attribute particular forms of action to the particular persons of the Trinity, albeit without suggesting that they are other than the acts of the one God. A familiar citation from Calvin makes the point: 'to the Father is attributed the beginning of activity, and the fountain and well-spring of all things; to the Son, wisdom, counsel and the ordered disposition of all things; but to the Spirit is assigned the power and efficacy of that activity'.[20] And part of the Son's 'ordered disposition of all things' is his truly suffering in the flesh for the sins of the world. It is the Son's particular office to become incarnate and suffer in the flesh, and too much stress on God the Father's suffering may detract from that.

That takes us to the heart of the doctrine of the Trinity. There is a relation, taking place in time, which both is and is not identical with the relation of the Son to the Father in the Spirit in eternity. It is identical, because what Jesus does in the flesh is the work of God the Father. It is not, because this is an authentically human action, which continues as the ascended Christ continues to be, through the Spirit, the agent of the relation of the world to God. That is why it is essential that our talk of God be tied not simply to the humanity of Jesus, but to what has traditionally been called the work of Christ. LaCugna is right to hold that it is not enough to draw analogies between God's being and our being. If we are to escape abstraction, we need

[19] Jürgen Moltmann, *The Crucified God. The Cross of Christ as the Foundation and Criticism of Christian Theology*, tr. R. A. Wilson and J. Bowden (London: SCM Press, 1974).

[20] John Calvin, *Institutes of the Christian Religion*, ed. J. T. McNeill, tr. and index F. L. Battles, Library of Christian Classics vols 20 and 21 (Philadelphia: Westminster Press, 1960), I. xiii. 18.

also to establish concrete links between God's being and action and ours.

The Gospel and the Triune God

The reasoning is that Christianity is gospel before it is theology, and theology is truly Christian if its account of the being of God is tied to divine action in Christ. Paul's account in 1 Corinthians 15.3 of the gospel he received is a good place to begin in elaborating elements of this truth. It has a number of focuses: the death of Christ for our sins according to the Scriptures, his raising from death and his appearances. If we take it in the light of the chapter as a whole, we shall see that beginning with the death of Jesus, the summary spreads out to include the whole economy of God's dealings with the world. 'According to the Scriptures' relates what happens to God's election of Israel, including as it does the universal covenant inaugurated in the promises to Abraham. The allusion to sin takes us into a yet wider context: the creation and its being deflected from its true course by sin and evil, summarized later in this chapter by the last enemy, death, whose reign will finally be ended by the risen Jesus. The chapter as a whole is dedicated to the resurrection, which shows that it is the lord of all creation who is at work through his renewing Spirit in what happens with and to Jesus. Finally, the appearances, especially if they are understood in the light of the descriptions of Jesus' rule later in the chapter, indicate what is credally expressed by means of the doctrine of the ascension of Jesus: that the history of this human being is not yet ended, but continues as the second Adam reigns until the end when he will deliver the Kingdom to God the Father, who will then be all in all (1 Cor. 15.20–28).

Implicit in this chapter is an account of what Irenaeus of Lyons called recapitulation. In Jesus, God recapitulates the human story, achieving the redemption of the lost creation by doing in triumph what Adam failed to do in defeat. As Adam failed to be the human being made in the image of God, so Christ, by becoming human, not only corrects what was wrong, but brings to perfection what was begun in the creation. In all this, Irenaeus works with a trinitarian conception of mediation. His well-known metaphor of the Son and the Spirit as the 'two hands' of God the Father enables him to show God as creator and redeemer of the whole world, not simply of its 'spiritual' dimensions. In opposition to the Gnostics, who denied at once the incarnation of Jesus and the importance of life in the body, he affirmed, for christological reasons both that Jesus was truly human and that human life in the flesh was of supreme importance. But he was unable to do this without considerable attention to the work of the second hand of God, the Holy Spirit.

Basil of Caesarea, in a characterization of the distinctive forms of activity of the three persons of the Trinity similar to that we have cited from Calvin, was able, while affirming that the Holy Spirit is 'inseparable and wholly incapable of being parted from the Father and the Son', to distinguish: 'the original cause of all things that are made, the Father; the creative cause, the Son; the perfecting cause, the Spirit'.[21] The Holy Spirit is, so to speak, the person of the Trinity to whom Scripture ascribes the eschatological action of perfecting the created order: of enabling it to become that which it was created to be. The strongly eschatological thrust of Irenaeus' theology, derives from the fact that he gives due attention to the activity of both of the 'hands' of God: the Son who involves himself fully in the material world and the Spirit who enables that world, through Christ and in the Church, to realize that which God would have it be. It is important to realize that, in distinction from the Gnostics, whose high God was far too lofty to be involved in matter except through the mediations of inferior deities, the two hands of God are God in action. It is thus through the thoroughly trinitarian structure of his theology that Irenaeus was able to do justice to God's creating and redeeming activity towards and in the world.

It is often said that Irenaeus' theology is an economic trinitarianism, and does not require a doctrine of the immanent Trinity. The same may appear to be the case with 1 Corinthians 15. Yet both require a 'space' between God and the world that allows God to be God, the world to be the world. Although it may be the case that others had later to draw out the implications of both the Bible's and Irenaeus' theologies for the being of God, there is no doubt that Irenaeus, who taught the eternal

[21] Basic of Caesarea, *On the Holy Spirit*, XV. 38.

divinity of both Son and Holy Spirit, laid, in dependence on Scripture, the foundation for later developments. His concern for a God who both allows and enables the world to be itself provides us with all the reasons for the importance not only of a theology of the Trinity, but for a doctrine of the immanent Trinity. For the world to be truly the world, it needs a God who is both other than it and who is able to love it for itself, because it is the world to which God has given being. That is the heart of the matter. Because God as Father, Son and Spirit is already, from eternity, a structure of love – of persons in communion – the world may be brought into relation with that God without having its own reality threatened or diminished. On the contrary, as we have seen, it is enhanced by being redeemed. The gospel implies a free and loving God; the doctrine of the Trinity allows us a glimpse into who the God is who meets us in Jesus Christ through the Spirit.

3

Eastern and Western Trinities: Being and Person. T. F. Torrance's Doctrine of God[1]

Something on the Sources

My first memory of Tom Torrance comes from a large student gathering in Bristol in 1963, when he shared the platform with, among others, Lesslie Newbigin. The congress was up to date for those days, with science and politics among the concerns, and our subject's address was, as might be expected, concerned with the former. But not in itself: the emphasis was on the necessity for scientist and theologian alike to show obeisance before the reality which they served. That introduces a theme central to Torrance's doctrine of God: that God's objective truth confronts us all with a demand which our subjective rationality may seek to encompass according to both God's and its limits, but which must never stray over those strict limits. The truth is prior to our appropriation of it. And a later memory is also definitive of the kind of theologian that Torrance is. It was a conference ordered around Rahner's book on the Trinity,[2] and an anecdote will illustrate the whole. One evening, towards the end of the conference, some of us, clever, no doubt, but inexperienced, were discussing our profound disquiet with some of Rahner's theology. We took it to Tom, who placed the whole thing in a somewhat wider context, before spending the

---

[1] First published in *The Promise of Trinitarian Theology. Theologians in Dialogue with T. F. Torrance*, ed. Elmer M. Colyer (Lanham, MD: Rowman and Littlefield), pp. 115–37.
[2] Karl Rahner, *The Trinity*, tr. Joseph Donceel (London: Burns & Oates, 1970).

night writing a response to the conference which summed up its proceedings magisterially, in a rounded paper which was later published, no doubt with minimal need for revision, as 'Towards an Ecumenical Consensus on the Trinity'.[3]

Many streams flow together into Torrance's doctrine of God, and to name them is to begin to understand something of its shape. Without doubt, the demand to be obeisant: before the reality of God is something that comes from the Calvinist inheritance, but it is a Calvinism modified in both a Scottish and a modern way. A number of nineteenth-century Scots, among them Edward Irving and John McLeod Campbell, reacted against what they believed to be the rigidities of the piety formed under the aegis of the Westminster Confession, and produced a theology designed to mitigate the effects of classic dual predestinarianism. McLeod Campbell is particularly important for Torrance. His pastoral motivation drove him to stress Christ's identification with the human condition and to push towards a theology of his universal significance. The incarnation is as significant for him as Jesus' death, which is understood truly as God's self-giving. This remains throughout Torrance's career at the very centre of his doctrine of God, and indeed of everything else.

The concern to ensure that God is truly given in Christ recurs in Torrance's early and continuing engagement with Karl Barth. For him, Barth is comparable only with Athanasius as the theologian in whom God's being and act are truly integrated. Barth's incarnational theology and attack on natural theology alike drive him, as Torrance understands him, not only to engage with the weaknesses of Calvin's tendency to posit a God hidden beyond Christ – a scholarly commonplace that Torrance accepts only with qualifications – but with a much more deep-seated Western tendency. From at least the time of Augustine onwards the modalist temptation to posit a God lying behind his acts has been one of the perennial pitfalls of our tradition, Catholic and Evangelical alike. (It is there that is to be seen the appeal to Torrance of Rahner's influential book, with its

---

[3] Now Chapter 4 of T. F. Torrance, *Trinitarian Perspectives. Toward Doctrinal Agreement* (Edinburgh: T&T Clark, 1994). Hereafter this work will be abbreviated TP.

critique of his own Catholic tradition's tendency to open a breach between the one God and the triune God.) Crucial for Torrance here is the figure of Athanasius, who can be said in some way or other to appear as a real presence in all of his thought. Part of his importance is to serve as the patristic forerunner of what Barth is in the modern age, although, as we shall see, that is only a part of a wide-ranging appeal.

Athanasius served Torrance as a theologian of God's being as Barth served as a theologian of his act – though the greatness of both is that they integrated the two – and it would be difficult to exaggerate the importance for him, in all aspects of his work, of the principle of the *homoousion*. '[T]he *homoousion* helps us to discern and makes us regard the Incarnation as falling within the Life of God himself and as thus providing the real ontological ground on which we think inseparably together the doctrine of the one God and the doctrine of the triune God.'[4] However, that is to leap ahead. Before we come to the One and the Three, we must pause to examine something of the basis and method of the doctrine of God which is so central to this theologian's work. The basis of the doctrine of God is to be found in the gospel of Jesus Christ and the worship of the Church which responds to it and lives by it. If we may suspect that a touch of intellectualism is sometimes near the surface of this theology, that impression is always qualified by the firm evangelical and missionary orientation of Torrance's thought. In that sense, his missionary origins have never left him, for all his writing about God breathes a concern that the truth and rationality of the gospel be communicated in and to the world.

Theology's task is to essay a rational account of the creed of the Church while remaining deeply entrenched in the gospel. It is at this, epistemological, level that the thought of Michael Polanyi has exercised a deep influence. The scientist-philosopher, along with Einstein, is central to Torrance's attack on dualism, another recurring theme of his writing. Dualism is that which distorts the Christian knowledge of God and, indeed, has seriously incapacitated all the thought of the West. Two aspects of what is a broad-based syndrome are at the heart of Torrance's concern. The first is the division between the

[4] TP, p. 81.

world of sense and the world of intellect. Against this, Polanyi's teaching that human agents indwell the world of their experience, an insight which Torrance sees to derive from the teaching of the Fourth Gospel, is crucial. Modern intellectual life is vitiated because it is dualistically deprived of its basis in material being. A philosophy of the necessity of the human mind's continuity with the material world not only has Christian origins, but is essential for the integration of thought and experience without which neither natural nor theological science can operate. In line with this insight, and alongside Torrance's insistence on the rationality of both God and the theology of the Trinity, is a concern to integrate the empirical – a word which appears often in the writing – and the conceptual. We might say that it generates a realist parallel with Kant's essentially idealist epistemology. Theological concepts must have a corresponding empirical purchase if they are not to fly dualistically off into a theology which is not rooted in the gospel.

The second dualism is parallel with that between mind and matter, and is between the being and act of God. Certain forms of the 'Latin Heresy'[5] have entrenched in the tradition the breach we have already met between the act of God – what he does – and his being – what he is. It is not too much of an exaggeration to say that Torrance's trinitarian theology is a sustained attempt to overcome that dualism. And at the centre of the enterprise of overcoming that dualism is the Nicene doctrine of the *homoousion*. A word count of Torrance's theology would almost certainly place this at the head of the major theological concepts which he employs, so that it is accordingly the more difficult to give succinct expression to the wide-ranging use to which it is put. One could almost say: that where Barth's theology of the Trinity is centred essentially on a theology of revelation, Torrance's is centred on the *homoousion*. That is not to suggest that his is not also a theology of revelation, nor that there are not major methodological parallels with Barth. The level we have already mentioned, the level of the experience of the gospel, is indeed the level of revelation. But where Barth places the threefold shape of the divine self-revelation, indeed

[5] T. F. Torrance, 'Karl Barth and the Latin Heresy', *Scottish Journal of Theology* 39 (1986), pp. 461–82.

christologically grounded, Torrance places a more firmly christological and incarnational centre.

This is where the patristic influence is the strongest, and it takes form in a more definite use than is to be found in Barth of the concept of the divine economy, by which is meant: 'the orderly movement in which God actively makes himself known to us in his incarnate condescension and his redemptive activity within the structures of space and time . . .'.[6] The allusion to space and time reminds us of the apologetic, perhaps better missionary, thrust of Torrance's theology, for as long ago as his definitive study of the incarnational relation of God to space and time he argued that God's movement into time in the gospel both (historically) created the conditions for modern science and demonstrates (in the present) the scientific and theological falsity of a dualistic view of God and the world.[7] Crucial here to his reading of theological history is the view that under the impact of revelation Athanasius and others developed conceptions of the relation of God to time and space which transformed the whole of culture, crippled though the developments were in early modernity by the dualistic mechanism of the Newtonian tradition.[8] Again and again we are reminded: the gospel of the economy shapes not only the Christian world but the world of culture as a whole.

The Triune Economy

To explain the epistemological and ontological function of the *homoousion* we must understand that Torrance goes beyond his modern teacher in drawing a firm parallel between natural and theological science. According to him, the former is based on everyday experience, and represents a development of the rationality already inherent in it. The first, experiential, level is

[6] T. F. Torrance, *The Christian Doctrine of God, One Being Three Persons* (Edinburgh: T&T Clark, 1996), p. 92. Hereafter this work will be abbreviated CDG.

[7] T. F. Torrance, *Space, Time and Incarnation* (London: Oxford University Press, 1969).

[8] T. F. Torrance, *Transformation and Convergence within the Frame of Knowledge. Explorations in the Interrelations of Scientific and Theological Enterprise* (Belfast: Christian Journals, 1984), Chapter 1.

thus already incipiently scientific. 'At the ground or primary level of daily life, our experiences and cognitions are naturally and inseparably combined together.'[9] The second or scientific level is that wherein conceptual integration is made of the first level. Essential for Torrance's general epistemology is that the second arise out of the first: 'their function is to enable us to grasp and to understand common experience from the intelligible relations *intrinsic to it*, but which are not themselves directly experienced'.[10] The third level is the meta-scientific (or second scientific) at which 'we seek to deepen and simplify the organisation of basic concepts and relations developed at the scientific level'.[11]

In theology there is a movement that is parallel, but not identical, to these three levels: from, we might say, the experienced gospel to a rational account of the truth of the gospel's God. The *homoousion* operates at all three levels, and in fact is crucial for their integration. At the first level is 'the ground level of religious experience and worship' – and we may notice that Torrance is less reluctant than Barth to speak of experience in such a way – which is experience of 'the Lord Jesus Christ clothed with his gospel', trinitarianly construed. This is 'incipient theology'.[12] The second level is concerned with the 'appropriate intellectual instruments' with which to give a primary theological account of the experienced gospel.[13] This is the level of the economy, and it is here that the *homoousion* is the hinge. It enabled, we might say, rational sense to be made of the God who made himself known in Jesus Christ. 'That is to say, the *homoousios* was harnessed to the Gospel of salvation proclaimed in the New Testament and linked ... to their belief "in one God the Father Almighty, Maker of heaven and earth ...".'[14] The rational achievement is that: 'The *homoousion* crystallises the conviction that while the incarnation falls within the structures of our spatio-temporal humanity in this world, it also falls within the Life and Being of God ...', and so is 'the

[9] CDG, p. 84.
[10] CDG, pp. 84f, emphasis added.
[11] CDG, p. 85.
[12] CDG, pp. 88f.
[13] CDG, p. 91.
[14] CDG, p. 94.

ontological and epistemological linchpin of Christian theology'.[15] Accordingly, the historic and enduring significance of
the Council of Nicaea consists in the fact that it entrenched in
the Church the christological orthodoxy, which was established
beyond all peradventure by Athanasius, that the Son of God is
equal in godhead with the eternal Father. Arianism is cor-
respondingly the most dangerous heresy, because it calls in
question the reality of revelation at both divine and human
levels.[16]

All this makes clear that the *homoousion* of the Son with the
Father is crucial in the development of Torrance's theology. It
represents God's contingent historical freedom to be fully present to the world in Christ and it drives the whole development.
Yet it is not enough for a doctrine of the Trinity unless the
homoousion of the Holy Spirit is also established. Two aspects of
Torrance's pneumatological thesis must here be mentioned.
The first is that, although the divinity of the Spirit belonged to
the tradition of the Church's faith, it was not until half a century
after Nicaea that the conceptual development and elaboration,
parallel to that of Christology, took place, momentum already
having been provided by Athanasius and Gregory of Nazianzen
in particular. Second, the epistemological role of the Spirit's
homoousion is essential for the development of the doctrine of
the immanent Trinity. Positively, it enables a move to be made
from God's economic action to his eternal being; negatively, it
prevents us from reading up into God the kind of causal
connections that are characteristic of the created world; our
knowledge of God must remain spiritual.[17]

Before coming to the third level, let us pause to consider
Torrance's theology of the economy, for that is what we are
concerned with here. The function of the *homoousion* in this
development is to obviate any hint of subordinationism in the
relation of the persons of the Trinity. This has losses and gains.
On the debit side is the fact that it downplays what came to be

---

[15] CDG, p. 95.

[16] T. F. Torrance, *The Trinitarian Faith. The Evangelical Theology of the Ancient
Catholic Church* (Edinburgh: T&T Clark, 1988), p. 119. Hereafter this work will
be abbreviated TF.

[17] CDG, p. 97.

called the monarchy of the Father. We shall come later to Torrance's relation to the Cappadocian Fathers, and concentrate here on how this affects his interpretation of some of the earlier theologians. In introduction, we must say that there is clearly an element of *economic* subordination – to be strictly distinguished from *ontological* subordination*ism* – in the Scriptures. The Son obeys the Father, does the Father's work and will hand over the Kingdom to the Father, and so on (to combine elements of the Fourth Gospel's Christology with that of 1 Corinthians 15.24–8). The concept of monarchy denotes the fact that the Son and the Spirit are mediators of the Father's work and rule. This is clearly expressed in Irenaeus' conception of the Son and the Spirit as the 'two hands' of God, but it is not that which Torrance tends to draw upon, but rather the bishop's – equally real, but less prominent – insistence on the true divinity of the hands. Rightly or wrongly, the authority of Athanasius is played against the view that the Son and the Spirit mediate the Father's kingly rule: 'the formula "one Being, three Persons" . . . carried with it a doctrine of the *Monarchia* . . . as identical with the one indivisible being of the Holy Trinity'.[18] We shall return to this question of whether the monarchy is that of the Father or of the whole Trinity, which is a central one for all trinitarian theology.

On the credit side of Torrance's development is that what we can call, with due qualification, a homogeneous view of the persons in the economy – homogeneous in the sense that even at the economic level there is no doubt at all about their full and equal deity – ensures that the move between economy and immanent or eternal Trinity is made less problematic than it is in some accounts. If the Son and the Spirit are economically equal to the Father, there is no difficulty in the anti-Arian task of attributing to them full and eternal divine status. Even here, however, there is a complication, as an illuminating comparison with Barth will indicate. In Barth, there is an element of subordination in the economy, in the sense that the Father commands and the Son obeys. However, this economic subordination is then, so to speak, read up into the eternal Trinity, where the economic subordination becomes, without being taken away, also and at once an immanent equality of being. So

---

[18] TF, p. 10.

it is that Barth can say, on the basis of christology, that it is as godlike to be humble as to be exalted: that there are within the being of God elements of commanding and obeying, of super-ordination and subordination.[19] This will serve as a useful way of understanding the ways in which Torrance is similar to and different from his great teacher, because what we can call the *homoousian* drive of his thought operates to minimize such elements and to stress the complete equality of the action and divinity alike of the three persons.

The 'homogeneity' of the persons of the economic Trinity is expressed in a stress on the co-givenness of all three persons in God's reconciling and revelatory activity. Torrance argues that although there is not a doctrine of the Trinity as such in the New Testament, the whole triune God is given in Jesus Christ. 'It is the mutual relation between the incarnate Son and the Father that provides us with the ground on which we are given access to knowledge of the one God in his inner relations as Father, Son and Holy Spirit.'[20] The point is stressed strongly: 'in the New Testament this revelation of the mystery of God toward us is revelation of God as Father, Son and Holy Spirit in his *whole-ness* . . .'[21] To put the matter in the terms we have been using, the *homoousion* enables us to understand that in Jesus Christ clothed with his gospel we have access to the whole God, Father, Son and Holy Spirit, all co-equally divine. The economic Trinity gives access to the eternal God as he is in himself.

The Eternal Trinity

Discussion of the immanent Trinity is so complex and contro-verted a matter that we shall need at the outset to specify the main questions to be asked. The first concerns the basis of the move from economy to theology. By what right does thought move from history to eternity, from action in time to being in eternity? The second concerns the function which the doctrine

---

[19] See especially Karl Barth, *Church Dogmatics*, eds G. W. Bromiley and T. F. Torrance (Edinburgh: T&T Clark, 1957–1975), 4/1, §59. 1.

[20] CDG, p. 42.

[21] CDG, p. 43.

performs. A number of recent trinitarian theologies have denied, or virtually denied, the need for a distinction between economic and immanent Trinity – between God's historical act and eternal being – perhaps most influentially Catherine Mowry LaCugna. For her, ontology is the enemy. 'There is neither an economic nor an immanent Trinity; there is only the *oikonomia* that is the concrete realization of the mystery of *theologia* in time, space, history and personality.'[22] Why, we must ask, does our theologian insist on the necessity of a proper and rigorous doctrine of the God's being, in distinction, but also inseparable, from his act? The third question concerns the meaning and relation of the two central concepts, being and person. It is here that modalism is always the threat, especially in the West. Torrance is one of those theologians whose relation to Augustine is relatively critical – he likes to quote Barth's characterization of the great Western theologian as 'sweet poison' – and clearly wants his own Western inheritance to be deeply transformed by the thought of the Eastern Fathers. The fourth question concerns the place of the particular persons within the being of the Trinity, and that brings us to the heart of the difference between the East and the West. What, in particular, are we to make of the Western addition to the creed, that the Spirit proceeds from the Father *and the Son*, the *Filioque*? Karl Barth accepted and defended this doctrine, by appeal to the economy of revelation, among other factors.[23] What does Torrance make of the judgement of his teacher in this regard? We shall approach the four questions one by one.

The Move from Economy to Theology

On what basis and with what justification do we move from the second, economic level, to the third? Torrance's answer is that thought is *compelled* to go further because of the nature of what is given at the second level, and again the *homoousion* is the reason:

---

[22] Catherine Mowry LaCugna, *God for Us. The Trinity and Christian Life* (New York: HarperCollins, 1991), p. 223.
[23] Barth, *Church Dogmatics*, 1/1, §12.2.

for it enables us to deepen and refine our grasp of the self-revealing and self-communicating of God to us as Father, Son and Holy Spirit, in such a way that our thought has to move from the secondary level in which we have to do with the economic Trinity to the tertiary or higher theological level where we have to do with the ontological Trinity . . .[24]

The necessity so to move is, it must be stressed, rational rather than mechanical. If the theologian is to be true to what is presented in experience, then certain conclusions cannot be evaded without falsifying the empirical and conceptual implications of our Christian experience. Here, without doubt, Torrance is following the method, though not in every respect the content, of Barth's great treatise on the Trinity. If revelation is truly God present to the world, then it is *God* present to the world, and what is given in time *is* the saving presence of the eternal God. Because it is the truthful God with whom we have to do, we know that he is giving us himself and not an external manifestation whose internal structuring may be different. The whole of Torrance's strategy is thus to strengthen and elaborate in terms of his patristic concept the insights that he had received, clothed in rather more nineteenth-century language, from Karl Barth.

The Function of the Distinction Between Economy and Theology

It was the achievement of Athanasius in particular to have distinguished between the being and the will of God. God is always the triune God, but not always creator, because while the Son comes from his being, the world is, *ex nihilo,* the product of his will. Athanasius' linking of creation and incarnation as both equally works of the divine will demonstrate the freedom of God. 'They tell us that he is free to do what he had never done before, and free to be other than he was eternally . . .'[25] The matter at stake becomes especially clear in Torrance's

---

[24] CDG, p. 95.
[25] TF, p. 89.

discussion of Rahner's so-called rule, that 'The "Economic" Trinity is the "Immanent" Trinity and the "Immanent" Trinity is the "Economic" Trinity.'[26] He justifiably accuses Rahner of abstraction, an abstraction which takes the form in this case of the classic idealist mistake of confusing the order of knowing with the order of being, so that:

> there is being confused a movement of logical thought from one doctrine of the Trinity to another, and a movement of understanding and devotion from God in his economic self-revelation to us in space and time to God as he eternally is in his inner divine life. The confusion between the two movements seems to be apparent when Rahner states that the 'Immanent' Trinity is 'the necessary condition of the possibility of God's free self-communication'. Does this not involve a confusion between a necessary movement of thought (a logical necessity) and the kind of 'necessity' arising from the fact that God has freely and irreversibly communicated himself to us . . .?'[27]

Against this, Torrance's more nuanced expression is that of Barth, albeit in this instance expressed in Rahnerian terms. There is an identity of outer and inner, because the self-communication in the Son and the Spirit is the self-communication of God; and yet it is because God is triune in himself, 'that he is free to communicate himself as Triune in the economy of salvation.'[28]

Being and Person

It is often said, oversimplification that it is, that in the East discussion of the Trinity moves from the three to the one, whereas in the West the reverse is the case. The real difference, however, tends not to be in the starting point but in the way in which the oneness and threeness of God are weighted in relation to one another, and whether, as often happens in the West,

---

[26] TP, p. 79, citing Rahner, *The Trinity*, p. 22. The original is in italics.
[27] TP, p. 80.
[28] TP, pp. 79–80f., citing Rahner, *The Trinity*, p. 102.

the oneness outweighs the threeness and makes the persons functionally indistinguishable to all intents and purposes. (That is, of course, another version of Rahner's complaint about the divorce of the doctrine of the one God from that of the triune God that we have met above.) In the case of our subject, the one and the three are interrelated from the very beginning, because the use made of the *homoousion* ensures that both are co-given from the outset. Indeed, the move from economy to theology has the effect of ensuring that God's threefold revelation shapes the treatment of his eternal being. It is in this light that we must approach our third question.

Torrance begins his definitive treatment of trinitarian theology with the being of God. Once again, Athanasius is the dominant authority. He had already been drawn upon in the earlier *The Trinitarian Faith* for his contrast between static and impersonal Aristotelian being and dynamic trinitarian being. The triune God is a philanthropic God, a borrowing from Athanasius that Torrance uses from time to time.[29] This God is 'intrinsically and intensely personal', the ever-living God,[30] '*personal, dynamic and relational Being*'.[31] Much, however, hangs on how this relationality is construed, and the key is to be found in the concept of *perichoresis*, which supplements that which can be obtained with the help of the *homoousion*. Where the latter stresses the utter reality of the presence of God in and to time and space, the former enables us to see that the whole God is given in the economy. *Perichoresis* refers to the mutual indwelling and coinherence of the persons of the Trinity, and 'serves to hold powerfully together . . . the identity of the divine Being and the intrinsic unity of the three divine Persons'. Interestingly and unusually – for the concept normally performs the function of showing how three distinct persons can yet constitute one God – Torrance moves from *perichoresis* to person and not the other way round, arguing that *by virtue of* the concept of *perichoresis* there developed a new concept of the person in which 'the relations between persons belong to what persons are'.[32]

[29] E.g., TF, pp. 91, 147.
[30] CDG, p. 121.
[31] CDG, p. 124.
[32] CDG, p. 102.

Because *perichoresis* characterizes the historical revelation of the one God, its meaning is derived primarily from the economy, rather than in reflection on the relation of the eternal persons. It is the reason that we can speak of God being personal in his eternal being, and here reference is made to the claim of Hilary of Poitiers that God is not solitary.[33]

For his construing of the meaning of one being in three persons, in general, Torrance prefers Gregory of Nazianzus to Basil of Caesarea and Gregory of Nyssa because of the apparent traces of Origenist subordinationism in the latter two Cappadocians. As is well known, Basil did not speak explicitly of the *homoousion* of the Spirit, either for tactical reasons deriving from the nature of the dispute in which he was involved or because he was still infected with the Origenist disease, as Torrance tends to suspect. He is therefore rather ambivalent about Basil's achievement, often crediting him with a crucial defence of the Spirit's divinity, while criticizing him for failing to make the final step to an explicit affirmation of the Spirit's *homoousion*. What does he then see to be so important in the later Gregory's position? Here a brief review of the use he makes of two theologians whose contributions are almost as important for him as Athanasius' – Gregory of Nazianzus and John Calvin – will profit our enquiry.

The achievement of Gregory of Nazianzus is, for Torrance, twofold. First, he rejected any element of Origenist ontological hierarchy in the being of God. He numbers Gregory among those who understand God and his work 'in the light of his undivided activity as Father, Son and Holy Spirit', and he cites in this context his saying, 'When I say God, I mean Father, Son and Holy Spirit.'[34] Second, Gregory had a more adequate conception of the person than Basil, rejecting as he did the latter's notion of the person as '*tropos hyparxeos* (mode of being or mode of existence)'.[35] The importance of this question is so great that we must pause to examine some of the ramifications. Two recent developments have brought it to the fore. First is critical discussion of Karl Barth's appeal to the *tropos hyparxeos* as

[33] TF p. 90.
[34] TF, p. 93.
[35] TF, p. 27.

expressing more adequately what the concept of the person once served to denote.[36] Second – and it is related – is the increasing literature on the concept of the person and the necessity of its redemption, rather than abandonment, if some of the deep problems of both Church and world are to be addressed. While Barth rejected the concept on the grounds of its irremediable individualism, in recent discussion it has been argued that used *of God* it provides a major weapon against the distortion of *our humanity* in modern anthropology. One of the emphases it enables theology to make is on the ontological compatibility of the one and the many in both instances. In the case of God, it means that to speak of the *koinonia* or communion in which the being of God consists provides a concept of divine oneness in which the individuality of the particular persons is also stressed, because Father, Son and Spirit in their interrelatedness make God to be the God that he is. This bears not only on our belief in God, but on the nature of what it is to be a created person, unique and particular yet bound up with the other in patterns of relational being and living.[37]

We can therefore agree with the rejection of the notion of the person *as tropos hyparxeos*. Theologically, it almost certainly fails to avoid at least the suspicion of modalism, even in Barth's most careful formulation. Therefore we must look with especial care at what Torrance makes of Gregory's, and indeed of Calvin's, formulation of the concept. Of Gregory he writes as follows:

> [T]he Persons are not just modes of existence but substantial relations subsisting intrinsically in the eternal Being of God . . . The term 'Father' . . . is not a name for being (*ousia*) but for *the relation that subsists* between the Father and the Son.[38]

And of Calvin's view that persons are subsistences in God's being, Torrance writes that they 'are to be understood as more than distinctive relations, for they really subsist . . . .'.[39]

---

[36] See, for example Alan J. Torrance, *Persons in Communion. Trinitarian Description and Human Participation* (Edinburgh: T&T Clark, 1996).

[37] See Christoph Schwoebel and Colin Gunton, eds, *Persons, Divine and Human. King's College Essays in Theological Anthropology* (Edinburgh: T&T Clark, 1992).

[38] TP, p. 27, emphasis added.

[39] TP, p. 28, cf. CDG p. 127.

Really subsist, we may ask, but as what? There are two problems with this development, first whether it is fair to accuse Basil of identifying the persons as modes of being; and second whether 'relation' is an adequate way of describing the person. In a passage cited by Torrance, Basil clearly attributes to the Spirit more particularity than that: 'the Spirit is living being [surely better translated "*a* living being"] from which his kinship with God becomes disclosed, while his ineffable mode of existence . . . is preserved'.[40] In that passage, the Spirit is neither a mode of existence nor a relation; rather, he is a person existing in a certain relation – *his* mode of being – with the Father. For Basil the persons are not relations; rather, persons are constituted by their relations to one another. It must therefore be asked whether it is not rather the case that the Cappadocians held not that the *tropoi* were persons, but that they referred to the way in which the persons were distinctly themselves, something in which Torrance himself shows little interest. Without a distinction between persons – as the ones who are each particularly what they are by virtue of their relations (*scheseis*) to one another – and the relations between them, the danger is that their particularity will be lost, as has been the case notoriously in the West with its excessive stress on the principle that the acts of God *ad extra* are undivided. It is significant that one of Torrance's few appeals to Augustine is in support of the notion that persons are relations, and that is surely a Western, not Eastern, way of putting it.[41]

What, then, is the relation between the being and the persons? That is to say, how are being and persons related in the doctrine of the immanent Trinity? Torrance here revises the Cappadocian teaching that *ousia* refers to the being of God in general, hypostasis to the particular persons who constitute God's being, and especially its 'recourse to the dangerous analogy of three different people having a common nature'.[42] I am sure that he is right about the latter, but let us look carefully at the way he himself states the relation:

In precise theological usage, *ousia* now refers to 'being' not

[40] TF, p. 218.
[41] TP, p. 29.
[42] CDG, p. 125.

simply as that which is but to what it is in respect of its internal reality, while *hypostasis* refers to 'being' not just in its independent subsistence but in its objective otherness. . . . [*H*]*ypostasis* denotes being in its 'outward reference'.[43]

An almost identical point is made in *Trinitarian Perspectives*: '*ousia* denotes being in its internal relations, while *hypostasis* denotes being in its inter-personal objective relations . . .'.[44] I am not sure quite what to make of these formulations. Do they perhaps run the risk of confusing the denotation of a term with its connotation? The obvious meaning of the distinction between the concepts is that which the Cappadocians teach: that *ousia* refers to God's being generally – to God's *oneness* – while hypostasis refers to the particular persons of which that being is constituted, his *threeness*. This is what Torrance in fact elsewhere says: 'the three divine Persons in their Communion *are* the Triune Being of God'.[45] The two terms are, accordingly, chiefly *denoting* terms, picking out different aspects of the one divine being. However, when it comes to connotation – to what the terms distinctly mean – should we differentiate between inner and outer in the way that Torrance does? He cannot intend the modalistic teaching that God is outwardly – in the persons – one thing, and inwardly, in his unified being another. But if not, what is the point of the distinction between inner and outer? Do not being and person both refer to God both outwardly – in the economy – and inwardly – in the immanent Trinity? Surely there is no relational being of God which is not that of the three persons in mutually constitutive *perichoresis*?

The particular persons and their relations

Torrance's fairly conventional treatment of the three persons of the Trinity follows the pattern that might be expected in the light of the developments so far. To the Father is attributed, according to the pattern of the creed, the act of creating, and therefore power. But, and here the *homoousion* again makes its presence felt, this is not mere or sheer power, but the power of

---

[43] CDG, p. 130. The latter expression is attributed to G. L. Prestige.
[44] TP, p. 131.
[45] CDG, p. 124.

God made known in what God actually does. 'The *homoousion* tells us that the sovereignty of the Father is identical with the sovereignty of the incarnate Son, and the sovereignty of the incarnate Son is identical with the sovereignty of God the Father.'[46] As we have seen, it follows from Athanasius' distinction between the being and will of God that while God is eternally Father, he is not eternally the creator, for creation is, as the first act of his sovereignty, the act of his freedom. The doctrine of God the Son is precisely correlative with this, and marks the place where Torrance's apophatic theology of language comes to clearest expression. The relation between eternal Father and eternal Son, being a spiritual relation, bursts the limits of the analogy which it represents. Patristic appeal to biblical language of light and radiance prevented 'any projection into God of the creaturely or corporeal ingredient in the terms "father", "son", "offspring" . . .' and yet 'also had the effect of making clear that as light is never without its radiance, so the Father is never without his Son or without his Word'.[47] The language remains rational and explicatory, but within the strict limits set by the nature of God's spiritual being.

Similarly, in line with what we have already seen, detailed discussion of the person of the Spirit is fairly brief, with Torrance concentrating on his function of ensuring that we conceptualize the truly spiritual nature of God. It is consistent with the drive of Torrance's thought to stress the way in which the being of the persons inheres in the being of the one God:

> [T]he Holy Spirit himself is to be thought of as the ever-living two-way Communion between the Father and the Son in which he is no less fully God than the Father and the Son. Through sharing equally in the one living Being of God, in an essentially *spiritual and onto-relational way*, the Father, Son and the Holy Spirit form and constitute together in their distinctive properties in relation to one another the natural Communion . . . and indivisible Unity of the Holy Trinity.[48]

Like Augustine, therefore, Torrance conceives the Spirit as the bond of love between the Father and the Son.

---

[46] CDG p. 205.
[47] TF, p. 121.
[48] CDG pp. 126–7.

What, then, does he make of what has some claim to be the crucial ecumenical crux, at least so far as relations between East and West are concerned? The *Filioque*, as is well known, was the occasion, some would say cause, of the breach between the Orthodox and Roman Churches. It was the occasion because of the West's one-sided political action of adding the offending clause to the creed. Torrance's main contribution, and it is a major one, is to seek to bring together the divided Churches by adopting a position which precedes and so relativizes their differences.[49] In Athanasius' teaching of the coinherence of the three persons is to be found the proof that the question should not have arisen in the way that it did. What we might call the *homoousial* revelation shows us the coinherence of all three persons in all that happens. It follows that they are also coinherent in being. 'Thus for Athanasius the procession of the Spirit from the Father is inextricably bound up with "the generation of the Son from the Father which exceeds and transcends the thoughts of men".'[50] In effect Torrance is saying that the solution is to be found in the doctrine that the procession, coming as it does from the being of the Father rather than from his person, involves the whole of the Godhead in such a way that a choice between the two positions should not be required.

Through Western Eyes?

All the questions which should be asked of this consistent, creative and important doctrine of God centre in some way on the relation between the one and the many. As always in these matters, a small emphasis in one area of theology affects all the other dimensions. As we have seen, there are some questions which can be asked about the interpretation of the Fathers, though anyone who ventures to engage with Professor Torrance's formidable learning must proceed with care. Accordingly, the following items will mainly take the form of a series of questions, and they all centre in some way on the query as to whether the immense stress on the *homoousion* does not

[49] It can, and below will, be argued that underlying the *Filioque* are questions of far more than ecumenical importance alone.
[50] TF, p. 235.

run the risk of flattening out the particularities, so that divine *being* tends to be stressed at the expense of the divine *persons*. Another way of putting it would be to ask whether the Eastern Fathers have been read rather too much through Western eyes. To be sure, this is to simplify overmuch what are highly complicated issues, as another glance at the historical provenance of this theology will make all too evident. One of the interesting features of Torrance's work has been his ecumenical work with the Eastern Orthodox. Despite what some may expect, Christians in the Reformed tradition are often able to engage with Orthodox theology in ways not so readily available to the Catholic tradition. The reason is that John Calvin, despite his heavy dependence upon Augustine, was also a careful reader of the Eastern, including the Cappadocian, Fathers, especially in matters trinitarian. What we find in Torrance is a reopening of a major historical conversation. My query is whether Torrance is still reading our common Fathers rather too much through Augustinian eyes, and I hope that the following questions will serve to clarify what is at stake at this important time in Christian history.

1. One key to Torrance's theology is a vision in some ways more patristic than biblical. Whether that be the case, it is remarkable how little exegesis of Scripture, as distinct from the Fathers, is to be found in the major treatments of trinitarian themes. It is also the case that – and in this our subject is scarcely different from other theologians – texts appealed to tend to be those supporting the tendency we have already noted, to bring the economic Trinity as close as possible to the immanent. Do the apparently subordinationist texts of 1 Corinthians 15 and some of those in the Fourth Gospel receive the attention they perhaps need if the subordinationist elements of the economic Trinity are to be adequately correlated with the necessarily and rightly egalitarian note in the treatment of the immanent Trinity? They at least appear to be counter evidence to the central thesis, and therefore require careful interrogation.

2. Can we not see in the reading of the Eastern Fathers the dominance of a rather Augustinian eye? We have seen that for Torrance the divine *monarchia* is that of the whole Trinity. The question we must ask of him is whether Athanasius supports his position as clearly as he is claimed to. He is too good a scholar

not to cite the crucial evidence, and the following piece is crucial. In it, God is identified by Athanasius as 'the all-holy Father of Christ beyond all created being'. This is then glossed to mean that:

> When Athanasius applied the term *ousia* to speak of the Being of God the Creator and of God the Father of Christ . . . it is 'being' understood in the light of the truth that the Son and the Spirit are each of one and the same being or *homoousios* with God the Father; or . . . that the fullness of the Father's Being is the Being of the Son and of the Spirit.[51]

Is there a subtle move here from the *homoousion* to something more than that? Does the final move, that 'the fullness of the Father's Being *is* the Being of the Son and the Spirit' (my emphasis) follow from what has gone before? May it not at least be asked whether both Athanasius and the Cappadocian Fathers express the particular being of the three persons of the Godhead rather more strongly than that?

3. The strength of the patristic concentration is revealed in the ecumenical importance of the theology. The Fathers are an authority which all branches of the Church have in common, despite the lamentable neglect of them in some places, and here Torrance's achievement is quite remarkable, able as he is to bring together theologians from a wide spectrum of background and confession. The question to be asked concerns his tendency to limit discussion too much to the realms of piety and churchmanship, the discussion of science excepted. And the point can be sharpened. The engagement with science, of immense importance as that is, is very much at the level of epistemology and ontology. When we come to more broadly human and social concerns, the trumpet gives a somewhat less certain sound. Do not let me be misunderstood: Torrance has written on ethical and social matters, with authority. But it seems to me that his armoury would have been stronger had other themes been treated in his work, and if, for example, there had been rather more engagement with the work of another important ecumenical figure, John Zizioulas, despite – or perhaps because of – their continuing differences

[51] CDG, p. 116.

over central matters of trinitarian construction (Zizioulas being more of the school of Basil than of Gregory of Nazianzus). Torrance shares with Zizioulas the judgement that the Fathers contributed centrally to the development of a new concept of the person.[52] Discussion of this, however, is for the most part rather limited, particularly with respect to what it might mean for human personhood. For it is there that our culture is in desperate need. I need not repeat here the often enough rehearsed contention: that modernity cannot do justice to the being of the human person because it has an impoverished theology.[53] Oscillating between collectivism and individualism – which represent ultimately one and the same failure – it calls desperately for an understanding of the person not as *a relation*, but as one who has his or her being *in relation to* others. This trinitarian and *ethical* insight flows from a theology of the Trinity in which both the one and the many are given due and equal weight. If Barth is right that all good dogmatics is also ethics, might we not expect this component of theology to be somewhat more strongly represented at this very place?

4. There is another place where discussion of things trinitarian is broken off where further development might have been of interest, and it is in a cognate realm. The solution of the problem of the *Filioque* is of far more than immanent churchly or ecumenical concern, and in two areas in particular. The first is the deep-seated weakness of the Western tradition on the doctrine of the Spirit. The reason is trinitarian. If the Spirit is conceived to proceed from the Son as well as from the Father, he easily comes to be treated as subordinate to the Son, and is therefore effectively reduced to the margins, as functionally appearing to do little more than apply Christ's work in the Church or to the individual believer. It is no accident that, in reaction to this impoverishment, outbreaks of Pentecostal and millenarian enthusiasm, which often over-emphasize the Spirit

---

[52] John D. Zizioulas, 'On Being a Person. Towards an Ontology of Personhood', Schwoebel and Gunton, eds, *Persons, Divine and Human*, pp. 33–46.

[53] Colin E. Gunton, *The One, the Three and the Many. God, Creation and the Culture of Modernity. The 1992 Bampton Lectures* (Cambridge: Cambridge University Press, 1993).

at the expense of the Son, have marked the history of Western Christianity from early times.

Corresponding to this weakness of our tradition, as its *alter ego*, so to speak, is a failure to do justice to the full humanity of the incarnate Son of God. Here, we must be careful to specify what exactly is the point of the question to our author. As always, there are resources in Torrance's work which are waiting to be developed. One of his papers which has long continued to work in my mind is that on 'The Mind of Christ in Worship. The Problem of Apollinarianism in the Liturgy'. The thesis of this magisterial paper is that the human Christ has effectively been written out of the liturgy of the Western Church. Here the theme is taken up of the human priesthood of the ascended Christ present in the worship of the Church.

> [S]ince he is God become man, who in becoming man was made Priest, it is humanity which is the sphere of his priesthood, and it is the fulfilment of his priestly ministry as man offering himself on our behalf which becomes the focus of our worship of the Father.[54]

This is christologically, and therefore trinitarianly, important, for the neglect of the Holy Spirit and the underplaying of the human life and ministry of Jesus, and especially its continuation in the ascension, are simply two sides of the same coin. Yet while the humanity of Christ is affirmed and used theologically in Torrance's work, it is surprising how little interest is shown in the *Christusbild*, the detailed Gospel presentations of the life, death, resurrection and ascension of Jesus. This is particularly marked in treatment of the eternal Sonship of Christ, but is muted even in the discussion of the incarnate Lord. This may, to be sure, be to ask too much, and it might be better to say that here is a question left over for later generations to develop in the light of issues that have recently become prominent.

The second ramification of the *Filioque* requiring consideration is the equally deep-seated failure of the Western tradition to avoid modalism of some kind or other. The problem of modalism in the context of the doctrine of the double

---

[54] T. F. Torrance, 'The Mind of Christ in Worship. The Problem of Apollinarianism in the Liturgy', in his *Theology in Reconciliation* (London: Geoffrey Chapman, 1975), pp. 139–214 (pp. 175–6).

procession is the problem of that which ultimately unifies the world and our experience. From the days of the Greeks onwards, the Western mind has sought the basis of experience and reality in the One, whether that one be the God of Israel and Jesus Christ, Heraclitean flux, the Parmenidean or Plotinian One, or the many variations on them that have appeared in philosophy and theology since. The perennial question, as Coleridge especially among modern thinkers has argued, is whether the unity of things be lodged in some impersonal principle – ultimately some monism or pantheism – or in the personal, triune God of Scripture. And the perennial temptation of the Western mind has been to seek for the unity of things in some deity or divine principle over and above the triune revelation. We have seen that Torrance's whole theological calling has been dominated by the establishment of the latter: that the only unity of things is to be found in the almighty triune creator, the one made known in his involvement in the created world in his Son and Word.

The problem of the dual procession is the related one of whether it subverts from within this personal and trinitarian integration of things. Now, I do not wish to adjudicate here on the dispute between, on the one hand, John Zizioulas' view that the only way of maintaining a truly personal basis for reality is by making the Father the source of all things, especially the source or *aitia* of the triune communion; and, on the other, Torrance's view that in some way or other we must understand the triune communion as a whole to be the metaphysical source of unity.[55] The problem rather is whether the double procession ineluctibly encourages the development of a modalist tendency in theological thought. The point is this. If the Father is the one from whom the Son is begotten – in the Spirit – and from whom the Spirit proceeds – indeed, through the Son – our enquiries come to an end. There is a final, if mysterious, explanation for the way things are. But suppose that the Spirit does come from the Father *and* the Son. Can we avoid at least toying with the question of the reality which gives the Father and the Son *their* underlying unity? In other words, a double procession is an invitation to seek a deeper cause than the Trinity, and thus a

---

[55] See the discussion by Alan Torrance, *Persons in Communion*, pp. 283–306.

modalism, even though it may not necessitate it, because while there remain two apparently ultimate principles, however unified in communion, discontented minds will seek that which underlies them. And surely there is a case for saying that some such temptation must explain why it is so difficult for Western minds not to tend to a modalism of some kind.[56] That is not to suggest that Torrance, any more than Barth, commits the heresy of modalism; it is rather that if its underlying causes are to be removed, more attention perhaps needs to be paid to the concrete ways in which the particular persons of the Trinity present themselves to our experience in the economy of creation and salvation.

Conclusion

In recent years, studies of the Trinity have appeared in ever-increasing, numbers, in some ways remarkably different from one another, but most of them responding to a real change in theological atmosphere. When I first entered the profession, the dominant names among Torrance's contemporaries and near contemporaries were for the most part critical, if not actively dismissive of the doctrine of the Trinity. One can recall, for instance, the considerable impact of a paper written by Maurice Wiles in 1957 doubting the biblical basis of the doctrine.[57] And far worse rationalist critiques of the orthodox

[56] This is not to suggest that the East does not have its own and entirely parallel problems, which also derive from a tendency to platonize the deity. We are very near to the problem, isolated in a celebrated paper by Dorothea Wendebourg, of the way in which the later development of Cappadocian trinitarianism fell away from its begetters' identification of the being of God with the persons. The problem is that the doctrine of the divine energies interposed in some way between the being and the persons of God, leading to what she has called 'The Defeat of Trinitarian Theology' (Dorothea Wendebourg, 'From the Cappadocian Fathers to Gregory Palamas. The Defeat of Trinitarian Theology', *Studia Patristica* 17.1 (1982), pp. 194–8). See TF, p. 72 for Torrance's version of this very point, or at least something similar, and his note 70 for references to his earlier treatment of the concept of the energies.

[57] Maurice Wiles, 'Some reflections on the Origins of the Doctrine of the Trinity', *Journal of Theological Studies* NS 7 (1957), pp. 92–106. Some of Wiles's points would hold against the particular formulations of Barth, but Torrance's more directly patristic development might be less liable to the critique.

tradition were, did we but know it, just over the horizon. To our subject must go much of the credit for refusing to succumb to the loss of confidence in mainstream Christian theology after the last war and for maintaining steadily and faithfully the vision of the classic doctrine of God. The interest in his work shows signs of increasing, and promises that the achievement will be a lasting one.

4

'And in one Lord Jesus Christ . . . Begotten not Made'[1]

The Perennial Problem: Arianism

Arianism was perhaps the twentieth century's favourite heresy, and is among the most appealing of them all. Teaching that Jesus Christ is in his being in some way less than fully divine, it appears to have support from Scripture. There have been numerous recent studies of Arius himself, and they include attempts to defend him, on various grounds.[2] I believe that they fail, but that does not affect the position I want to develop, which is to construe Arianism as a perennial type of approach to Christian doctrine, just as one can similarly construe Gnosticism, even if Irenaeus was wrong in detail about the particular teachings of his various opponents. Certain heresies are, so to speak, archetypal as attractive solutions to difficulties that are intrinsic to the faith, and will therefore continue to appear in every generation. Various symptoms of the particular disease with which we are concerned can be identified, the best known being found in the Arian slogan, 'there was when he was not': that the Son, the second person of the Trinity, has an origin which is in some way posterior to that of God the Father. The

---

[1] Previously published in *Pro Ecclesia* 10 (Summer 2001), pp. 261–74; and *Nicene Christianity. The Future for a New Ecumenism*, ed. Christopher R. Seitz (Carlisle: Paternoster Press, 2002), pp. 35–48.

[2] Maurice Wiles, 'In Defence of Arius', *Working Papers on Doctrine* (London: SCM Press, 1976), pp. 28–37; R. C. Gregg and D. Groh, *Early Arianism* (London: SCM Press, 1981); Rowan Williams, *Arius. Heresy and Tradition* (London: Darton, Longman & Todd, 1987).

ontological aspects – considerations to do with God's being – are theologically crucial, for corresponding to a reduction of the Son's eternity there is also one of his ontological status. In some marked respect he is less truly divine than God the Father. The error of this is that it detracts from his saving significance, for if he is not fully divine his capacity to be saviour from sin and death is called into question. Against Arianism was directed the doctrine of the eternal begottenness of the Son: that God the Son's being the Son of the Father was not a temporal process, as is the case with all instances of created fatherhood, but is eternal.

A reduction in Jesus Christ's saving significance is precisely what Arius' twentieth-century representatives desire, for implicit in much modernist critique of ancient theology is the supposition that we do not really require saving, because in some sense we are intrinsically able to save ourselves; because in some way we are already implicitly or potentially divine. That is why the fate of Christianity in the modern Western world depends upon a secure hold on the Nicene inheritance. Without it, just as ancient Christianity would have disappeared, had Arius conquered, into the mass of ancient religiosity, so today the Church would likewise become just one version of modern body, mind and spirit paganism – as some no doubt wish it to become. It is at this place that study of antiquity profits us, for it is precisely where modern thought contains a restoration of certain ancient philosophical assumptions that it is driven to Arianism.

I approach a discussion of the ancient evidence with the work of an influential Anglican theologian of an earlier generation. It is to Maurice Wiles's credit that, even if he comes to the wrong conclusion on its basis, his setting out of the early development is clear and scholarly.[3] All true scholarship is on the

---

[3] In point of fact, Wiles does reveal a crucial failure to note one piece of evidence. He offers evidence that the Cappadocians, like Augustine after them, failed to attribute any functional distinctions between the economic work of the three persons of the Trinity, but fails to give attention – to cite one example – to Basil, *On the Holy Spirit*, XV. 36 and 38. While affirming the unity of the one God, he says that we must also distinguish: 'the original cause of all things that are made, the Father; . . . the creative cause, the Son; . . . the perfecting cause, the Spirit'.

side of the angels, even if we ultimately conclude on its basis that something from the past has to be rejected. For the fact is, as Wiles has shown, that there were two aspects of the development of the doctrine of the eternal generation of the Son of God which, far from serving to undermine the heresy, were actually fraught with Arian threat. 'In the first place the original use of the concept of generation to describe the relation of the first two persons of the Trinity was not very closely linked to an understanding of them as Father and Son.' The tendency in the Apologists for the word 'Logos' to be preferred to 'Son' is a symptom of the first of our problems, for, although Wiles does not note this, it introduces a tendency to depersonalize the relationship, preferring, that is to say, rational to personal categories in expounding the relationship between the Father and the Son. If that is an oversimplification, a clearer view of the problem is given by the kind of appeal to Scripture that was used to support the Apologists' case. Proverbs 8.25, 'before all the mountains were settled in place, before the hills, I was given birth', was, as Wiles notes, 'of primary importance'.[4] Not only is this full of Arian possibilities – there manifestly was when wisdom was not – but its dominance also dangerously limits both the range and the type of the Old Testament evidence that can be called upon. This is a question to which we must return. Another aspect of the same set of problems raised by the Apologists is that the orientation of the discussion was to the eternal Trinity at the expense of the revealed or economic. Now, to be sure, our topic has to do with the eternal Trinity, with who the Father and Son are eternally, and what is their relation. But once the conception breaks free from the economy, from what happens in time, the dangers of abstraction present themselves in full force. And that takes us to the second set of problems raised by the early development and noted by Wiles.

For this, we move into a later century, to the contribution of Origen of Alexandria, who is much praised even by orthodox historians of dogma for his development of the doctrine of the eternal generation of the Son. The price that was paid, however, is this: Origen's primary defence of the doctrine lies in an a priori appeal to divine immutability, almost always a bad form

---

[4] Wiles, 'Eternal Generation', *Working Papers*, pp. 18–37 (p. 19).

of argument, rather like the 'he must have . . .' appeal so popular in modern biographers who wish to impose their own interpretation of their subjects, and particularly speculate about their sexuality, in the absence of evidence. In like manner, Origen is not really interested in the evidence of the relation between the Father and the Son as it is revealed in the biblical narrative, but in what 'must be' the case. In the crucial section of his *De Principiis* he defines 'the only-begotten Son of God' as 'God's wisdom hypostatically existing'.[5] He continues: 'And can anyone who has learned to regard God with feelings of reverence suppose or believe that God the Father ever existed . . . without begetting this wisdom?'[6] As Wiles shows, however, this kind of argument offered assistance to Arians in the respect that it failed to guarantee the uniqueness of the Son, only establishing his eternity. Origen's other a priori appeal, to God's omnipotence, led him to suppose that not only the Logos but also the creation – or an aspect of it – was eternal.[7] Notice by contrast the emphatic language of the creed, which might have been developed to counter it: 'in *one* Lord Jesus Christ'.

This consideration raises for us another question to which we must give attention: the nature of the language we are using. To say that Jesus Christ is begotten is to use a metaphor, for clearly, whatever else is the case with his being begotten in time in the womb of Mary, he is not there *eternally* begotten. To say that God the Father is the negation of this – that he is unbegotten – is to contrast the ways of being of the Father and the Son, their τροπος ὑπαρχεως. It is to specify an inner-trinitarian difference, and remains metaphorical in the respect that its use is transferred from the finite to the infinite realm. It was, however, the further and also metaphorical use of the term 'unbegotten' that muddied the waters. G. L. Prestige – to whose scholarship Wiles makes appeal – points out that Clement of Alexandria and Origen use the word originally meaning 'unbegotten' (ἀγεννετως) 'in the sense of "absolute", implying eternity,

---

[5] The problems of this are immediately apparent. Origen continues: 'I do not think that our mind must stray beyond this to the suspicion that this hypostasis or substance could possibly possess bodily characteristics . . .'

[6] Origen, *On First Principles*, tr. and ed. G. W. Butterworth (London: 1936, new edn Peter Smith Publishers, 1985), 1.2.2.

[7] Wiles, 'Eternal Generation', pp. 24–5.

causation, and transcendence of finite limitations'.[8] He is, however, far too optimistic in supposing that the development represents a gain both in precision and theologically. For to use 'unbegotten' to characterize the relation of creator and creation confuses two concepts which, as Athanasius well knew, must be distinguished in this context. One pairing, unbegotten–begotten, is best used, as we have seen, to conceive the relation between the Father and the Son; while the other, uncreated–created, that between God and the world. If the two are confused, we shall be faced with confusions of the kind we observed to arise in the case of Origen's development. Our credal expression – begotten not made – makes it clear that the Father–Son relation must be understood in the framework of the first pairing, unbegotten–begotten. This is because we are here concerned with the relation between eternal persons, whereas the latter pairing is concerned with the relation between eternal creator and the creation which is not eternal. To use 'unbegotten' of the creator rather than of God the Father runs the risk of confusing the issue.

Why is this so? We saw that Arianism raises two related problems. The first is that God the Son is in some way less eternal than God the Father; the second that he is also in some way less fully divine. It is possible to affirm, as we have seen, that the Son is eternally begotten, and still to deny that he is unique. It can happen when the first of the two pairings we have met is confused with the second. Against that, we have to say, first, that the Son is eternally begotten: which is to say that he is not only the product of the Father's eternal love but also in some way defines that love. To ask who God is is to receive the answer, he is the one who is the love of Father and Son in the Spirit – though for now we must leave on one side the third person of the Trinity. On the other hand, second, to ask what the creation is is to invite, Christianly, a significantly different answer. The creation, like the Son, is the product of God's eternal love; but it does not form part of that love's definition. To be God, this God cannot but be both Father and Son (at least); he does not similarly have to be creator. It is to ensure, in a way that Origen did not, that the Son belongs necessarily to our understanding of the being

[8] G. L. Prestige, *God in Patristic Thought* (London: SPCK, 1952), p. 51.

of God that our concept is needed. To see how this is to be understood we must return to some of the questions so perceptively raised but wrongly answered by Professor Wiles.

The Biblical Centre

First we must ask the question of what kind of justification for our credal confession is given by, or can be sought from, Scripture. It is apparent to anyone reading Athanasius' diatribes against the Arians that at stake is not which texts from Scripture are used but the way in which they are used. Between Arians and Athanasians lies a matter of theological hermeneutics, of what is made of Scripture. The lesson for our purposes is that proof-texting is not enough, and it must be acknowledged that there is some doubt as to whether Scripture supports the credal confession directly or without great labour. We have seen already that appeal to Proverbs 8 is highly dangerous, because whatever wisdom is in that place, it is not co-eternal with God. The same may even be said – though admittedly far more questionably – of appeal to the prologue of John's Gospel. There is some dispute about the meaning of μωνωγενες in John 1.18, and whether it supports the kind of absolute identification of Jesus with the eternal Son of God which the creed affirms. It seems to me fairly obvious that it does, and that it clearly connotes something special, even unique. As one commentator argues, it is related to the word ἀγαπετως used of Jesus at crucial times of his ministry, specifically his baptism and transfiguration.[9] But that suggests, at the very least, that we must go beyond any single proof-text or texts and examine the broader context in which it must be understood, that of Scripture as a whole.

The function of the crucial episodes of baptism and transfiguration in the Gospels is clear. At baptism, Jesus' sonship is affirmed by the Father through the Spirit. During his ministry, this affirmation is tested, first through temptations and trials of various kinds and then specifically at Caesarea Philippi in the further temptation, mediated to Jesus through Peter, not to go

---

[9] G. R. Beasley-Murray, *John. Word Biblical Commentary* (Nashville: Nelson, 2nd edn, 1999), p. 14.

through with the specific responsibilities of sonship which have
been imposed on him by his Father. Peter, like the devil in the
wilderness, suggests that Jesus can be Son other than through
the way of sacrifice. The reiterated ἀγαπετως at the transfiguration confirms and reinforces the original designation. Jesus'
decision to go unarmed into the realm of the enemy is ratified
by his Father. Similarly, at the death of Jesus – the fulfilment of
his earthly calling – as it is described in Mark's Gospel, the
words of the centurion place further confirmation on the lips
of a Gentile. But the words in the Greek remain ambiguous, as
are John's if we really wish to be sceptical. 'Surely this man was
– a – Son of God'? (Mark 15.39). Even here, therefore, the texts
do not of themselves provide the uniqueness that we need, so
that we must proceed to examine something more of the
character of the sonship that is presented in these and other
passages.

One key to this phase of the enquiry is to be found in the fact
that a crucial deficiency of Origen's defence of the eternal
begottenness of the Son is its lack of appeal to Jesus, in whom he
is not really very interested.[10] Indeed, we have to confess that
many of the Fathers do not concern themselves overmuch with
the fact that he is a Jew indicated by his name, the roots of
whose meaning are to be found only in the Old Testament. It is
as faithful Israel that Jesus works out his sonship in a recapitulation of Israel's story, beginning, as we have seen, with a new
wilderness temptation, a new testing in which this time a faithful
sonship is realized, raising a cry of affirmation even from the
lips of the Gentile observing the end of the ordeal. This son is
faithful and obedient, learning obedience in what he suffers as
a man. We may not construe our credal confession of his eternal
sonship apart from this. Yet, on the other hand, neither may we
understand him simply as a man, for his sonship is not so
limited. To develop the wider dimensions, we must return to

---

[10] Here, as in other places, he sails far too close to the wind of Gnosticism.
'This abstraction [the Gnostics'] from Jesus to the Christ, and then back again
to ourselves, is a movement which has been repeated over and over again in
subsequent theological speculation and sermonizing. It is the second and
more important reason why gnosticism is to be identified as the archetypal
heresy.' Douglas Farrow, 'St Irenaeus of Lyons. The Church and the World',
Pro Ecclesia 4 (1995), pp. 333–55 (p. 337).

Israel. Robert Jenson has recently reminded us of the centrality of Israel's sonship in the Old Testament:

> We see the way in which the narrative identification of God by his involvement with Israel displays a mutuality of *personae* whose differentiating relations are between God and Israel *and* somehow between God and God . . . God is identified *with* Israel in that he is identified *as* a participant *in* Israel's story with him.
>
> Having seen these structures, we may then also note that prophets could explicitly evoke the Lord's relation to Israel as a relation of father to son, although their use of this language is rare . . .[11]

What we learn from this is something of the interaction of the eternal and the temporal already with Israel. Everything that takes place here is, indeed, the work of the eternal God, but because it is not achieved apart from Israel, neither can the being of Israel's God be construed without it. But there is a complication.

Israel may be the son of God, but she is not so eternally in the way that our creed affirms of Jesus,[12] so that we have to end this appeal to Scripture by saying something of what here is new, also. We return to John 1.18, where 'no one has ever seen God' almost certainly contains a reference to God's words to Moses in Exodus 33.20: 'you cannot see my face, for no one may see me and live'. With this Israelite, things are decisively different. The μονογενες Son of God ἐχεγεσετω, exegeted, the Father: set him forth in time. That is surely part of the burden of the Fourth Gospel as a whole: that those who see Jesus, and are later educated into his story by the Holy Spirit, *have seen* the Father. 'In many and various ways God spoke to us through the prophets, but in these last days' – and observe the eschatological note which is so often absent from the later patristic treatments, though not from Irenaeus – 'he has spoken to us through his

---

[11] Robert W. Jenson, *Systematic Theology*, vol. 1, *The Triune God* (New York and Oxford: Oxford University Press, 1997), pp. 76–7. The language may be rare, but it comes in significant places, for example Exodus 4.22: 'tell Pharaoh . . .: Israel is my first-born son'; and compare Hosea 11.1.

[12] As Jenson also sees, describing Israel as the people created by God's word. Jenson, *Systematic Theology*, vol. 1, p. 68.

Son', writes its author to the Hebrews. And this is a son to fulfil, indeed, but also to exceed anything seen or spoken by the prophets: 'whom he appointed heir to everything, and through whom he made the universe' (Heb. 1.1–2). Paul had earlier engaged in a similar, and surely related, contrast of Jesus and Moses, speaking as he does of 'the light of the knowledge of the glory of God in the face of Christ' (2 Cor. 4.6).

The burden of all this is that we must extend our notion of Jesus' sonship to include more engagement with the relation between Jesus and his Father as it is worked out in the time of his ministry. Jesus is not only obedient Israel, but the eternal Son of God become, in Luther's words, the proper man. The relation between Jesus and the Father who affirms his sonship is also a relation between God and God, and this taking place of God in time is to be found in the verbs which describe what happened. Central are those which indicate sending and sacrifice: that God the Father sends and gives up his Son for the sins of the world (Gal. 4.4; Rom. 8.32). Perhaps most suggestive here is the placing in parallel, in Philippians 2, of the divine sending and the obedience of the second Adam. The one who was in the form of God both emptied himself to human estate and was obedient to death on the cross. The verbs express both a divine and a human obedience, whose meanings are inseparable. But theologically that is the source of problems as much as of solution, and that takes us to the second set of questions raised by Wiles's analysis. If the eternal Son is only given in and with time, by what right do we abstract or project to eternity and speak of one who is eternally begotten? And what is the meaning of the metaphor in which the relation of Father and Son is expressed?

From Economy to Theology

Scripture, to recapitulate, gives us, across a broad range of its witness, the foundation for our credal confession. But it does not yet give us the fullness of the Nicene affirmation. All the texts we have adduced can be read in an Arian sense if we are determined enough, as some of our contemporaries appear to be. God may be in the verbs, because it is in and by them that time and eternity are given together, but the verbs remain temporal, lodged in time, and it does not of itself follow that from them we can read off an eternal begottenness. We have a foundation, but need to build upon it theologically if we are to move from economy to theology. A similar point can be made by saying that much of the language we have encountered could be given a subordinationist interpretation, that is, one which continues to hold that Jesus, even as Son, is subordinate in being to God the Father, and so in some way less truly God than he.[13] We must here concede that there is a sense in which the Son is indeed subordinate to the Father. As we have seen, he is Son as he is sent, given, obedient; as he is, in a certain respect, though certainly not in others, passive.[14] It is in his suffering that his effective action lies. Two questions have to be pursued. First, could he not have done all the things attributed to him while remaining less than fully divine? Second, do we need to move thus from the economy to theology, from time to eternity? Much recent trinitarian writing has argued that we do not really need a doctrine of the immanent Trinity.[15] Do we, likewise, need a doctrine of the eternal begottenness of the Son?

The first question has been answered definitively by Athanasius, and the shape of his answer will enable us to answer the second also. Much of his argument in *Against the Arians* tends, to be sure, to be rather a priori and to appeal too much to proof texts. But its achievement is in showing beyond all peradventure that Jesus could not have done all the things attributed to him had he been less than fully divine. Underlying everything is, it seems to me, an assurance based not on a priori questions about what Jesus could have done, but on what he did in fact do. Athanasius has a deep sense of human sinfulness and the fallenness of the whole creation, and this derives from his prior conviction that what has in fact happened can only be the work of one who is fully God. It is here that the theology of *On the Incarnation of the Word* is in many ways more helpful to our case

---

[13] In Origen's terms, as god rather than *the* God.

[14] Indeed, such a concession goes some way to obviating those tendencies, especially strong in Western theology, that render the three persons of the Trinity functionally identical.

[15] For recent unsatisfactory attempts, Catholic and Protestant respectively, to minimize or abolish the doctrine of the immanent Trinity, see Catherine Mowry LaCugna, *God for Us. The Trinity and Christian Life* (New York, Harper-Collins, 1991) and Ted Peters, *God as Trinity. Relationality and Temporality in Divine Life*, Louisville: Westminster/John Knox Press, 1993).

than the polemics of the later work. Athanasius believes that Jesus Christ is the mediator of creation, returning to his creation to restore the created order to its maker and so enable it to fulfil its original purpose. In turn, that founds his belief in the eternal divinity of the Son, and accordingly his later defence of the doctrine of eternal begottenness. The real basis of our credal confession is to be found in what God has in fact achieved through the life, death and resurrection of his Son, the one through whom he created and upholds the world.

For Athanasius,

> transgression of the commandment was turning them [human beings] back to their natural state, so that just as they have had their being out of nothing, so also, as might be expected, they might look for corruption into nothing in the course of time.[16]

The return to nothingness which was the natural result of sin could be prevented only by an act of grace of the original creator:

> Now, if there were merely a misdemeanour in question, and not a consequent corruption, repentance were well enough. But if, when transgression had once gained a start, men became involved in that corruption which was their nature . . . what further step was needed? or what was required for such grace and such recall, but the Word of God, which had also at the beginning made everything out of nought?[17]

The chief reason for the move from economy to theology, from what happened to an account of the being of the eternal God whose economy it is, is Athanasius' conviction, which was that of Irenaeus also, that the Son of God is mediator not only of redemption but of creation also. Perhaps here, at the risk of complicating matters, I should pause to say something about Athanasius' awareness of a matter which has been with us from the beginning: the metaphorical nature of the language which is being used. '[T]he divine generation must not be compared

---

[16] Athanasius, *On the Incarnation of the Word*, 4, ed. E. R. Hardy, *Christology of the Later Fathers*, Library of Christian Classics vol. 3 (London: SCM Press, 1954), p. 59.

[17] Athanasius, *On the Incarnation* 7, *Christology*, pp. 61–2.

to the nature of men, nor the Son considered to be part of God . . .'[18] This is part and parcel of his recognition that it is one thing to be creator, another to be creature. His firm hold on the distinction enables him, as is well known, to distinguish also between God's being and his will, what God is and what he does freely in relation to that which is not himself. There is a case for saying that the very distinction between creator and creation became possible only because of Christology, and, indeed, the very Christology which was sketched in the previous section. Because the action of the man Jesus is also so unselfconsciously identified in Scripture as also the action of God, it carries in itself connotations of God's freedom over against the world. It was such an interpretation of Scripture that gave Irenaeus his cutting edge and authority against the Gnostics who were gnostic because they confused the creature with the creator. This is our safeguard against Arianism, also. In making the Son of God a hybrid, something between the creator and the created, Arians offend against the absolute rule, that it is one thing to be God, another to be a creature. That paradox is here twofold: first that by putting this man, and this man alone, on the side of the creator we maintain the integrity of the creation; and we can do it while remaining true to a confession of his full humanity.

How can this be? The key must be found in the words of the confession we are considering: Jesus Christ, not Logos or even Son, but Jesus of Nazareth who is also the Christ of God, the one Lord. What claim are we making? Essentially, that all of God's action, whether in creation or in the redirection of that creation gone astray, is achieved by Jesus Christ. As we have seen, there is a tendency in the tradition to play down the 'Jesus' part of the action, but we cannot do that if we are to be true to the biblical places we have visited. The only-begotten Son is also the lamb who takes away the sin of the world. The one who is the object of the worship of heaven in Revelation is the lamb bearing the marks of slaughter upon him. It is not a Logos with no relation to Jesus whom we confess but 'One Lord Jesus Christ . . .

---

[18] Athanasius, *Against the Arians*, 1.28; ET in *Nicene and Post-Nicene Fathers of the Church* II, eds P. Schaff and H. Wace (Edinburgh: T&T Clark; Grand Rapids: Eerdmans, 1991).

Begotten not Made'. Jesus of Nazareth, the one who was begotten in time, *is* also and at the same time the one who is eternally begotten. But what is the meaning of that 'at the same time'? Here is the place at which our categories simply fail to encompass the mystery, for we have to say two things which appear to be contradictory: that he is Son quite apart from and in advance of being Jesus of Nazareth – for Jesus of Nazareth has a begetting in time – and yet he is not Son apart from being Jesus.

Irenaeus puts this as well as it can be put:

> [God's] only-begotten Word, who is always present with the human race, united to and mingled with His own creation, according to the Father's pleasure, and who became flesh, is Himself Jesus Christ our Lord, who did also suffer for us, and arose again on our behalf, and who will come again in the glory of His Father, to raise up all flesh . . .[19]

Notice that there is an identity statement – 'God's only-begotten Word . . . *is* Jesus Christ' – alongside one of historical action – 'united to and mingled with His own creation'. Everything depends on how we hold the two in tension. Here we face a twin peril. On the one hand, as we have seen, we play down the human Jesus' part in all this; on the other, we project this Jesus into eternity, and make no distinction at all between time and eternity, leaving ourselves once again only the economy.

Something on the Point of It All

Why do we need thus to stretch our categories to breaking point? The reason is that if we are to speak truly of the God we confess, we must make Jesus Christ in some way intrinsic to his being, and that requires insisting that he is eternally begotten. This involves holding to the traditional practice of understanding the persons of the Trinity in terms of their relations of

---

[19] Irenaeus, *Against the Heresies*, 3.16.6. This ought surely to dispel all the nonsense that Irenaeus' is only an economic trinitarianism, and that the 'evil' of ontology came in only with Nicene theology. Irenaeus of Lyons, *Against the Heresies*, ET in *The Anti-Nicene Fathers*, eds A. Roberts and J. Donaldson (Grand Rapids: Eerdmans; Edinburgh: T&T Clark, 1989), vol. 1.

origin, of where they, so to speak, come from within the being
of the triune Godhead.[20] Wolfhart Pannenberg is perhaps the
more interesting of recent theologians to have questioned
the theological adequacy of the practice.

> When scripture bears witness to the active relations of the
> Son and Spirit to the Father, it is not good enough to treat
> these as not constitutive for their identity and in this respect
> to look only at the relations of begetting and proceeding (or
> breathing), viewing solely the relations of origin, which lead
> from the Father to the Son and Spirit, as applicable to the
> constitution of the persons.[21]

While agreeing with the first half of that contention – that we
have to take into account the biblical characterization of the
actions of the persons – I wish to deny the second. It seems to
me that in general the Fathers were right to concentrate their
account of the biblical relations in the so-called relations of
origin. For the purposes of referring to the distinctive τροποι
ὑπαρχεως of the persons of the immanent Trinity they
serve very well. Indeed, to introduce the economic actions into
a definition of the eternal being of the persons is to muddy the
water by confusing – as distinct from distinguishing – the relation of the economic and immanent Trinities. The following
theses are designed to demonstrate the point:

1. The purpose of developing a notion of the eternal Son of
God is that it enables us to speak of one who is God in a different way from God the Father. The point is often enough made,
especially in recent theology, that too great a stress on the indis-
tinguishability of the actions of God *ad extra* leads to the effective redundancy of the doctrine of the Trinity. The solution to
that problem is not to be found in post-Rahnerian programmes
to collapse the immanent Trinity into the economic, but rather
to show in what ways the Father, Son and Spirit are to be distinguished in the mode of their actions in the world. The distinguishing mark of the Son's action in the world is that he is
sent by, given by and obeys the Father even at the cost of his life,

---

[20] This discussion assumes an essentially Eastern approach, in contrast to the
Western tendency to conceive the persons in terms of relations of opposition.

[21] Wolfhart Pannenberg, *Systematic Theology*, vol. 1, tr. G. W. Bromiley
(Edinburgh: T&T Clark, 1991) p. 320.

not heteronomously, as being *merely* commanded, but as realizing his obedience in the freedom of the Spirit who maintains
him in truth, by which must be understood maintaining him in
right relation to his Father.

2. The point of the notion of Jesus Christ's eternal begottenness is that it enables us to characterize the kind of relationship
that subsists between the two persons we have so far considered.
It also enables us to do justice to the undoubtedly subordinationist elements of the biblical record which we have noticed:
the Son is sent, is given, obeys and, indeed, expresses his eternal
sonship in temporal or economic subordination. His eternal
sonship is the other side of this agency. Pannenberg is right,[22] it
seems to me, in seeking to retain the distinctive subjecthood of
the Son; but wrong in basing it in his self-distinction from the
Father. That attributes to the Son an autonomous initiative that
he simply does not have. His proper human autonomy derives
rather from the freedom, given by the Spirit to be the kind of
subordinate Son that he is. It is this which justifies the Fathers in
limiting their descriptions of the inner trinitarian relation to
relations of origin in the way that they do. To say that the Son is
eternally begotten is to point to a particular kind of personal
relation, which is like that between a created father and son but
must be construed only on the basis of what happened in the
conception, birth, ministry, death, resurrection and ascension,
all realized in and by the Spirit of God, of the actual man Jesus
of Nazareth.

3. All this means that we cannot do justice to the notion of
eternal begottenness without some attention to the doctrine of
the Spirit also. One of the many good reasons for rejecting the
doctrine of the *Filioque* is that in the economy, the Son is also
the gift of the Spirit, who is the one by whose agency the Father
begets Jesus in time, empowers his ministry and raises him from
the dead. To speak of the Spirit's work also in terms of self-
distinction, as Pannenberg does,[23] gives the Trinity a tri-theistic
air, for the Spirit is only himself as one of the two hands of the
Father, his eschatological power and energy, albeit a distinctive

[22] Pannenberg, *Systematic Theology*, vol. 1, p. 319 n. 183, recording his
disagreement with Robert W. Jenson.
[23] Pannenberg, *Systematic Theology*, vol. 1, p. 315.

concrete particular, a person.[24] We should beware of mere projection, but can at least ask whether it is right to suggest that, because the Spirit is the agent of the begetting of Jesus in the womb of Mary, he is also the agent of his eternal begottenness. The Son is the kind of eternal Son that he is by virtue of the way in which he is related to the Father by the Spirit in the eternal triune love. In view of the fact that there is nothing that is not at once and in different ways the act of the whole Trinity, something like it needs to be said. It might be rather near to Augustine's doctrine of the Spirit as the bond of love, but I hope that it says more than that, particularly about the Spirit's being the focus of God's movement outwards. The Trinity locked up in itself, to use Rahner's characterization of much post-Augustinian trinitarianism, by conceiving the Spirit as the closure of an inwards-turning circle, militates against a link between the Spirit's being in eternity and his action in the world.[25] In the gospel stories, accordingly, we must conceive the Spirit as the one who indeed maintains the Son in truth as his being the particular human being that he is: the only one who, after the Fall, is enabled to be in true relation to God the Father and so truly human.

4. We thus achieve a trinitarian *perichoresis*. The Father who begets and the Son who is begotten are together one God in the κοινωνια of the Spirit. They are one because the Son and the Spirit are, in a sense, though as God, subordinate in the eternal ταχις as they are in the economy. But in another sense they are not subordinate, for without his Son and Spirit, God would not be God. So Athanasius: 'for, whereas the Father always is, so what is proper to his essence must always be; and this is his Word and His Wisdom'.[26] It follows that the distinctive personhood of each – their being each what they are and not someone else – derives first from the constituting action of the Father, but also from the responsive action of the Son and the particularizing action of the Spirit. Accordingly, in both the mutuality and

[24] I owe the latter point to Shirley Martin to whom I am grateful for a number of comments on this paper that have assisted in its preparation for publication.

[25] '[A] Trinity which is absolutely locked within itself – one which is not, in its reality open to anything distinct from it . . .' Karl Rahner, *The Trinity*, tr. Joseph Donceel (London: Burns & Oates, 1970), p. 18.

[26] Athanasius, *Against the Arians*, 1. 29.

reciprocity but also the distinctive particularity of the three persons consists the eternal love of the one God. In other words, it is thus possible to maintain an Eastern – and scriptural – sense of the monarchy of the Father without succumbing to an ontological hierarchy which renders the Son and the Spirit as less than fully divine.

Why, finally, do we bother with all this? Both because it is true and because our salvation hangs upon it. The second part of the answer is second because it is secondary, because if the credal confession is not true, we are still in our sins, and the assumption of Christian theology is that we are not: not that we do not sin, but that because of Christ our sins no longer define who and what we are. And so a final word about truth. I have said once or twice that in saying that Jesus Christ is begotten we are using a metaphor. In popular parlance – and we must remember that the word metaphor is often used metaphorically these days, to refer to things other than linguistic change – to say that something is metaphorical is to say that it cannot really be true. The truth, however, is quite the opposite. Just as for Kierkegaard nothing important, nothing, that is, that concerns our relation to eternity, can be said without paradox, so it is also with metaphor. Nothing truly interesting can be said, and certainly nothing interesting about the relation between God and the world, without some kind of metaphor. And that takes us back to the place where we began. It is the Arians who are the literalists, who will not allow language to be stretched to speak of eternity. Polanus, the late sixteenth-century Calvinist, put it thus: 'what the Fathers say, that the Father begat the Son of His essence, is to be taken metaphorically, because he did not do so outside of his essence . . . as the Arians once used to say'.[27] Because he, the Word become flesh, *is* the truth, it follows that created things, and that includes our words, can also be true; and that is one reason why we must continue to work at our theology.

[27] Heinrich Heppe, *Reformed Dogmatics, Set out and Illustrated from the Sources,* tr. G. T. Thomson (Grand Rapids: Baker, 1950), p. 122.

5

The Holy Spirit who with the Father and the Son together is Worshipped and Glorified[1]

Divine Being and Action

The God of biblical faith is a God of particular action. Israel, Jesus and the Church are at once typical of the way God works in the world, and more than merely typical, for they determine our understanding of how his acts take place. It is also the case that the creeds were formed in a particular historical development, though in this case the development is more ambiguous. It is possible to read the development of the creeds in a suspicious way, especially when you remember some of the political contexts, with the Council of Nicaea assembled for the peace of the Roman empire as well as – some would say more than – for the well-being of the Church. But for the most part it is perhaps as Barth liked to remark, *hominum confusione, dei providentia*: by human confusion and divine providence. The creeds emerge out of a particular story of worship and life, of thought and dispute. They develop out of the struggles of the Church to be itself, and to communicate its gospel in the world of which it was a part. Only by beginning there can we begin to learn how we should be the Church in the strangely similar world of which we are a part. (Of course, everybody says how different and unique the modern world is, and that is true also. I shall return to that point at the end.)

The emergence of the affirmation, '. . . the Holy Spirit who with the Father and the Son is worshipped and glorified' was by

---

[1] Previously published in *Fire and Wind. The Holy Spirit in the Church Today*, ed. Joseph D. Small (Louisville: Geneva Press, 2002), pp. 21–36.

75

no means a straightforward matter. From one point of view, there seems to be very little difficulty, if we listen to Scripture, of concluding that the Spirit of God is divine. All the things the Spirit does are things done by God: he breathes over the waters of creation, inspires the prophets and the Church, raises Jesus from the dead and is poured out on the Church at Pentecost, in anticipation of the very end of all things. It is worth noting that according to one difficult saying of Jesus, sin against the Spirit – the Spirit of truth – is the only unforgivable sin (Matt. 12.31). We might say – and I want to stress this point – that very often for Scripture the Spirit is God being eschatological. For the New Testament especially, wherever the Spirit is, there the conditions of the last times are anticipated: in the Church being led into all truth, in the anticipation of the communion of the last days, in all kinds of ways in which the end is promised and anticipated – above all, of course, in the resurrection of Jesus. The Spirit is the one, as the Eastern Orthodox tradition likes to stress, who raised Jesus from the dead, in fulfilment of the promise inherent in Ezekiel 37.1–14. This eschatological note can also be illustrated from Romans 8 and from Paul's description of the Spirit as the 'down payment' – a monetary image speaking of the first instalment and guarantee of final redemption (2 Cor. 1.22, 5.5; Eph. 1.14). But perhaps the most interesting and extended illustration is to be taken from the book of Revelation. 'I, John . . . was on the island of Patmos because of the word of God and the testimony of Jesus. On the Lord's day I was in the Spirit . . .' (Rev. 1.9–10). Being in the Spirit means, perhaps most obviously but also dangerously, being in an inspired state – dangerously, because we are always in danger of mistaking the Spirit of God for a force or an experience of some kind.[2] But I think that John means much more than that. It is the significant, for it refers to worship, and it is through sharing mysteriously in the worship of his separated fellow-Christians that John is enabled also to share the worship of heaven and the

---

[2] The suppositions that this book is reference to the Lord's day that is both a consummate literary product which draws on a long tradition of language and imagery and the product of some kind of ecstatic experience are by no means in conflict with one another. The processes of deep learning and inspiration involved are wonderfully illustrated by J. Livingston Lowes, *The Road to Xanadu* (Boston and New York: Houghton Mifflin, 1927).

vision of what is both happening now and is going to happen at
the end. The Holy Spirit reveals to the seer at once the present
and the future as it shapes the present, but only as a function of
the communion of the Church in which he is enabled to share.

In that light, it seems far easier to see the Spirit as divine than
it is to see the man, Jesus of Nazareth, as such. A man is, for
Scripture in general, fairly obviously not divine, and that is why
to confess Jesus, the crucified teacher and prophet, as Lord and
God (John 20.28), is on the face of it far more difficult than to
understand the Holy Spirit to be divine. Indeed, it has been
suggested that perhaps the one attempted definition of God in
the New Testament is that 'God is Spirit' (though whether 'God
is love' is also a kind of definition and how it coheres with this is
an interesting question).[3] And yet what might appear to be
obvious was not, for the most part, historically the case. It was
'for the most part' because the second-century theologian,
Irenaeus, to whom we shall return, described both the Son and
the Spirit as the 'two hands of God', God himself in action, and
clearly believed in the eternal divinity of the Spirit.[4] But
Irenaeus was untroubled by considerations that troubled others –
that is his unique genius – and after him it came to seem to
some far from obvious that the Spirit was equal in rank with the
Father and Son. It was not until after the full divinity of the Son
of God had been established with much agony and argument
that a similar process of discernment was applied to the Spirit.

Here, we need to distinguish two aspects of the problem. The
first concerns the being of God. Is the Spirit a distinct person
within God's being? The difficulty here lay in the fact that the
world in which all this was hammered out tended to think in

---

[3] '. . . the Bible's closest approach to a definition of the divine nature, that
"God is Spirit". Robert W. Jenson, *Systematic Theology*, vol. 1, *The Triune God*
(New York and Oxford: Oxford University Press, 1997), p. 146. That, of course,
is what Hegel also thought, and might be queried in the light of another near
definition, if it is, from earlier in that same chapter, that God is love, 1 John
4.16.

[4] 'Now what has been made is a different thing from him who makes it. The
breath, then, is temporal, but the Spirit is eternal.' Irenaeus, *Against the Heresies*,
5. 12. 2. This is particularly important in view of the still repeated canard that
Irenaeus was only an 'economic' trinitarian. ET in *The Ante-Nicene Fathers*, eds
A. Roberts and J. Donaldson (Grand Rapids: Eerdmans; Edinburgh: T&T
Clark, 1989), vol. 1.

hierarchies, in layers, so that it was almost impossible for theologians – and here we must exercise historical imagination – not
to suppose that God the Father is fully divine, the Son rather
less so and the Spirit even lower. The shape of the problem as it
developed can be seen in the work of Origen of Alexandria in
the third century. For Origen, God the Son was a second God,
derivatively divine, we might say, and the Spirit was the highest
of the creatures, sent by God to sanctify the believer.[5] We must
beware of dismissing this too easily. The point about these theological problems is that because they concern the being of God,
there is no simple solution. The complexity is apparent if we
again refer to the scriptural characterization of God. It is almost
a commonplace of New Testament scholarship that when the
New Testament speaks of God, *simpliciter*, it usually can be taken
to be referring to God the Father. Similarly, there are respects
in which Jesus and the Spirit are subordinate to the Father. In
John's Gospel, for example, Jesus subordinates himself to the
Father: he is sent to do the Father's work, to obey his will in
Gethsemane and later to ask the Father to send 'another com-
forter' the Spirit. Similarly in 1 Corinthians 15, the point of
Jesus' ministry and reign at the Father's right hand is, at the
end, to hand all things over to God the Father, so that God may
be all in all. What is technically called 'subordinationism', the
teaching that the Son and the Spirit are in some way less divine
than God the Father, *seems* to have some support in Scripture, so
that from one point of view it is not obvious that some form of
subordinationism is wrong. It seems a very satisfactory way to
guarantee God's unity, something essential to the faith, for
there is but one God and one gospel.

   There is, however, a second side to the question – as always in
theology! – and a brief outline of that will take us to the very
heart of the matter. Christianity is what it is because it is a
gospel, and that gospel implies, requires, that God act in and
toward his world. And the problem is this. If we attribute particular actions in the world to the Son and the Holy Spirit, as

---

[5] For evidence that this may not necessarily be the case with Origen, see
David Rainey, 'The Argument for the Deity of the Holy Spirit according to St
Basil the Great, Bishop of Caesarea', M.Th. thesis, Vancouver School of
Theology, 1991, pp. 11–13, especially to *On First Principles*, 1.3.7.

when the book of Acts says things like, 'It seemed good to the Holy Spirit and to us', is that effectively to divide up the action of God? Can we really say that the Father does some things, the Son others and the Spirit yet others?[6] This problem comes to a head in some of the creeds, for example the Apostles' Creed: 'I believe in God the Father, the maker of heaven and earth . . . and in His only Son, who was incarnate . . .' This raises the question of what is called modalism: that Father, Son and Spirit are different modes of the one being of God. And the problem with that is that it suggests that the real God is an unknown something lying behind the three agents but not really like any of them.

As in all theology, we are on a knife edge, or, we might say, a narrow path with precipices on each side. On one side, we deny the unity of God, and make it appear that there are three gods; on the other, we cause the distinctions of the three to disappear into some underlying undifferentiated deity.[7] On the whole, our Western tradition has tended to the latter, so to stress the unity of God's action that it becomes difficult to do justice to its diversity. This is partly responsible for some prominent features of church life over the centuries. First, we have not known what to make of the Spirit's action, and tended to depersonalize it, speaking rather of 'grace' as a sort of fluid poured into the person (that is the 'Catholic' tendency); or (the Protestant side) we have identified the Spirit's action with warm feelings, subjective inspirations and the like – a sort of religious fix. Second, we have notoriously neglected the work of the Spirit in our life and thinking, and that is why there have been outbreaks of Pentecostal church life and belief which serve as a just reproach to the one-sidedness of the Western tradition.

We therefore need as clear as possible an understanding of both aspects of our theology of the Spirit: of the Spirit's part in a unified conception of God's action and of the distinctive character of his action. For the first, I do not think that we can do better than hold to Irenaeus' straightforward characterization

---

[6] We speak, for example, of the Holy Spirit 'indwelling' believers, but what sense does it make unless we relate this action to that of the Father and the Son?

[7] Which we can, as a result, call with equal validity mother and daughter, in contradiction of Scripture, than which we then presume to know better.

of God's action in the world: the Father works, as we have already heard, by means of his two hands, the Son and the Spirit. That is not as inappropriate to the 'spiritual' nature of God as may appear. When you use your hands, to greet someone or to write a letter, it is you who are doing it. 'God's right arm has gained the victory . . .' That is not mere metaphor, but a metaphor that conveys a great and important Christian truth. Our God's action is not immediate but mediated action. Immediate action would overwhelm and depersonalize, if not worse; recall the story of Moses wishing to see God's glory (Exod. 33.19–23). The incarnation provides our chief model of mediation. God's actions in Christ are sovereign and achieve their end, but they respect our createdness and personhood. But the incarnation happens through the Spirit, too, and in that respect God's actions in the Spirit serve to bring about those things God purposes in Christ. In sum: all divine action, whether in creation, salvation or final redemption is the action of God the Father; but it is all equally brought about by his two hands, the Son and the Spirit. And these hands do not act separately, like someone holding a baby in one hand and trying to bang in a nail with the other – though I fear that our talk of the Spirit might sometimes suggest that. The Spirit works through the Son, paradigmatically as Jesus' ministry was empowered by the Spirit. All is the unified action of the one God, the one God of Old Testament confession, mediated in this twofold way.

How, then, do we achieve our second aim, of doing justice to the distinctions, the differences, between the persons? Let me approach that by outlining a further complication. It is not in every way a bad thing that we do not speak much about the Spirit. It is sometimes said that the Spirit is the self-effacing person of the Trinity. Think especially of John's Gospel, where the Spirit is sent to witness, to draw human beings to Jesus, and through him to God the Father. That 'self-effacingness' is even, though in a different way, the case with Jesus in that Gospel, who is sent to do the Father's work. Compare also the apparently offensive saying recorded by Mark, and altered in other accounts: 'Why do you call me good? There is none good – except God alone' (Mark 10.18). Jesus indeed effaces himself so that he may point us to his Father, but he does not efface himself in the same way as the Spirit does. The Spirit's characteristic action is self-effacing, because the Spirit is the one who enables people and things to be themselves through Jesus Christ. We are called to proclaim Jesus Christ, not, or at least not in the same way, to proclaim the Spirit – and that is perhaps where some Pentecostalist emphases are wrong. The Spirit is the one who enables us to present Jesus Christ in our teaching and to live in his way, so that there is a sense in which it is truer to say that we speak *from* than *about* the Spirit. And yet we do need to know from whom we are speaking. If the Spirit is a person, then we need to identify, to mark out the being, of the kind of person with whom we have to do.

We have, then, but begun our differentiation of the three persons of the Trinity, and need to be more specific. If we are to identify a person, to say something about specific character-istics, something more general needs to be said. And that is something Irenaeus did not really do, tending simply to place the two hands side by side. To go the next stage, let us consider observations about the Spirit by two later theologians, and first Basil of Caesarea, who speaks of: 'the original cause of all things that are made, the Father; . . . the creative cause, the Son; . . . the perfecting cause, the Spirit'.[8] John Calvin is remarkably similar: 'to the Father is attributed the beginning of activity, and the fountain and well-spring of all things; to the Son, wisdom, counsel and the ordered disposition of all things; but to the Spirit is assigned the power and efficacy of that activity'.[9] It is Basil who makes, I think, the most important point. To say that the Spirit is the perfecting cause of creation is to make the Spirit the eschatological person of the Trinity: the one who directs the creatures to where the creator wishes them to go, to their destiny as creatures. Where the Spirit is, there do the creatures become that which God creates them to be. (In our case, it means our freedom: 'where the Spirit of the Lord is, there is liberty', 2 Cor. 3.17.) That, we must remember, happens only

---

[8] Basil of Caesarea, *On the Holy Spirit*, XV.36 and 38.

[9] John Calvin, *Institutes of the Christian Religion*, ed. J. T. McNeill, tr. and index F. L. Battles (Philadelphia: Westminster Press, 1960), Library of Christian Classics 20 and 21, I. xiii. 18. Cf. John Owen, *Of Communion with God the Father, Son and Holy Ghost, each Person Distinctly, in Love, Grace and consolation; or The Saints' Fellowship with the Father, Son, and Holy Ghost Unfolded*, Works vol. 2, p. 16: 'the Father doeth it by the way of *original authority*; the Son by the way of communi-cating from a *purchased treasury*; the Holy Spirit by the way of *immediate efficacy*'.

through Jesus Christ, so that we are distinguishing, not separating what the three persons do. But the allusion to Basil takes us back towards the track that is the main one for this chapter: can we say, and in what sense, that 'the Holy Spirit . . . with the Father and the Son together is worshipped and glorified'?

The Problem in Historical Context

It has already been noted that after Origen there was always in the Church a temptation to rank the three persons of the Trinity on a descending scale. This was done, let me repeat, for the best of reasons: to maintain the unity of God and to do justice to the fact that the Son and the Spirit are in certain respects subordinate to the Father. After all, the Son obeys and the Spirit is sent, subordinate functions in that they are ordered by the Father to certain forms of action. In our modern obsession with equality, we tend to think that subordination is a bad thing, but that is wrong. It is only as humble that Jesus is divine, as Barth never tired of pointing out, only as the Church serves her Lord that she is truly the Church. The temptation then as now was to assume that this must be wrong, and to conclude that because the Spirit is sent by the Father, he cannot be as divine as he. About a century after Origen, Athanasius of Alexandria wrote a series of letters in defence of the divinity of the Holy Spirit. His opponents were known as the Tropici, because they argued that when we speak of the Spirit as divine, we are using only a figure of speech. It is merely, they argued, honorific, as when one Hollywood actress tells another that her performance was divine. (At least, it did when language like that was modish.)[10]

The Tropici, like so many of the protagonists in this struggle, were resolute defenders of the unity of God. The trouble was that they defended an abstract and unbiblical conception of divine unity. The Bible's God is rich and various in his personal being, and it was this that Athanasius was concerned to defend. Just as it was often argued that God the Son was fully divine

[10] The arguments of this group bear a remarkable similarity to some proponents of today's 'metaphorical theology', arguing as they do on the basis of a unity of God underlying the apparent plurality that one can in effect project on to deity such attributes as appear to suit the needs of the day.

because he brought salvation – and only God could do that – so it was argued by Athanasius that only God can make holy, so that if the Spirit makes holy, the Spirit must be God. (Calvin makes a similar point about the Spirit's work in creation: 'in transfusing into all things his energy, and breathing into them essence, life, and movement, he is indeed plainly divine'.[11]) This led Athanasius to attempt to do justice to the two things we have been exploring, the unity and the diversity of God's action. In his earlier arguments against the Arians he had already tried an explanation, rather different from the one Basil was to use, but complementing it: 'one God, the Father, existing by himself according as He is above all' (what we call 'transcendent') 'and appearing in the Son according as he pervades all things' (immanent) 'and in the Spirit according as in Him He acts in all things through the Word'.[12] Stressing, on the other side, the unified activity of God, he says that the Spirit is the energy of the Son, 'as realising and giving actuality to the power of God'.[13] As Theodore Campbell says, there is here both equality and subordination.[14] Because the Spirit is God in action, he is equally divine; but because he is sent by the Father, he is only such *as subordinate.*

Basil faced a similar problem, and it took the form of a challenge to the very expression I am addressing: 'who with the Father and the Son together is worshipped and glorified'. He was criticized for the apparently contrary forms of benediction that he was using in worship. One, more characteristic of the worship of the early Church, said: 'Glory to the Father, through the Son and in the Holy Spirit.' That implies the account I have been recommending: as God's action in the world is mediated through the Son and Spirit, so is our response in worship and life. In worship, we are brought to the Father by the Spirit through the Son. The other form, however, went rather differently: 'Glory to the Father with the Son together with the Holy Spirit.' It raised objections, because it seemed to imply an absolute equality of the three persons, something which, as we have

[11] John Calvin, *Institutes* I. xiii.14.

[12] Athanasius, *Against the Arians*, 3.15.

[13] Theodore Campbell, 'The Doctrine of the Holy Spirit in the Theology of Athanasius', *Scottish Journal of Theology* 27 (1974), pp. 408–40 (p. 427).

[14] Campbell, 'The Doctrine of the Holy Spirit', p. 429.

seen, parts of the tradition found very hard to accept. One can put the theological problem quite simply: we are enabled to worship by the Spirit; can we also be said to worship the Spirit, the one through whom we worship? Basil's opponents, this time with a different name, the Pneumatomachi – the 'Spirit fighters' – put forward similar arguments to those of the Tropici, concentrating on the argument that the Spirit is nowhere explicitly called divine in Scripture.[15]

Basil's great treatise on the Spirit was designed to contend that we can, nevertheless, so describe the Spirit. His argument is the classical one: from the Spirit's activities. If God is given through the Spirit, then God is what you get. He argues: the Spirit can be blasphemed; according to the Old Testament he fills the universe, and can yet be present in particular places; he intercedes, is described as Lord and remission of sins is granted through him.

> He is called Spirit, as God is Spirit . . . He is called holy, as the Father is holy and the Son is holy . . . not as being sanctified, but as sanctifying. He is called good, as the Father is good and He who was begotten of the Good is good . . . He is called Paraclete, like the Only begotten, as He Himself says, 'I will ask the Father and He will give you another comforter.'[16]

Is it right to use both of Basil's doxologies? Why not? In so far as the Son and the Spirit share the Father's divinity, they are equally to be given that which only God should receive, at least receive absolutely: worship and honour and glory. But in so far as they are his two hands, we recognize also that they are at the same time the mediators to us of God the Father's being and action. In a certain respect, we can draw a parallel with our understanding of the doctrine of Christ. Inasmuch as Christ is both God and man, he is at once our Lord and the one who shares our condition so that we might come before God forgiven and renewed: both one of us and the one who is the object of our praise and worship. The reason why we can similarly do both in the case of the Spirit is given by the great

---

[15] This was something of a commonplace. In his fifth Theological Oration, Gregory of Nazianzus also acknowledges that the deity of the Spirit is not clearly and explicitly taught in Scripture.

[16] Basil, *On the Holy Spirit* XIX, 48.

Puritan theologian of the Holy Spirit, John Owen. 'The *divine nature* is the reason and cause of all worship; so that it is impossible to *worship any one* person, and not worship the *whole* Trinity.'[17] You cannot have one without the other two, and therefore they are worshipped together. There is, according to Owen, a distinction of persons according to their *operations* – what we can call their originating and mediating activity – but not as to their being objects of worship. 'So that when by the distinct dispensation of the Trinity, and every person, we are led to worship . . . any person, we do herein worship the whole Trinity; and every person, by what name soever, of Father, Son or Holy Ghost, we invoke him.'[18]

When we come now to ask what is the point of it all, we shall pursue the two aspects of our topic that we have met, the being and action of God, one by one.

The Point of It All?

God's Being

The strength of Basil's argument that we worship God the Spirit with the Father and the Son is this: if the Son and the Spirit are as truly God as God the Father, then all three together are worshipped and glorified. In one respect, that is all the Church is for: to praise the one who made us and has rescued us from the domain of darkness into his glorious light. The Christian life is first of all one of thanks and praise to God simply for what he eternally is, just as at our best we love our fellow human beings simply for what they are. That is in no way inconsistent or apart from saying that our worship also makes much difference in how we live our lives on earth. We need to know that it is one thing to be God, quite another to be a creature: to know what the distinction is, because that determines where are our priorities, those things we hang our lives on. And for our purposes the crucial factor is that there are no intermediates between God and the world: nothing created that we should

[17] Recall the word 'together' in our credal formula.
[18] Owen, *Of Communion* pp. 268–9. I owe this reference to Kelly Kapic.

half worship, or treat as a privileged way to God. We worship the triune God, and no other.

Here, the function of the doctrine of the Spirit is to show that God is complete in himself, as the particular kind of God we worship: the perfecting cause in respect of God's eternal being as well as of his creation. First, there is an eternal communion of love that we call the triune God. The Spirit perfects the divine communion by being the dynamic of the Father's and Son's being who they distinctly are. God's being is, therefore, perfect in itself, but, second, is at the same time of such a kind that its very character provides the basis of God's movement out into the world to create, to redeem, and to perfect. God is no lonely monad or self-absorbed tyrant, but one whose orientation to the other is intrinsic to his eternal being as God. God's work 'outwards' is an expression of what he is eternally. The Spirit, we might say, is the motor of that divine movement outwards, just as the Son is its focus and model (*eikôn*). Augustine called the Spirit the bond of love between the Father and the Son, but this is in danger of leading us to think of God as a kind of self-enclosed circle. The medieval, Richard of St Victor, provided the basis of a correction by making it possible to suggest that the Spirit is the focus of a love beyond the duality of Father and Son, of a love outwards to the other.[19] The Spirit's distinctive inner-trinitarian being is oriented not on inwardness, but on otherness: as perfecter both of the eternal divine communion – in which there is real distinction, *otherness* – and of God's love for the *other* in creation and redemption.

It is this God, as Father, Son and Spirit, whom Christians worship, and we worship a God who is as such distinguished from every other principle of lordship or object of worship. That is the point of Basil's second doxology, 'Glory to the Father with the Son together with the Holy Spirit.' But we worship in a world which has numerous other objects and focuses to which to attribute absolute value. There are a number of candidates for divine status in our world, and that is where it is peculiarly like the ancient world in which Basil and his

---

[19] Richard of St Victor, *On the Trinity* III, 19–20; *Richard de Saint-Victor: De Trinitate* (Paris: Librarie Philosophique J. Vein, 1958), ET Richard of St Victor, *On the Trinity*, Book 1, tr. Jonathan Conser (1999).

colleagues did their theology: in the words of Paul, 'there are gods many and lords many' (1 Cor. 8.5). Our age has two in particular, the self and the earth: the god within and the god in nature (in the end, they come to the same thing). But there is no god within; only a mess. The self is our problem, not our solution. There is likewise no god in the earth, except the one that having given us life, can offer us only death, not the resurrection of the dead.[20]

In sum, to ask what the doctrine of the third person of the Trinity achieved, in its development in Basil and the other Cappadocians, is to enquire your way to the completed doctrine of the Trinity – complete at least in its confirming of the absolute distinction, begun in Irenaeus two centuries before, between the creator on the one hand and that of the creation on the other. To say that there is an absolute difference in being between God and the world is to say: look out, up even, not in or down, if you want to know the real source of our being and meaning. To look into the self or the earth is to put your trust in that which cannot save. The doctrine of the Trinity is the Church's resource against idolatry, against worshipping anything other than the one who by the eternal Spirit raised Jesus from the dead.

God's Action

But if you ask, how this is to take shape in worship and life, then you need Basil's other doxology: through the Son and in the Spirit. There is no God within, but there is the Son who comes alongside us in mercy and judgement. There is no God in the earth, but there is the Spirit who comes, through that same Son, to transform our personal being into that which it was created for, a living sacrifice of praise and thanks to God the Father. The Pauline blessing speaks of the communion of the Holy Spirit, and I think we can take this to mean the communion with God that the Holy Spirit gives (2 Cor. 13.14). John Owen again: 'And

[20] We are today too much inclined to put our faith in politics also. Just after the present British government was elected, someone at a conference in Australia opined that there seemed to be new hope for Britain: 'Tony Blair'. My reply was instant, sceptical and biblical: 'Put not your trust in princes . . .' (Ps. 146.3).

truly for sinners to have fellowship with God, the infinitely holy God, is an astonishing dispensation.'[21] That is what all are offered through the Spirit now, in the present. Perhaps the great expression of this in Scripture is Eph. 2.18: 'For through [Christ] we both' – Jew and Gentile – 'have access to the Father in the one Spirit.' Listen also to 1 John 1.3: 'our fellowship – *koinonia* – is with the Father and with his Son, Jesus Christ'.

In one sense, that communion is an end in itself, just as the life of the triune God is quite complete without there being a world. Yet just as the Spirit, as we have seen, is the focus of God's creation and love of the other, so the distinctive personal action of the Spirit is to prevent us from being content with that communion, but to share it with the world. The mission of the Spirit, his sending by the Father through the Son, is to create communion in the Church, and in so doing to prevent the Church from remaining content with its own fellowship. Speaking of the Fourth Gospel's teaching on this topic, Francis Watson writes:

> The movement of the Spirit towards Jesus' followers includes them within the scope of Jesus' relation to his Father, thereby gathering them together in *koinonia* with one another. But it also has the effect of directing them outwards, turning them towards the world. The comfort that the Spirit brings is not the comfort of communal self-absorption, for it is the role of the Spirit to bear witness to Jesus in the world, and to enable Jesus' followers to do likewise (15.26–7, 16.7–11).[22]

Conclusion

For Basil, as we have seen, the chief work of the Spirit consists in making the Church holy: hence the 'Holy Spirit', whose action is, in the New Testament, often concentrated on the Church. That is something we need to relearn today, and it takes us back near to where I began, with the fact that the final, eschatological,

---

[21] Owen, *Of Communion*, p. 7.

[22] Francis Watson, 'Trinity and Community: a Reading of John 17', *International Journal of Systemic Theology* 1/2 (1999), pp. 167–83 (p. 182). In a recent article it was argued that Britain would now be a gentler place if churches had built up their communities rather than spending their energies trying to persuade Mrs Thatcher to change her policies. Iain Murray, 'Faith Healing' in *The Spectator*, 9 October 1999, pp. 22–4.

book of the New Testament, becomes possible through the work of the Spirit on the Lord's day. Worship, communion, the fellowship of the last days, all these are the gifts of God the Spirit as he relates his chosen people to God the Father through the one who became man and died for us. If nothing else comes out of this essay, I hope it will be a conviction that we need to recover again a sense of the Church as the holy people of God, called first and last to praise his – threefold – name in all the ways that it can be done: formal worship, holy living and the proclamation of the gospel in all the world. We shall not perform that mission unless we learn again what it is for the Church to be God's distinctive and holy people in a world that for the most part seeks and worships gods and lords other than the one triune God of Scripture. One of the things that recent reappropriation of our Jewish heritage is teaching us also is the importance of Torah, of God's dispensation for those who are chosen to be his holy people on earth – the people who are different because he is different. Holiness is the gift of the Spirit, and, as Calvin knew so well, the Spirit works in part through the law that God has given to be a guide to our life on earth, through the routines of worship and behaviour that we learn among the people of God. The Fathers were not all that far out in concentrating on the Spirit as the one who sanctifies.

Yet there is also a weakness in the ancient account, located in its perhaps too restricted concern with sanctification. It is now fashionable to extend the Spirit's action to the created world as a whole, especially in view of our ecological worries. Although, as I have suggested, there are in that dangers of idolatry, so that we must be cautious, yet there are positive points to be made.

First, let us return to Basil: the Spirit is the one who perfects all God's creating action, and that is why Calvin, for example, is quite happy to attribute all right human action in the arts and politics to the action of the Spirit.[23] Wherever there is truth and

---

[23] Calvin, *Institutes* 2.2.12–17. It is also noteworthy that Basil at times platonizes the Spirit, takes him out of the realm of the material creation. ' "Holy Spirit" is a name peculiarly appropriate to everything that is incorporeal, purely immaterial, and indivisible' (IX. 22) – like raising Jesus from the dead? we might enquire. 'Now the Spirit is not brought into intimate association with the soul by local approximation. How indeed could there be a corporeal approach to the incorporeal?' Irenaeus would, I think, conceive otherwise, as did Owen. See the final words of the passage cited in note 8 above.

right is done, there is indeed the perfecting Spirit. But, second, perfection is, after the fall, or however we wish to characterize the sway of sin, death and the devil,[24] achieved only through the incarnation, life, death and resurrection of the Son of God. Perfection comes only by salvation, and that means that things become what they are only by being brought back into right relation with God through Jesus Christ. The Spirit is the one who restores through Christ the direction of things to their proper end. And the call of the Church, her mission, is to remind the world that, as the priests of nature, human beings are called to enable the world to be itself – which means to praise the one who made it. In that service, and in the gift of God the Spirit alone, is all true art and science, political and natural alike.

Finally, a brief return to the point made at the beginning about our distinctive modern situation. In many ways our world is very like that of the early Church: pluralistic, hedonistic, moving perhaps towards the death of a civilization. The way in which it is different is that, as Robert Jenson has pointed out, this is the first culture to have rejected the gospel after once having, apparently, accepted it. That makes our mission all the more complex and difficult. How do you communicate the gospel in a world which is effectively inoculated against it? How do we, like the early Church, outthink and outlive the decadent civilization around us? A large part of the answer lies in the one whose being and action we have been exploring, so that it seems to me both right and necessary that we should pray: 'Come, Holy Spirit', come and lead us into the truth that is Jesus Christ, the only Son of the Father, full of grace and truth.

---

[24] See here Carl Braaten and Robert Jenson, eds, *Sin, Death and the Devil* (Grand Rapids: Eerdmans, 1999).

PART 2

Triune Divine Action

6

Creation: (1) Creation and Mediation in the Theology of Robert W. Jenson. An Encounter and a Convergence[1]

Mediation

'The first proposition [of a doctrine of creation]: that God creates means that there is other reality than God and that it is really other than he.'[2] That lapidary statement of one of the fundamentals of the Christian faith introduces our question, for if God and the world are ontologically other, some account of their relation – some theology of *mediation* – is indispensable.[3] Specifically, the notion is necessary because Christian theology is devoted to the articulation of a gospel involving divine action in and towards the world. It could be said that mediation broadly conceived has been crucial for Robert Jenson's theology from the very beginning, for he has always brought into contrast two ways in which the gospel has been conceived to be mediated. The matter can be put culturally, from the point of view of his self-understanding as a consciously American theologian. What is America's theological weakness today? It is that,

---

[1] Previously published in *Trinity, Time and Church. A Response to the Theology of Robert W. Jenson*, ed. Colin E. Gunton (Grand Rapids: Eerdmans, 2000), pp. 80–93.

[2] Robert W. Jenson, *Systematic Theology*, vol. 1, *The Triune God*; vol. 2, *The Works of God* (New York and Oxford: Oxford University Press, 1997, 1999), vol. 2, p. 5. (Later references in this chapter to the work will appear in parentheses as *ST* 1 or 2, followed by the page reference.)

[3] From such a generalization, indeed, further generalizations follow: that the differences between the so-called theistic religions and, and indeed, the differences within the varieties of Christian theology, consist at least in part, of differences of mediation.

having rejected a robust view of the divine ordering of history –
as, for example, it is represented in Jonathan Edwards' pre-
destinarian theology of providence – it has opted instead for
what Jenson calls 'religion', by which is meant a form of mediation opposed to that given in the gospel.[4] In that it is an
attempt to escape, 'outwards' from time into a timeless eternity
it denies the affirmation of created time made real in the
incarnation of the Word. In this form, religion is a concept
appropriated from the early Barth and employed in a searching
diagnosis of the American condition. 'Religion' is America's
fate and problem, the stumbling block before its acceptance of
the gospel and has its basis in the Greek contribution to the
complicated fabric of Western thought. It is the attempt of the
soul to transcend its temporal framework to a timeless realm
above and beyond.

The beginnings of Jenson's theological authorship – about
the time when I had the privilege of being set by him on the
route at once of postgraduate research and Barth scholarship –
were developed in engagement with Barth, and especially with
his understanding of mediation as it emerged in his various
treatments of the relation of eternal God and temporal world.
Barth's christological and trinitarian conception of mediation
generates an affirmation of created reality in contradiction of
Hellenism's tendency to that reality's implicit relativization by
timeless eternity.[5] Yet both of Jenson's books devoted to Barth's
theology uncover tendencies in him which work against the
project. Christologically, there is a danger that Jesus Christ will
become less a concrete historical reality than a timeless platonic
form,[6] trinitarianly, divine timelessness threatens to subvert the
doctrine of divine eternity as representing the affirmation of
created time.[7] The problem is that the shape of a doctrine of

---

[4] Robert W. Jenson, *America's Theologian. A Recommendation of Jonathan Edwards* (New York and Oxford: Oxford University Press, 1988).

[5] What is the student, as yet unacquainted with Robert Jenson, to expect from an entry in the 1967 Oxford University lecture list entitled, 'The Trinity as an Anti-Religious Doctrine'? Not what turned out to be the case!

[6] Robert W. Jenson, *Alpha and Omega. A Study in the Theology of Karl Barth* (New York: Thomas Nelson, 1963).

[7] Robert W. Jenson, *God After God. The God of the Past and the God of the Future, Seen in the Work of Karl Barth* (Indianapolis and New York: Bobbs Merrill, 1969).

God's eternity may threaten the very media of revelation from which Barth's starting point was derived. In that respect, if not in others, Barth is classically Augustinian, and something that can only be mentioned here is that Jenson is one of the several seminal theologians of our time who has pointed to the importance of the Cappadocian Fathers as sources for the reappropriation of trinitarian insights that the West had for the most part neglected.[8]

That a concern for the true being of the creation in relation to God has been a continuing interest is indicated by the fact that it reappears in more recent writings also, for example in connection with Jenson's query to Edwards' theology of creation. '[T]o say that "God himself, in the immediate exercise of his power" is the creatures' sole support and coherence, were we to take the proposition without trinitarian differentiation, would surely threaten the distinct reality of creation' (*ST* 2, p. 41). The reason is that an authentically Christian theology must make two affirmations which so easily slip into contradiction of one another: that, first, God is the sole creator, and indeed, sole lord of what happens within that creation's history subsequent to its creation; and that, second, as creator and redeemer he is at the same time the one who gives to that creation its proper *Selbständigkeit* or relative independence, a subsistence which it receives from its relation to God. That is apparently to want to have one's cake and eat it. Are the two claims incompatible? It is one reason for the modern world's rejection of the gospel that it has come to the conclusion that this is indeed the case. To affirm the world, and especially to establish the freedom of the human agent within that world, it has been thought necessary to deny God. That is almost an axiom of modern atheism, and indeed of much that affects to be a Christian response to it. Yet the fall into Arminianism which characterizes both American culture and much of the Church's response to the apparent dilemma is for Jenson to take precisely the wrong route out of the morass. Effectively, it is atheism, for it denies divine lordship, and therefore the reality of the Bible's God.

---

[8] Robert W. Jenson, *The Triune Identity. God According to the Gospel* (Philadelphia: Fortress Press, 1982).

Christology

As has already been suggested, Jenson's approach to the situation is firmly trinitarian, and his is a trinitarianism predicated on the claim, developed from Barth, that in Jesus Christ we meet God, and that Jesus is the only eternal Son that there is. This is not, as some have taken it to be, a denial of an eternal or 'immanent' Trinity. Indeed, the fact that some commentators accuse him of denying that reality,[9] others of conceding too much to traditional doctrines of divine eternity,[10] is indication of the fact that here we encounter a more careful revision of the tradition than meets some eyes. The crucial focus is christological: that there is to be no positing of a 'logos asarkos', a kind of double of the incarnate Christ who provides a route back into timeless eternity – a God behind God, in some way undetermined by the triune shape he takes in history. 'What in eternity precedes the Son's birth to Mary is not an unincarnate *state* of the Son, but a pattern of movement within the event of the Incarnation, the movement to Incarnation, as itself a pattern of God's triune life' (*ST* 1, p. 141).

What has caused the most widespread dissent from this position is its essentially Lutheran character, which is in an interesting way parallel to the later Bonhoeffer's movement beyond the Christology of his teacher. It is no accident that the sharpest disagreement has come from commentators aligned to a more Reformed conception, whose tradition of the so-called 'Calvinist extra' – which seems to me in essence also Athanasius' position[11] – necessarily drives them to a stronger affirmation of, if not a logos asarkos, at least a sharper distinction between the states of being of the eternal Son and the incarnate Lord. That I share in the dissent – as Jenson has himself commented, confessional disagreements continue to mark the way in which the problems take form for all of us – will I hope make possible some clarification of what is at stake. What is agreed between us

---

[9] Ellen T. Charry *By the Renewing of your Minds. The Pastoral Function of Christian Doctrine* (New York and Oxford: Oxford University Press, 1997), pp. 124f.

[10] Ted Peters, *God as Trinity. Relationality and Temporality in Divine Life* (Louisville: Westminster/John Knox Press, 1993), pp. 144f.

[11] Athanasius, *On the Incarnation of the Word*, 17, ed. E. R. Hardy, *Christology of the Later Fathers*, Library of Christian Classics vol.3 (London: SCM Press, 1954).

is that a trinitarian mediation of creation is indispensable to a Christian systematic theology. What is not is the form that the christological centre should take. Let us then review Jenson's Christology as it appears in his recent *Systematic Theology*.

Immediately apparent is that this takes a more monophysite than dyophysite interpretation of Chalcedon, after the tradition of Luther himself. Indeed, Jenson would have wished that 'from two natures' had been preferred by the Council to 'in two natures' (*ST* 1, pp. 131–2). The reason is that the substance of the new relation to God achieved by the incarnation can be conveyed only by stressing the one hypostasis in a way precluded by the typical usage of later Western Christology with its dangerously dualistic separation of the 'natures'. Jenson's sympathy with certain Eastern trends is clear:

> Cyril's followers who remained within the imperial church went on to produce an interpretation of Chalcedon that made it say what, in their view, it should have said. By a strong version of the communion of attributes, they made the one hypostasis to be the 'synthetic' agent of the whole gospel narrative, both of what is divine in it and of what is human in it, and they identified the eternal *Logos* as himself this hypostasis. (*ST* 1, p. 133)

The continuities with later Lutheranism are clear: 'The incarnation given, what we call the humanity of Christ and the deity of Christ are only actual as one sole person, so that where the deity of the Son is, there must be Jesus' humanity, unabridged as soul and body' (*ST* 1, p. 203).

But must there? While the doctrine of the communion of attributes does not necessarily lead to Feuerbach – although historically it did – it does have grave consequences for the doctrine of the humanity of Christ. It must be conceded that almost anything is to be preferred to the double agency encouraged by Leo's formulation – anticipated as that is, it must be recalled, also in the writings of the Eastern Fathers before Cyril[12] – so that surely Jenson is right to deny house room to the

---

[12] See, for example, Athanasius' attempt to show that as man Jesus was ignorant, as the divine Word he was omniscient, in *Against the Arians*, 3. 42ff; ET in *Nicene and Post-Nicene Fathers of the Church* II, eds P. Schaff and H. Wace (Edinburgh: T&T Clark; Grand Rapids: Eerdmans, 1991).

suggestion that 'the "natures" may, in context of the total document, be taken as each a distinct agent of its part of the gospel narrative' (*ST* 1, p. 132). Yet a strong version of the communion of attributes would seem inevitably to offend against Chalcedon's 'without confusion'. Given the asymmetry of the relation between creator and creature, the communication of attributes is likely to eventuate in the effective submerging of the human Jesus in the action of the divine, as is also unavoidably the case with the application of *perichoresis* to the two natures.[13] If Christology is to provide a matrix for an understanding of the relation between creator and creature, must not more be done to ensure the distinct reality of Jesus' humanity as the eternal Son become incarnate? If Jesus is a *creature* – to be sure, not in an Arian sense, but as *verus homo*[14] – must not an account of his humanity contain something more than an assertion that this is a function of the one hypostasis? I am not suggesting that there is none given in *Systematic Theology*, but that its tendency is to downplay the necessary otherness of Jesus and the Father at the expense of their necessary relatedness. In other words, while it can be conceded that 'the idea of the *Logos's* human nature speaking on its own has a rather too Antiochene ring' (*ST* 2, p. 159), may it not yet be objected that more effort should be devoted to demonstrating that the Logos speaks *as human*?

Considerations similar to those pertaining to the *incarnate* apply also in the account of the *incarnation*. If there is too strong an *identification* of the incarnate with what, however unsatisfactorily, we call the pre-incarnate Word – and here the argument hangs in part on the relation of John 8.58 ('before Abraham was, I am') and that Gospel's Prologue ('the Word became flesh') (*ST* 1, p. 139) – once again the 'space' of Jesus' humanity is in danger of being invaded. Jenson here cites a crucial passage from Irenaeus: 'The Word of God, who is the Saviour of all and the ruler of heaven and earth, *who is Jesus*, who

---

[13] What is appropriate for the three equal persons of the Trinity is far less satisfactory when applied to the asymmetrical relation between God and man. See Leonard Prestige, 'ΠΕΡΙΧΩΡΕΩ and ΠΕΡΙΧΩΡΗΣΙΣ in the Fathers', *Journal of Theological Studies* 29 (1928), pp. 242–52.

[14] Colin E. Gunton, *Christ and Creation. The 1990 Didsbury Lectures* (Carlisle: Paternoster Press and Grand Rapids: Eerdmans, 1993), Lecture 2.

assumed flesh and was anointed by the Father with the Spirit, *was made to be Jesus* Christ [emphases added].'[15] As with the Fourth Gospel, much depends on how the apparent tension in the two statements – of identity ('who is Jesus') and temporal realization ('was made to be Jesus') – is to be resolved. We shall return to Irenaeus when we come to discuss the mediation of creation.

The point of all this is that differences between Christologies generate differences in the conception of the mediation of creation. But here I want to emphasize that these christological questions are the sharpest I want to ask of Robert Jenson's theology in this chapter, because after the antithesis between a 'Lutheran' and a 'Reformed' approach, I shall hope to move not to an easy synthesis, but to an attempt to relativize the differences between us in an account that will allow the large amount of common ground to be revealed. By thus beginning with our greatest difference, I shall hope to move into a positive conversation – aided by an actual oral one at a recent conference which has helped me to see where the heart of the matter of mediation is to be found. And it is encapsulated in the question Jenson himself asked of Barth, 'You wonder where the Spirit went?'[16] The humanity of the Word is most satisfactorily articulated where attention is given to his relation to his Father as it is mediated by the Spirit, and this plays little part in the *Systematic Theology*.[17] My contention is this: when in his account of mediation Jenson makes room for pneumatology, there the differences between us begin to be relativized.

---

[15] *ST* 1, p. 140, citing Irenaeus, *Against the Heresies*, 2.4.3.

[16] Robert W. Jenson, 'You Wonder Where the Spirit Went', *Pro Ecclesia* 2 (1993), pp. 296–304.

[17] This has been achieved in Reformed theology without conceding to Antiochene dualism. I do not wish to repeat here accounts of the way in which John Owen and his successors, within a fundamentally Calvinist christological framework, have sought to ensure, pneumatologically, a stronger doctrine of Christ's humanity. But their historical context is worth indicating. Owen's work was written in face of Socinian charges that christological dogma effectively abolished the humanity of Jesus, and these cannot be answered unless more effort is put into showing that, while Jesus is the eternal Word, he is so only as fully human, like us in all things, sin apart. See Alan Spence, 'Inspiration and Incarnation: John Owen and the Coherence of Christology', *King's Theological Review*, XII (1989), pp. 52–5.

Creation

In a summary of a recent paper by Robert Jenson on the doctrine of creation, I wrote as follows:

> Professor Jenson articulates the main affirmations of the doc-
> trine [of creation] in a number of points . . . [They] together
> guarantee what some theologies . . . do not always adequately
> safeguard, that what we are concerned with in the doctrine of
> creation is not a timeless relation between God and the world
> but one which requires a notion of the relation between the
> eternal and time that better guarantees the reality and
> importance of the latter.[18]

That takes us to the place where this chapter began, Jenson's
assault on the divine timelessness which is characteristic of
religion. What is distinctive, however, about his formulation of
the doctrine emerges in two passages from the paper being
introduced:

> I can now jump to my central assertion, which is merely the
> converse of these considerations: for God to create is for him
> to open place in his triune life for others than the three
> whose mutual life he is. John of Damascus again: 'God is . . .
> his own place.' In that place, he *makes room*, and that act is the
> event of creation.[19]

It follows that:

> The triune God is precisely not a sheer point of Presence, not
> even the one at the center of the turning circle from which all
> things are equally present. And therefore, whether we want to
> talk about God's 'time' or not, creation is not a problem for
> God and the posit of time imposes no strain on the character
> of being. God is roomy; he can make room in himself if he
> chooses; if he so chooses the room he makes we call time; and
> that he creates means that he so chooses.[20]

---

[18] Colin E. Gunton, 'Introduction', *The Doctrine of Creation* (Edinburgh: T&T
Clark, 1997), pp. 1–15 (p. 6).

[19] Robert W. Jenson, 'Aspects of a Doctrine of Creation' in Colin E. Gunton,
ed., *The Doctrine of Creation*, p. 24, citing John of Damascus, *The Catholic Faith*,
13. 9–11. Much of this exposition reappears in *ST* 2, pp. 25–8.

[20] Jenson, 'Aspects of a Doctrine of Creation', p. 27.

The complexities of our topic are to be found in the fact that we are here in the realm not simply of the relation of eternity and time, but also of infinity and space. We are, furthermore, in the realm of metaphor, which, to repeat what should not, but does, require repeating, is in no way to suggest that we are in the realm of mere construction or projection. Metaphors are the necessary means of our interaction with the world, the necessary means of widening our grasp of what it is to be a creature of the good God in the world he has created and redeemed. In that respect, some are true and some false, and in this particular context, the truth of the metaphor of roominess consists, at least in part, in its counteracting of the dogma, amounting for much of the tradition almost to an axiom, that the creator of space is necessarily non-spatial. Barth, as is well known, was among the first in this particular field of combat. 'God is spatial as the One who loves in freedom, and therefore as Himself . . . God possesses His space. He is in Himself as in a space. He creates space.'[21] Because God lives in a dynamic order of trinitarian space, he is able to create a world which has space to be the world.

In this light, let us explore how the notion of God's 'roominess' is articulated trinitarianly in the *Systematic Theology*. Our chief question concerns the way in which it is made to imply that creation takes place in some way *within* the being of God. Of particular moment is the relation between pneumatology and freedom. 'The Spirit is *Spiritus Creator* as he frees the Father from retaining all being with himself, and so frees what the Father initiates from being the mere emanation it would have been were the Father God by himself' (*ST* 2, p. 26). The work of the Son in this is that 'he mediates between the Father's originating and the Spirit's liberating' (*ST* 2, pp. 26–7, cf. p. 45) 'thereby to *hold open* the creatures' space in being' (*ST* 2, p. 27). In this way, a notion of creation not only as taking place within God but also of creation as externalization begins to make an appearance. While I do not want to suggest that this in any way subverts the notion of creation as the opening up of space for creatures within the divine being, that 'withinness' is carefully

---

[21] Karl Barth, *Church Dogmatics*, eds G. W. Bromiley and T. F. Torrance (Edinburgh: T&T Clark, 1957–1975), vol. 2/1, p. 470.

qualified, as a juxtaposition of the two following passages
suggests:

> God makes narrative room in his triune life for others than
> himself . . . Thus as we 'live and move and have our being' in
> him, the 'distention' within which we do this is an order
> *external* to us, which therefore can provide a metric that is
> objective for us . . . (*ST* 2, p. 34, my italics)

And:

> To be a creature in specific relation to the Father is to be a
> motif in the orchestration that occurs when God's musicality
> opens *ad extra* . . . God opens otherness between himself and
> us, and so there is present room for us. (*ST* 2, pp. 39, 47)

The *ad extra* is significant. May we not here cautiously draw a
parallel with a point made by a commentator on Berkeley's
teaching that ideas (that is to say in our context, created things)
exist only *in* the mind of God and the minds of finite beings, to
the effect that the 'in' should not be taken literally?[22] It must be
cautious because of the insistence on creation as in some sense
within God's being. Yet the balance between internality and
otherness is well summarized in this fine passage:

> The Father's love of the Son is, we have seen, the possibility of
> creation. Insofar as to be a creature is to be other than God,
> we may say that the Father's love of the Son as other than
> himself is the possibility of creation's otherness from God . . .
> Moreover, we now also see why we had to say that time was the
> 'room' God made for us in his life: did not God set us other
> than himself, did he not make space between him and us, all
> time would just be *his* time and there would be no 'accom-
> modation' in him . . . 'That place is called God's place that
> more fully participates in his energy and grace.'[23]

The question is this: is there a difference between saying, as
Barth tends to say, that there is an analogy between God's

---

[22] 'The phrase "in the mind" should not be taken in the literal sense – as, for
instance, "the apples are in the basket"; it should be taken more in the sense of
"I shall keep you in mind".' David Berman, *George Berkeley. Idealism and the Man*
(Oxford: Clarendon Press, 1994), p. 39.
[23] *ST* 2, p. 48, citing John of Damascus, *The Orthodox Faith*, I.13.17–18.

spatiality and that of the world he creates, and saying with
Jenson that created space is in some way within God? The
answer to that is, we have just seen, not necessarily. In his argument with the Gnostics, Irenaeus argued that anything that God
does not contain must necessarily contain God, and so be God
itself.[24] And yet must not the metaphorical containing also allow
for an element of externality, in the sense of an otherness which
is established by God so that the creature shall be authentically
itself? The necessity is to express the relation so as to be true to
Athanasius' principle that, 'a work is external to the nature, but
a son is the proper offspring of the essence'.[25] And so we are
ready for the limning of possible convergences.

Convergences?

At stake in all this is the way in which we shall conceive the
relation of God and the world realistically but – to use the
politically correct, questionable, but here useful, jargon – non-
oppressively. It is agreed between our representative 'Lutheran'
and 'Reformed' positions that the Trinity is the indispensable
key. We probably also accept Coleridge's argument that in the
end there are only two theological possibilities, pantheism or
trinitarian theism, with only the latter allowing that 'space'
between the creator and the creation which ensures at once the
Selbständigkeit of the created order and its continuing dependence upon God for everything that is and takes place. Where we
differ in this conversation is to be found in the different ways,
shaped or determined by different Christologies, of construing
the spatial metaphors with the help of which the God–world
relation is conceived. The one trinitarianly mediated doctrine
takes different forms because the Christologies are different.

As we have seen, Jenson expresses the matter in the spatial
language of 'withinness'. What I have identified as a Lutheran
Christology has a tendency to stress the divine Christ, so that to
say that God creates 'in' Christ is to suggest that what happens

[24] Irenaeus, *Against the Heresies*, 2.1.2. ET in *The Anti-Nicene Fathers*, eds A.
Roberts and J. Donaldson (Grand Rapids: Eerdmans; Edinburgh: T&T Clark,
1989), vol. 1.
[25] Athanasius, *Against the Arians*, 1. 29.

'in Christ' must also be said to happen 'within' God. One could speculate here about the extent of Hegelian influence in modern Lutheran Christology, Jenson's and Pannenberg's alike. To go the whole Hegel is to push the 'withinness' in a pantheist direction, and this both Jenson and Pannenberg, with their less realized eschatology, remain well short of committing.[26] Yet it remains a permanent danger of the language of within, as the history of theology shows only too well. How can what is within God, it is asked, fail to be part of God? We have seen something of Jenson's answer, and we must retain in mind the fact that we are here in the realm of a metaphor in terms of which the continuing relatedness of the creation to God is being construed.

On the other side, the stress in the Calvinist tradition – Barth interestingly excepted – is on a greater distinction between the divine and the human in Christ, and so a tendency to conceive creation as externalization: as God's creation of something 'outside' himself, and so with a stress on its otherness. The danger here is that without a strong pneumatology the outcome will be the excessive separation of God and the world, corresponding to Nestorianism, that in fact came to be deism. One can be over schematic, but perhaps it is not too much of a simplification to say that each tendency seeks to conceive the relation-in-otherness of God and the world, the first stressing the relation, the second the otherness – again, in parallel with their corresponding christological emphases.

However, the important feature held in common is that on both sides of the divide a genuinely trinitarian conception of mediation is being sought. Here we return to the question of 'religion'. At the beginning of the chapter, I suggested that Jenson is opposing one form of mediation, that of what we might call the revealed gospel to the conception implicit in religion of the creature's autonomous movement into eternity, 'from below'. The point may be made more sharply. The

---

[26] The reference to Hegel, though seriously meant, is also designed to enable me to cite my favourite Jenson footnote, repeatedly quoted to students to this day. 'Hegel's only real fault was that he confused himself with the last judge; but that is quite a fault.' Robert W. Jenson, *The Knowledge of Things Hoped For. The Sense of Theological Discourse* (New York: Oxford University Press, 1969), p. 233.

religion that began, at least so far as our culture is concerned, in Greece – and indeed may be a form of that which is universal apart from those places where the Bible's God has made his presence felt – is more a quest for immediacy than a form of mediation; indeed, it is a denial of the necessity of mediation. Kierkegaard's attack on Hegel is in this respect a defence of the necessity of christological mediation against the immediacy which would make the human in some way continuous with, perhaps ultimately identical with, the divine.

In that light, the seriousness of the differences between the two conceptions of trinitarian mediation which I have been comparing can at least be mitigated. So long, on the one hand, as the being of creation 'within God' is not construed as implying continuity; and so long, on the other hand, as creation as externalization is not conceived in such a way as to rule out the continuing presence to, and capacity of God for immanence within, the created order, both traditions are aiming at the same outcome. But how best is the relation between immanence and transcendence to be preserved? My preference would be to say that the creation takes place within *Christ*, rather than within God *simpliciter*. To confine the spatial metaphor to Christ is to take up a hint from Colossians 1.16 in order to make the point that the place where the relation between God and the world is both realized and understood is the person of him who is the externalization in the world of the one who mediates all the Father's creating and redeeming action. This, it must be stressed, is not a matter of proof-texting but of attempting to ensure that the general relation between God and the world is focused in the particular place where their relation takes paradigmatic and determinative form.[27]

The outcome of this account of the differences between a Lutheran and a Reformed orientation on the doctrine of creation is that we are enabled to see that in certain respects the two traditions are seeking to reach the same kind of conclusion. This is not to recommend the sentimental modern relativism that all routes lead to the same place, but to suggest that shared

[27] For this conception, and its background in Athanasius, see Colin E. Gunton, *The Triune Creator. A Historical and Systematic Study* (Edinburgh: T&T Clark and Grand Rapids: Eerdmans, 1998), pp. 142–3.

– credal rather than confessional! – interests in some way lead us, because of our different historical and ecclesial formation, to different conclusions that, although they cannot be left undiscussed, should not be the occasion of personal or ecclesial alienation either. There are, and there will continue to be, ways of conceiving the same problem which can, but ought not to be allowed to, appear as antithetical, as leading to accusations, respectively, of pantheism and deism. Are not the most fruitful encounters often between those whose fundamental commitment to the God and Father of our Lord Jesus Christ allows wide scope for differences even in things sometimes thought essential?[28] And is this not an eschatologically oriented approach of the kind of which Jenson might approve? Whatever the answer to that, and I am not predicting its outcome, we can surely agree on one characteristically Reformed principle: *Soli deo gloria.*[29]

---

[28] It is, to give a personal example, a blessing for research students to have a supervisor whose theology is different enough to keep them on their intellectual toes.

[29] I am most grateful to Shirley Martin, who read an earlier draft of this chapter, and made some important queries and suggestions, to its considerable improvement.

7

Creation: (2) The Spirit Moved Over the Face of the Waters. The Holy Spirit and the Created Order[1]

Biblical Matters

As scarcely needs to be remarked, there has been much specula-tion and controversy about the meaning and relation of the first two verses of Genesis. Following Wenham and most of the ancient tradition, it seems to me that verse 1 – 'in the begin-ning, God created the heavens and the earth' – simply describes the first act of divine creation. Verse 2 therefore forms part of the process of creation after this first act. In turn, it has three also disputed aspects, and, again, I shall generally follow Wenham:

1. What is the nature of the 'total chaos' which characterizes things at this stage? It is ' "chaos, disorder," most frequently of the untracked desert where a man can lose his way and die. . . . This frightening disorganization is the antithesis to the order that characterized the work of creation when it was complete.' It is 'coupled with "void" where, as the context shows, the dread-fulness of the situation before the divine word brought order out of chaos is underlined.'[2] Is it necessary, then, to speak of a staged creation even here? It seems so. All is so far from being complete that even after the basic division of heaven and earth has been made, rank disorder characterizes the situation. It is not that God is bound to operate in this way, as some recent

---

[1] Previously published in the *International Journal of Systematic Theology* 4 (2002).
[2] Gordon J. Wenham, *Genesis 1–15, Word Biblical Commentary* 1 (Waco: TS, Word Books, 1987), pp. 15f.

theologies seem to suggest, any more than, after Augustine, we must hold that he must have created everything instantaneously, with the reference to time merely a way of accommodating the matter to our finite understanding. It is rather – and this is a key to a theology of the Spirit – that God creates a world which requires time both to be and to become what it is created to be.

2. Second, it seems to be the case that even if the preferred translation of 'ruach elohim' is 'wind' rather than 'Spirit', the reference is to the 'powerful presence of God moving mysteriously over the face of the waters ... hovering and ready for action'.[3] We should note even at this stage that, as in the New Testament, the Spirit is understood to be the power of God in action over against that which is not God. Terms like the power or glory or energy of God 'are widely recognised as frequently serving as circumlocutions for the Spirit' in the New Testament, so that we can rightly find pneumatological references in many places where the Spirit is not explicitly named.[4] We can thus discern a measure of continuity between New Testament usage and this mysterious prolegomenon to the successive days of creation.

3. Third, according to Wenham, notions of a bird-like Spirit brooding over or incubating an egg are simply unjustified, over-influenced as they are by attempts to feminize the translation in some way.[5] As we shall see, they can be made to work, but the point is this. Whatever traces of mythical language may still remain in this chapter, they are relativized by the overall stress

[3] Wenham, *Genesis*, p. 17.

[4] D. Lyle Dabney, ' "Justified by the Spirit": Soteriological Reflections on the Resurrection', *International Journal of Systematic Theology* 3/1 (2001), p. 49.

[5] Basil in *Hexaemeron* II.6 shows that he is as aware as some recent commentators of the Syriac translation of our verse. An unnamed Syrian has informed him that it is: 'more expressive, and that being more analogous to the Hebrew term it was a nearer approach to the scriptural sense. This is the meaning of the word; by "was borne" the Syrians ... understand: it cherished that nature of the waters as one sees a bird cover the eggs with her body ...' Basil understands this to mean, 'prepared the nature of water to produce living beings: a sufficient proof for those who ask if the Holy Spirit took an active part in the creation of the world'. Basil of Caesarea, *Homilies on the Hexaemeron; The Father of the Church, vol. 46*, tr. A. C. Way (Washington, DC: Catholic University of America Press, 1968).

to be found on the absolute sovereignty of God over that which he calls into being and shapes. The chaos does not represent limits on what he can do, but is simply a way of speaking of that which has to be done before the world can be that which it is created to be. We are in the realm of elusive, uncontained, mysterious and utterly sovereign power.

Only with the benefit of hindsight can we read this whole passage in a trinitarian way, and yet surely we may and must. But that is not our concern at present, which is to visit two other texts which may suggest that although in one respect God's creating work is finished at the end of the sixth day, in others it undoubtedly is not. Not only is the divine 'rest' of the seventh day the preface to further labours – explicitly suggested in the Fourth Gospel: 'My Father is always at work . . .' (John 3.17) – but there are other signs that there are things still to do. The first is to be found in the instruction in Genesis 1.28 to man to 'subdue' the earth. Are there suggestions, as is sometimes argued, that the chaos continues to bear upon the creation, so that the human task is to repel something that threatens the created order even before sin plays its disruptive part? We do not have to go so far as Barth in suggesting that the threat of nothingness is almost directly consequent on the divine creative activity,[6] but must be aware that the creation is not yet completely as God would have it be; that in eschatological perspective there is something still to do, and that this involves at least the overcoming of a measure of continuing disorder or at least absence of what we can call eschatological order and freedom. Does an element of the chaos of verse 2 still remain, so that a kind of exorcism of the created order continues to be necessary? That would give a sharp focus to the continuing work that is implied in the divine command.

Our second relevant text is that containing the account of the garden in chapter 2. The existence of the garden would appear to presuppose that outside it things are not so ordered, for a garden is a piece of earth which is subdued to human purposes in a way that land beyond it is not. At the very least there is a task to perform, and the implication – realized in the expulsion of

---

[6] Karl Barth, *Church Dogmatics*, tr. eds. G. W. Bromiley and T. F. Torrance (Edinburgh: T&T Clark, 1957–1975), 3/3, §50, pp. 289–368.

Adam and Eve from the garden – may be that elsewhere things
are not so hospitable to the human race. In that regard, chapters 1 and 2 are saying much the same. The world is of such a
kind that it requires obedient human activity to enable the
achievement of that for which it was created. Creation is perfect
– 'very good' – but remains to be perfected, in part by faithful
human action.

What all this has to do with the doctrine of the Spirit we shall
explore later. Before doing so, let us review other Old Testament texts that appear to be more directly relevant. Psalm 33.6
– 'By the word of the Lord were the heavens made, their starry
host by the breath of his mouth' – places in parallel the Word
and the Spirit in such a way that it appears that for the writer
they are conceptually little different, however things may
appear in trinitarian retrospect. However, another Psalm of creation attributes to the Spirit a specific function, and it looks
forward to the later credal characterization of the Spirit as the
Lord and giver of life:

> When you take away their spirit they die and return to the
> dust.
> When you send your Spirit they are created, and you renew
> the face of the earth. (Ps. 104.29b–30)

This takes up the much noted verse describing the creation of
Adam in Genesis 2.7: 'The Lord God formed the man from the
dust of the ground and breathed into his nostrils the breath of
life, and the man became a living being.' The Lord's Spirit gives
the breath that is life, a theme to which we must give central
attention in any theology of the Spirit and the creation. It is
reinforced by an equally important reference which brings in a
more definitely eschatological note than we have so far met.
Punning on the various meanings of *ruach*, Ezekiel makes the
Spirit the source of eschatological life as well as what we can call
the life of the creation in general:

> 'Come from the four winds, O breath, and breathe into these
> slain, that they may live' . . . 'This is what the sovereign Lord
> says: O my people, I am going to open your graves and bring
> you back up from them . . .' (Ezek. 37. 9, 12)

Not only life, but resurrection life is the gift of the Spirit.

We can accordingly make a general distinction between two related functions of the Spirit according to these two characterizations of his activity. In Psalm 104 the emphasis is on the Spirit's maintaining of the creation, the everyday work, so to speak, of maintaining the processes of life and, indeed, death. The created order is finite, as are its inhabitants: they have their day, and when the Spirit is taken away from them, they die. In that respect, death is not a problem for Scripture, representing as it does God's ordained end for the time the creature has on earth. But in another respect death becomes an enemy, and this leads us to the second, eschatological activity of the Spirit. Here death refers to that which resists the creator's good dispensation for his creation, so that in Ezekiel we meet the promise of renewed life for that which has suffered the death which is not fulfilment but subjection to futility. The Spirit is therefore to be understood as the power of God by which he both upholds the life of the world and renews even that which has been subjected to futility.[7]

The eschatological note returns in one of the few direct treatments in the New Testament of the Spirit in relation to the created order. Does Romans 8.20 – 'the creation was subjected to futility, not by its own choice, but by the will of the one who subjected it' – contain a reference back to Genesis 3.17? 'Cursed is the ground because of you; through painful toil you will eat of it all the days of your life . . . until you return to the ground, since from it you were taken; for dust you are, and to dust you will return.' Apart, that is to say, from the Spirit's act of eschatological renewal, the destiny of the whole creation, man and nature alike, is futility and death. And, according to Paul, the justifying act of God in Christ is to renew the whole of the creation: 'that the creation itself will be liberated from its bondage to decay and brought into the glorious freedom of the children of God' (Rom. 8. 21).

The crucial lesson to be learned from Romans 8 and its background in Genesis 1–3 is that it is a mistake to treat what we can call the material creation or the natural world in abstraction from its being in some way ordered to the human race. Whether

---

[7] Should we summarize this by saying that the Spirit gives both life and eternal life?

or not this is 'anthropocentric' and ecologically incorrect, and whether indeed that matters, it seems to me the clear message of Scripture. Human beings have a specific calling in relation to the remainder of creation and it is that of dominion, of representing, mediating indeed, the rule of God the creation's Lord. The failure to exercise that calling is in some way responsible for the fact that the creation does not realize its calling, which is to share in the liberty of God's children. The exchange of liberty for slavery in one realm, the human, involves a bondage for the created world also. The work of the Spirit is in some central sense the key to liberation in both realms. 'Where the Spirit of the Lord is, there is liberty' (2 Cor. 3.17); what that involves for the non-human creation is the chief concern of this essay, but it cannot be treated without some account being given of the Spirit's role in relation to the human.

Dogmatic Considerations

The next task is to explore something of the general dogmatic questions which provide the context for our topic. The first concerns the situation in the light of which we approach the theology of creation: the relation of creation and redemption. In so far as we can know it at all, we cannot know the creation apart from its redemption. In that regard, the famous Thomist slogan, that grace perfects but does not abolish nature, remains one of the greatest over-simplifications to have won wide currency. It presents a false alternative, for to suppose that it is either a matter of perfecting or of abolition is to ignore the truth that something more than a mere perfecting is needed. Whether we are to speak of the fallenness of the whole creation or not, we must certainly speak of the fallenness of its human inhabitants; they, certainly, require redemption before they can be perfected, and there is much to be said for the view that their environment is, along with them, subjected to vanity. After the Fall, the Spirit works only in the context of opposition. Two considerations must therefore be maintained in tension. The first is that nothing can take away the essential goodness of the creation: 'that it is a slander on creation to charge it with a share in chaos because it includes a Yes and a No, as though oriented to God on the one side and nothingness on the other'.[8] Creation's fundamental and irrefragable orientation to God entails that we can appropriate Barth's characteristically rhetorical expression of the matter:

> It is true that in creaturely existence, and especially in the existence of man, there are hours, days and years both bright and dark, success and failure, laughter and tears, youth and age, gain and loss, birth and sooner or later its inevitable corollary, death. It is true that individual creatures and men experience these things in most unequal measure, their lots being assigned by a justice which is curious or very much concealed. Yet it is irrefutable that creation and creature are good even in the fact that all that is exists in this contrast and antithesis.[9]

The shadow thrown by the light – and we note that the list includes death understood as mortality – is simply an indication of what it is for creation to be finite. Alongside this, however, must come the second and patristic insistence that creation comes out of nothing, and in its fallen state bids fair to return there. There is, that is to say, no nature that *maintains itself* in being – the underlying suggestion of so many so-called natural theologies – but only a creation that is upheld against the inbreaking of chaos and death by the power – that is, the Spirit – of God.

Two further dogmatic points follow. The first is that we may explore the theology of the Spirit only through the lens provided by Jesus Christ. This is needed to save us from the kind of pneumatology of creation that attributes to the natural order itself either some intrinsic significance apart from those who have been granted dominion over it or some power to save itself apart from the incarnation. The word spoken in the beginning is, after all, the Word who became man first for human salvation and only after that for the reconciliation of all things. It may or may not be the case, as used to be claimed, that the Old Testament account of creation was written as a reflex, so to speak, from the experience of redemption in the Exodus and entry into the promised land. There is certainly much to be said for

[8] Barth, *Church Dogmatics*, 3/3, p. 299.
[9] Barth, *Church Dogmatics*, 3/3, p. 297.

the view that a confession of creation represents more of a universal element of Old Testament faith.[10] But the question is relativized by the fact that the Word through whom things came to be is also the one in whom the creation is upheld. There is neither nature nor grace apart from him, nor any understanding of the work of the Spirit in creation. Only in this light are Genesis and the other Old Testament texts fully revelatory of what it is to be a creature.

The second piece of dogmatic background follows from this, and it is the trinitarian. If we are to avoid the worst kind of anthropomorphism – of making the Spirit a kind of individual agent in relation to the created order – we must remember that his action is inseparable from that of the Father and the Son. However, so far as the doctrine of creation is concerned, it must be granted that the dogmatic tradition does not here give us as much assistance as it might. There are a number of Cappadocian sayings which form the basis of a pneumatology of creation, but they take us only part of the way. They are, however, worth citing. There is first the much quoted theologoumenon of Basil of Caesarea, distributing the Trinity's work *ad extra* to the three persons of the Trinity: 'the original cause of all things that are made, the Father; the creative cause, the Son; the perfecting cause, the Spirit'.[11] This gives us one essential element, the notion of the Spirit as the perfecting cause of creation. We shall follow this up later. And then there is the equally important corresponding point made by Gregory of Nyssa, stressing the corresponding unity of the divine action, that God's action begins with the Father, goes through the Son and is completed by the Spirit.[12] Our difficulty here concerns the fact that that is all we have. The Fathers do not give us much further assistance

[10] H. H. Schmid, 'Creation, Righteousness and Salvation: "Creation Theology" as the Broad Horizon of Biblical Theology', *Creation in the Old Testament*, ed. B. W. Anderson (Philadelphia: Fortress Press, 1984), pp. 102–17.

[11] Basil, *On the Holy Spirit*, XV. 38.

[12] 'Therefore, then, the Holy Trinity works every activity according to the manner stated, not divided according to the number of hypostases, but one certain motion and disposition of goodwill occurs, proceeding from the Father through the Son to the Spirit.' 'Gregory of Nyssa's *Concerning We Should Think of Saying That There Are Not Three Gods*, to Ablabius', *The Trinitarian Controversy*, tr. and ed. William G. Rusch (Philadelphia: Fortress Press, 1980), p. 155.

in expanding this matter. Even in his *Hexaemeron*, Basil makes little of the work of the Son and the Spirit, and the fact seems to be that from early in the tradition the doctrine of the Trinity appears to have played a minimal part in shaping the doctrine of creation.

One symptom of this is to be found in the main reasons given to establish the equal divinity of the Spirit. While both Athanasius and Basil do appeal to his creating function, it is the Spirit's enabling of human piety that plays the main role. The Spirit is the one who makes holy, went the favourite argument, and since only God can make holy, it must follow that the Spirit is divine. Nor does the Western tradition give much assistance. Augustine's conception of divine action tends to see it in unitary form: God the Trinity acts as simply as Trinity, and he is chary of attributing particular forms of action even to the Son, suspecting as he does even his predecessors' tendency to attribute the presence of God to the world in the Old Testament accounts to the Son. Aquinas picks up something of the Cappadocian attribution of perfecting to the Spirit, but he seems to mean by this chiefly the production of creatures who cannot but desire God as their end.[13] And yet, as always with this theologian, there are things worth hearing. The Spirit is the 'love with which the Father loves the Son', and as such the 'love with which the Father loves the creature by imparting its own perfection to it'.[14] 'In [created] things, the motion which is from God seems to be attributed properly to the Holy Spirit.'[15] Similarly, Luther by no means misses the importance of the Spirit as the giver of life, and indeed interprets Genesis 1.2 as an anticipatory revelation of the Trinity, though not the Trinity 'in so many words . . .; this was to be reserved for the teaching of the Gospel'.[16]

The Father creates heaven and earth out of nothing through

[13] Aquinas, *In Sent.* 14, 1, 1, c.
[14] I owe this reference to a conference paper by Bruce Marshall, 'What Does the Trinity have to do with Faith and Reason', Center of Theological Inquiry, Princeton, May 2001.
[15] Aquinas, SCG IV, 20 (no. 3571), cited by Bruce Marshall, *Trinity and Truth* (Cambridge: Cambridge University Press), p. 114.
[16] Martin Luther, *Lectures on Genesis Chapters 1–5, Luther's Works*, 1, ed. J. Pelikan (St Louis, MO: Concordia, 1958), p. 12.

the Son, whom Moses calls the Word. Over these the Holy Spirit broods. As a hen broods her eggs, keeping them warm in order to hatch her chicks, and, as it were, to bring them to life through heat, so Scripture says that the Holy Spirit brooded, as it were, on the waters to bring to life those substances which were to be quickened and adorned. For it is the office of the Holy Spirit to make alive.[17]

That allowed, Pannenberg is surely right to say that this aspect of things has never been adequately developed, with post-Reformation thought concerned almost exclusively with the Spirit's role in creating and maintaining faith.[18]

Christ and the Spirit

There are, it seems to me, two notes which need to be sounded more strongly than the tradition has mostly achieved: the christological and the eschatological. There is no Spirit without the Son, for we are concerned with the creating and providential action of the one God. Similarly, there is no adequate doctrine of the Spirit apart from the eschatological emphasis placed by Ezekiel and reinforced not only by Paul, but also in the whole New Testament presentation of the story and significance of the one who is the *eschatos*, the last as well as the first. We shall in this light explore our topic christologically through four focuses: the incarnational, the soteriological, the eschatological and the ecclesiological. What do these four gospel themes teach us about the work of the Spirit in relation to the created order?

First, the incarnation represents among other things a particular use of the created order by the Father through the Spirit, in forming a body of flesh for his eternal Son. It implies a reaffirmation and indeed concentration of the fact that God is imaged in the world by the human race, and that therefore the creation of the material world comes to a kind of climax here. (That is not to claim that the creation of man and woman

---

[17] Luther, *Lectures on Genesis*, p. 9.

[18] Wolfhart Pannenberg, *Toward a Theology of Nature. Essays on Science and Faith*, ed. Ted Peters (Louisville: Westminster/John Knox Press, 1993), pp. 126–7.

represents the goal of creation; that is surely to be found in the rest of the seventh day and its ultimate goal in the reconciliation of all things.) God the Father through his Spirit shapes this representative sample of the natural world for the sake of the remainder of it. The Word becomes not merely a human being, but, more broadly, flesh, *sarx*: human being which is what it is only in dependence on the Spirit of God. There is already an eschatological note, especially in Luke's characterization of the work of the Spirit in his first two chapters. Where the Spirit is, there is the end breaking into the present with the renewal of life signalled and begun by the conception of this particular child.

In the work of the incarnate Lord, empowered as he is by the Spirit, we see, second, the redemptive aspects of the incarnation. Sickness represents for the gospel writers the slavery of parts of the creation to forces that prevent them from becoming what they ought to be. This is particularly evident in the healings of those possessed by demons, phenomena which signal creation's bondage. 'If I by the Spirit of God . . .' (Matt. 12.28). But it can also be seen to apply more generally: 'a daughter of Abraham whom Satan has kept bound for eighteen long years' (Luke 13.16). Once again, an eschatological note is sounded. The healings and exorcisms are anticipations of the end, the beginnings of the kingdom that will have no end. This is the Father's work achieved by the Son in the power of the Spirit. The created order is exorcized of its demons, as is even suggested by the words Jesus used in the stilling of the storm. At the same time – and this reminds us of the consideration which has to be held in tension – creation's everyday praise of its Lord is also made clear, in the parables above all. Creation praises its maker, as it is; yet without healing it cannot praise its maker as universally as it should do. Creation as it was in the beginning is maintained in its essential goodness, which has, however, been subverted, so that while it can realize its purpose in particular ways, that is not yet the case universally. In sum, we must say that through his Son and Spirit, his two hands, the Father both prevents the creation from slipping back into the nothingness from which it came and restores its teleology, its movement to perfection.

We have seen that eschatological notes enough have already been struck in the first two topics, incarnation and redemption.

Wherever the Spirit is, there the true end of creation is anticipated. Yet, third, the most fully realized eschatology, and that
which reveals the meaning of the whole story until then, is the
resurrection. God the Father raises from death his Son through
the power of the Spirit, thus realizing for and in him the life of
the age to come.[19] We must emphasize the material dimensions
of the event. The one who breathed into Adam the breath of
life now raises the second Adam to new life by the transformation of his body not to bodiliness but to a new form of bodily
life. The Spirit is the Lord and giver of life, and this means both
the everyday life of the mortal and the transformed life of the
one whose mortality has put on immortality. The bearing of this
transformation is first of all on the destiny of the human being.
For Paul, the giving of the Spirit to the community that is the
Church is a guarantee of precisely this:

> . . . we do not wish to be unclothed, but to be clothed with
> our heavenly dwelling, so that what is mortal may be swal-
> lowed up by life. Now it is God who has made us for this very
> purpose and has given us the Spirit as a deposit, guaranteeing
> what is to come. (2 Cor. 5.4b–5)

Thus the new creation is both continuous with and a transformation of the old: 'sown . . . perishable, . . . raised imperishable;
. . . sown in dishonour, . . . raised in glory; . . . sown in weakness,
raised in power, . . . sown a natural body, . . . raised a spiritual
body [that is, one filled with the Spirit]' (1 Cor. 15.42–4).

All three aspects of the Jesus narrative come together in our
fourth focus, the ecclesiological, and in particular in the
Church's celebration of the Last Supper. While the historical
question of whether Jesus intended to form a Church, and of
what kind, is likely to remain disputed, it seems clear that in
calling twelve disciples he was concerned at least with a form of
culture in the broadest sense, a form of living together in
response to God's covenant mercies. What is not in doubt is that
his death, resurrection and ascension, resulting in the sending
óf the eschatological Spirit, eventuated in the forming of a
distinctive community gathered around him and dedicated to

---

[19] Romans 8. 11: 'the Spirit of him who raised Jesus from the dead'; 1 Peter
3.18: 'put to death in the body, but made alive by the Spirit'.

an – at least – fourfold form of life: 'the apostles' teaching and fellowship, . . . the breaking of bread and the prayers' (Acts 2.42). It is not an exaggeration to say that in a number of Paul's letters, especially perhaps the First Letter to the Corinthians, we see being hammered out before our eyes the distinctive form of culture that the Church was and is. Among the preoccupations of that book are discussions of sexual ethics, of the attitude to be taken to cultural forms of the city of Corinth – temples and law courts at the centre – and of the liturgical and social ordering of the life of the congregation. Together they focus the diverse forms of relationship that constitute a form of human culture: with God, with one another, with human beings outside the community and with the material world. For this letter, the forms of relationship all come to a head in the Church's celebration of the Lord's Supper which is, as Paul makes clear, to be understood in its ritual, liturgical and ethical dimensions at the same time and inseparably.[20]

This returns us to the other three themes of this section. There is, first, the incarnational – 'in memory of him', especially represented by the bread; second, the soteriological – the covenant sealed in his blood, the cup representing God's judgement; and, third, the eschatological – 'until he comes'. The Supper takes place in the bodily absence of the ascended Lord, between his resurrection and that of the end of time. But as the Fourth Gospel makes so clear, the bodily absence is the occasion of the sending of the 'other παρακλετος' who is the means of the Church's relation to the Father through the Son. Important for our purposes is the fact that the meal centres on natural things, which are also manufactured: the material world shaped by human hands. In all this it is important, it seems to me, that we at least question if it has been a mistake to concentrate so much energy and thought on asking whether and in what sense the bread and the wine become something else. It is surely the fact that they set forth the incarnational,

[20] See my ' "Until He Comes": Towards an Eschatology of Church Membership', *Called to One Hope. Perspective on the Life to Come. A Selection of Drew Lectures on Immortality delivered at Spurgeon's College*, ed. John Colwell (Carlisle: Paternoster Press, 2000), pp. 252–66. Also in *International Journal of Systematic Theology* 3 (2001), pp. 187–200.

soteriological and eschatological realities as bread and wine that makes them able to represent the Lord's achievement as it takes up into itself both the human and with it the rest of the created order. One of the things that has been lost in the development of the traditional sacramental view of the bread and wine is their representative function, an account of which can be found in Irenaeus above all. In offering worship through a Christ so represented, the Church offers not only itself as a 'living sacrifice, holy and acceptable to God' (Rom. 12.1–2) but also the whole created order, in anticipation of its final perfecting when all things are 'brought to a head in Christ' who 'ascended higher than all the heavens, in order to fill the universe' (Eph. 1.10, 4.10). It is the eschatological office of the Spirit that he is the one by whom the Father brings particular created things to perfection through the ascended Christ, beginning with the first fruits, his body incarnate, crucified and raised from the tomb.

Fragmentary Remarks on Culture and Life

To enquire what the Spirit does to the bread and wine in response to the prayers of consecration and epiclesis is, fortunately, beyond the scope of this work. But the fact that there is a complicated and at least threefold set of relations, the terms being the triune God, the gathered Church and the fruits of the earth means that it forms a suitable place to carry forward an enquiry into the relation between God the Spirit and the created order. The meaning of the created order here comes into particular focus through human action, and I shall therefore pursue the matter of the relation of the Spirit to the world first with some examination of the nature of human culture. By culture I mean neither high culture – though I shall make mention of it – nor culture in the sense sometimes used by social scientists of the symbolic worlds human beings develop, but something much more general. As nature is that which comes from the hand of the creator, so culture is all the things that human beings do to, with and in that created world. It is nature in some way affected or shaped by human hands, paradigmatically represented by bread and wine.

There are a number of advantages of looking at the matter in this way, and they have been prepared for earlier in the chapter.

To look at the Spirit and the created world in general in the light of Genesis 1 and Psalm 104 is relatively unproblematic. Complications begin to arise with the entry of sin into the world, so that the perfecting of nature is placed in the hands of those not only made in the image of God, but now also fallen, so that it is in what is made of nature by sinful (and sometimes reconciled) men and women that we can understand something of the Spirit's cosmic office. And, again, we shall have to bear our tension in mind. First, is that good things are done in all kinds of places which show that the work of the Spirit may be affected but is by no means constrained or constricted by the Fall. Here Calvin, the theologian of the Spirit, made the point well. More or less satisfactory forms of political order are often achieved by human beings, but that is not to be attributed to any inherent capacity – except perhaps in part to the remains of natural capacity given by God but extinguished by the Fall – but rather to the Spirit's overruling power.[21] So also is it with all human culture: where it is good, it is because it is enabled to be so by the power of the God who upholds all things in Christ. Second, however, it is the case that things often take place rather differently, as the history of politics and the pollution of the ecosystem only too well witness. Yet even when it becomes demonic, as we know that it can, culture is never outside the overruling power of God, but is sometimes allowed to take its destructive course, as, for example, Revelation 6 makes clear. I shall leave that on one side, as I am in this chapter concerned to speak not so much of fallen culture as of those places where the Spirit may rightly be discerned to be at work in the human activity. Yet it does remind us that after the Fall, the Spirit's work is achieved only against opposition.

That is why we must begin with some account of the communities of redemption, Israel and the Church, as forms of culture instituted by God. According to biblical witness, the shape of the two communities is determined by the covenants, divine acts by which human life is reoriented to the end for which it was created. Worship is at the heart of the calling of

---

[21] John Calvin, *Institutes of the Christian Religion*, ed. J. T. McNeill, tr. and indexed F. L. Battles (Philadelphia: Westminster Press, 1960), Library of Christian Classics 20, II. ii. 12–17.

both Israel and the Church, for in their cults human life in community and in the world is consciously ordered to God's historic acts in creation and redemption, and the creation's eschatological orientation restored. Specific forms of symbolic actions place human life in relation to God, human social order and the material world. The action of the Spirit is required if those actions and their social context are to achieve what they are designed to do. Mention has already been made of the Lord's Supper, in which the cultic action incorporates natural entities – the grain and the grape – which have been shaped by human cultural action. I want, riskily, to move from there to other more general forms of cultural action, which can perhaps be understood in the light of this ecclesial form of culture. One way of suggesting that it is not an unfounded risk is to be begin with another reference to our one New Testament source for our topic, Romans 8. In this, the pneumatological chapter of Romans, Paul begins with an account of life in the Spirit – of churchly culture – and proceeds to set this form of life in the context of the whole created order: 'in the hope that the whole creation will be liberated from its bondage to decay and brought into the glorious freedom of the children of God' (Rom. 8.21).

An orientation both to the Spirit and to the material creation is made explicit in Exodus 31, the account of the making of the tabernacle, of whose chief craftsman God says: 'I have filled him with the Spirit of God, with skill, ability and knowledge in all kinds of crafts . . .' (Exod. 31.3). As Gabriel Josipovici has noticed, the words 'Spirit of God' return us to Genesis 1:

> [T]he text itself makes the link between the Creation of the world and of the Tabernacle explicit, for after God has given his instructions to Moses and filled the craftsmen with wisdom, he orders Moses to remind the people to keep the Sabbath . . . 'for in six days the Lord made heaven and earth, and on the seventh day he rested . . .' (Exod. 31:17). The linguistic parallels between God looking at what he had done and Moses looking at the completed Tabernacle are striking: 'And God saw everything he had made, and, behold, it was very good' (Gen. 1:31); 'And Moses did look upon all the work, and, behold, they had done it as the Lord had commanded . . .' (Exod. 39:43). [And I here omit some of

Josipovici's examples, to end]: 'And God blessed the seventh day' (Gen. 2:3); 'and Moses blessed them' (Exod. 39:43).[22] In this instance, we are speaking of a craft given by the Spirit and exercised in the explicit service of the Lord. Do we have a licence to speak more generally of the work of human hands being attributable to the work of the Spirit? The concept of inspiration – of a breathing of the Spirit – is widely used of secular art also, and in different ways, not all of them necessarily compatible with biblical revelation. Yet it seems to me to be right to understand the mandate of Genesis 1.28 as not a permission but a command to so engage with the created order to enable it to join the human species in praise of its creator. We can call this the cultural mandate, the divine command to make something of the world. When this is done aright, it is because the Spirit enables it to be so done, simply because the Spirit is the agent by whom God enables things to become that which they are created to be.

Two points should be made here. The first is that we are on the way to developing a criterion by which we may seek to judge whether or not any given cultural activity or artefact is the gift of the Spirit, and that is whether it enables the creature, human and non-human alike, to join in praise of the creator by giving him glory. Clearly, many of the things which are claimed to be art would on this criterion, at best be bad art, at worst blasphemy of the creator, but that is not our main concern here. Second, and equally important, is the fact that the Spirit is free to enable those who by no means confess God's being and action to achieve the greatest of things. Barth's remarks about Mozart's theological achievement, though 'he does not seem to have been a particularly active Christian',[23] are well enough known, but recently I came across some words by a great writer who, without mentioning the Spirit, puts his finger on the heart of the matter:

> So we also, holding Art in our hands, confidently deem ourselves its masters; we boldly give it direction, bring it

---

[22] Gabriel Josipovici, *The Book of God* (New Haven and London: Yale University Press, 1988), p. 102.
[23] Barth, *Church Dogmatics*, 3/3, p. 298.

up to date, reform it, proclaim it, sell it for money, use it to please the powerful, divert it for amusement ... or else adapt it ... toward transient political or limited social needs. But art remains undefiled by our endeavours and the stamp of its origin remains unaffected: each time and in every usage it bestows upon us a portion of its mysterious inner light.[24]

That 'mysterious inner light', which shines through human cultural activity, even against the will of the agents, is the point of it all. 'The wind blows where it pleases. You hear its sound, but you cannot tell where it comes from or where it is going . . .' (John 3.8).[25]

But we cannot end there. The creed confesses the Spirit as 'the Lord and giver of life', and that reminds us that at the heart of our topic is that mysterious and indefinable reality we call life – that realm which, as Robert Jenson reminds us, is peculiarly that of the Lord.[26] We human beings are made, like everything else created, of the dust of the earth, and in that sense are constituted of the very same matter as all our fellow-creatures. But we share life with only some of them, and this suggests that what we have learned to call the biosphere is in some sense peculiarly the sphere of the Spirit's perfecting activity. It is worth noting that Barth took with a certain seriousness Schweitzer's thesis about respect for life, and that is relevant for an ethic of createdness, whatever problematic uses may

[24] From Solzhenitsin, in Robert K. Johnston, *Reel Spirituality. Theology and Film in Dialogue* (Grand Rapids: Baker Academic, 2000), p. 90. See also p. 91: 'Works which have drawn upon the truth and which have presented it to us in concentrated and vibrant form seize us, attract us to themselves powerfully, and no one ever – even centuries later – will step forth to deny them.'

[25] This does, I hope legitimately, extend the attribution of the Spirit's work rather beyond that of its context.

[26] 'All meals are intrinsically religious occasions, indeed sacrifices, and were so understood especially in Israel. For all life belongs intimately to God, so that the killing involved in eating – which we do not at all avoid by eating vegetables – is an intrusion into his domain. . . . Sharing a meal is therefore always a communal act of worship and establishes fellowship precisely before the Lord.' Robert W. Jenson, *Systematic Theology*, vol. 1, *The Triune God*; vol. 2, *The Works of God* (New York and Oxford: Oxford University Press, 1997, 1999), vol. 2, p. 185. I am also grateful to Shirley Martin for ensuring that I took this aspect of the topic with due seriousness.

sometimes be made of it.[27] But if we are to avoid a feeble descent into moralizing, we must return to the specifically eschatological dimensions of our topic. The Spirit as the perfecting cause of the creation is the one who enables things to become what they are created to be; to fulfil their created purpose of giving glory to God in their perfecting.

As we have seen, culture is one way by which we may be enabled by the Spirit to perfect the creature. In the realm of life, the matter is more complicated still. Both the development of crops and the husbandry of animals are clearly part of the human calling, and both involve interference in and alteration of the ecosystem. But when does the approach to the breeding of crops and the rearing of animals cease to show due respect for the life that they share with us? When is the killing of an animal properly called a sacrifice – an offering of praise to God – and when is it improper exploitation? How is a farm animal enabled to achieve its 'proper perfection'? It seems to me fairly obvious that much modern treatment of animals is exploitative rather than respectful. All life belongs to the Lord, and only with that in mind shall we be enabled by the Spirit to respect it appropriately. In his remarks on the theology of nature, Pannenberg claims that it is on the basis of the fact that God has breathed his Spirit into Adam that 'whatever the man called every living creature, that was its name' (Gen. 2.19).[28] There is, as a matter of fact, no explicitly pneumatological reference in those verses, and yet something of Pannenberg's point can be adopted. To name something is to enter into a particular kind of relation to it; and it is surely the gift of the Spirit that we may sometimes be rightly related to those creatures the Lord gave Adam to be his companions, though not his helpmeets and equals.

The question of human life is in some ways easier to approach, at least in general, despite the difficulties of particular cases. The Pope has rightly described much modern ethical practice as the culture of death, a culture which systematically

---

[27] Barth, *Church Dogmatics*, 3/4, p. 324: 'Life cannot for us be a supreme principle at all, though it can be a sphere in relation to which ethics has to investigate the content and consequences of God's command.' Cf. also pp. 349–50.
[28] Pannenberg, *Toward a Theology of Nature*, p. 154.

fails to respect the personal life that only God may give and take away. We are here in the eschatological realm, where ultimate issues are at stake, for the choice between life and death is an ultimate one. God not only breathes into his human creatures the breath of life, but he makes them to be like him, persons, whose beginning and ending are in his hands. As we have seen, the question of the Spirit and the created order comes to a head here, in this most problematical of all God's creatures, for what we do to each other – to babies in the womb, and we should avoid the depersonalizing word 'foetus', and to those on and near their deathbeds – is the measure of our treatment of the creation in general.[29] The promise, taken up by Luke (Acts 2) from Joel, that the Spirit will be poured out on all flesh surely refers to the human creation; but it does not follow that nothing can be learned pneumatologically about the world of life in broader compass. In the relation of God's Spirit to our spirits is mysteriously centred that which God has in store for his whole creation, so that with us it may be able to be perfected to his praise and glory.[30]

---

[29] See Michael Banner, *Christian Ethics and Contemporary Moral Problems* (Cambridge: Cambridge University Press, 1999), especially chapter 2.

[30] I am grateful to Shirley Martin for conversation during and after the writing of this chapter, and to Bruce McCormack, Francis Watson and Murray Rae for suggestions which have helped in its revision for publication.

8

Creation and Redemption: Christ, the Wisdom of God. A Study in Divine and Human Action

Human Wisdom

Despite recent claims of 'multiculturalism', Western culture involves largely a conversation – in the broadest sense of that word – between its classical and biblical heritages. As is well known, Christian theology is the fruit of a highly complex inter-action between the two worlds, still continuing, as is Western literature and art. Other voices may be entering the conversa-tion, but not yet so as to change the central questions. Part of the interest of our topic is that we are faced in it with a most suggestive paradox. On the one hand, in discussion of the con-cept of wisdom we see the closeness of the relationship between the classical and the biblical in Western thought; and perhaps that is not unrelated to the influence on the Old Testament of Near Eastern wisdom traditions. On the other hand, however, it is in Christology that the two traditions are most sharply div-ided. As Werner Elert showed, in contradiction of Harnack's famous thesis, orthodox Christology was able to emerge only as the result of a critique of certain, virtually unquestionable, philosophical dogmas about the nature of deity, so that in its essential claims, particularly those concerning God's involve-ment in the material world in Jesus of Nazareth, orthodox Christology contradicts the heart of the mainstream Greek philosophical tradition.[1]

---

[1] Werner Elert, *Der Ausgang der altkirchlichen Christologie* (Berlin: Lutherisches Verlagshaus, 1957). A leading thesis of Adolf Harnack's *History of Dogma*, 7 volumes (London: Williams and Norgate, 1899), is that patristic thought mostly represented the victory of Hellenism over the gospel.

Let us begin with the first arm of the paradox, the common-alities. Both ancient Greek and Wisdom writers mean similar things when they speak of wisdom as a way of human being in the world. Even allowing for the irreducibly theological orienta-tion of Hebrew wisdom, we can see clear parallels with the thought of the roughly contemporary Greeks. That is to say, the theological background of biblical wisdom talk is often precisely that – background only – as is illustrated by the oft-repeated observation, that although the God of Israel is not mentioned in the book of Esther, he is nevertheless everywhere present; or perhaps better by the fact, pointed out by Norman Whybray, that Ecclesiastes is only apparently an expression of Eastern pes-simism because the writer everywhere assumes the Israel's belief in God.[2] That is to say, there is something about the biblical God which enables a 'secular' account of human life to be given which is, as a result, comparable with the accounts given by similar non-biblical sources. By secular here I do not mean non-theological, but an account which enables the created world to be considered in its relative independence from its creator: as distinctively creation. When the wisdom literature describes human life in the context of the created world, it has things to say comparable with the parallel literature of other cultures.

What does the Old Testament mean by wisdom? In some way or other it is to do with life according to the way of being appropriate for one who is part of the created order of things. As is often pointed out, wisdom has a practical function. Although Greek wisdom is often contrasted with this by virtue of its more theoretical orientation, it remains true that both Plato, and perhaps even more the shadowy figure of Socrates lying behind him, were oriented to practice. We should not confuse the wisdom expected of the philosopher kings with the more narrowly conceived rationalism that has tended to succeed it in the world after the Enlightenment. The theoretical and the practical were not alienated into two distinct worlds, as has increasingly come to be the case. So it is with Aristotle: *phronesis* – if it is right to translate that as 'practical wisdom' – 'is a rational faculty (*hexis*) exercised for the attainment of truth in

---

[2] R. N. Whybray, *Ecclesiastes. New Century Bible Commentary* (London: Marshall, Morgan & Scott, 1989), pp. 27–30.

things that are humanly good and bad' – Pericles being his chosen example.[3] In respect, then, of the ineradicable interconnection of theory and practice, biblical wisdom and that of the ancient Greeks were close to one another, despite differences of emphasis.

Similarly, present day talk of wisdom involves a process of conversation between different traditions of construing precisely what is meant by the word.[4] One depressing fact is that since the Enlightenment the word has tended to fall into disfavour, to the advantage of a narrower rationalism, perhaps because it is too imprecise. In our time, wisdom is effectively replaced by reason, as, for example, in Kant's ethics, superficially similar though that is to Aristotle. (The deep difference, I think, is that Kant's ethical theory tends to be abstracted from the concrete context in a way it never was in Aristotle. Aristotle's practical wisdom is that of the citizen of the polis, Kant's that of the individual bourgeois who is only contingently related to other human beings.) One interesting example of the relative disfavour into which the concept of wisdom has fallen is to be found in T. S. Eliot's lament in *Choruses from 'The Rock'* for the loss of wisdom to knowledge and information. ('Where is the wisdom we have lost in knowledge? Where is the knowledge we have lost in information?' – over-quoted, no doubt, but for good reason.) Similarly, the recent *Cambridge Dictionary of Philosophy* contains, astonishingly, in view of the origin of the discipline, no entry under that heading. The reader looking for wisdom is urged to consult instead 'cardinal virtues', to which sixteen column lines are devoted.[5] But, despite this, the word does appear in modern philosophy, frequently enough, at any rate, for us to learn that juxtaposition of one recent philosophical and one theological use will demonstrate the continuing overlap of the classical and Christian.

I begin with a recent philosophical usage, confined, as we

[3] Aristotle, *Nicomachean Ethics*, tr. T. Irwin (Indianapolis: Hackett, 1999), 1140b 4–6.
[4] That is, if it is possible, as is extremely doubtful, whether we can, or indeed ought to want to achieve precision in the case of so open-textured and rich a concept.
[5] *Cambridge Dictionary of Philosophy*, ed. Robert Audi (Cambridge: Cambridge University Press, 1995).

might expect, to the human realm. Raymond Gaita writes that it is only in philosophy that people tend to limit their expression to

> ethical and spiritual *knowledge*. . . . We speak more commonly of the deepening of understanding and of wisdom. The wise are those who, as we sometimes put it, 'have something to say'. That does not mean that they have information to impart or a new theory to propound. It means that their authority depends upon our acknowledgement of their indi-vidually achieved lucidity about their experiences. Such lucidity is necessarily hard-won and necessarily won in the course of a life.[6]

That is by no means all there is to say, especially as Gaita's account comes out of a discussion of an example of remarkably saintly behaviour that he once met, but it provides a way of distinguishing between wisdom and other forms of human rela-tion to reality. It has to do with a breadth of human engagement with the world – not merely rational, scientific, or moral, but over a wide range of human being. The breadth implied by that characterization of wisdom is explicitly brought out by Daniel Hardy, who wishes to resurrect in modern terms the classical ideal as it was revived during the Renaissance, of

> 'a single sapientia which holds within itself "the knowledge of all things human and divine" [Cicero] and knows how to express them with all the persuasive powers of *eloquentia*'. . . . Wisdom in the positive sense designates not only the funda-mental ordering of reality, its *truth*, but the rightness of this ordering, its *goodness*.[7]

The relevance of the Renaissance is that it returned Europe to aspects of the classical ideal which had been submerged in Christendom's combination of the biblical and the philo-sophical. Especially in the later scholastics there emerged a

---

[6] Raimond Gaita, 'Response to Sue Patterson, "Dressing the Wounds of the People" ', in *Beyond Mere Health. Theology and Health Care in a Secular Society*, eds Hilary Regan, Rod Horsfield and Gabrielle McMullen (Kew, Victoria: Australian Theological Forum, 1996), p. 223.

[7] Daniel W. Hardy, 'The God who is with the World', unpublished paper, pp. 1, 3, citing C. Vasoli in *The Cambridge History of Renaissance Philosophy*.

tendency to abstraction, illustrated as that is in the unjust but
telling use of the word 'dunce' for the employment of excessive
logical subtlety at the cost of practical wisdom. Although it is
often seen as the root of the modern world's abandonment of
Christianity, in this respect the Renaissance also marks a return
to the essentially Christian notion of the close interweaving of
theory and practice.

The heart of the matter of wisdom as a practical as well as
theoretical ideal takes us to the place where the second arm of
our paradox begins to appear, in the deep differences between
the Bible and the Greeks. The difference, already scarcely con-
cealable, is to be found in different conceptions of the origin
and source of wisdom. Here, the story of Socrates is instructive.
Being told by the oracle that he was the wisest man in Greece
he, Popper-like, sought to falsify the hypothesis, only to be con-
vinced of its truth on the grounds that he alone realized his lack
of wisdom. His successors were less restrained, and, in a sense,
went to the opposite extreme, marking the essentially dualistic
or dialectical character of all Hellenism, undecided as it is
whether the human being is essentially base matter or divine
substance. In all classical philosophy, because of its inherent
instability, the one side of the dialectic is always giving way to
the other. That is to say, in place of Socrates' disavowal of wisdom, except in the most negative sense, his successors not only
divinized it but ascribed it to themselves, as human thinkers.
While wisdom remained a transcendental ideal, it came to be
seen as one open to the mind, to that part of the human being
which was continuous with the divine realm. Accordingly, divine wisdom could be attained by thought, because the human
soul already contained a spark of the divine wisdom. Wisdom
for this strain of Hellenism was thus a focus of the essential
continuity between the human and the divine.

That is where the difficulties begin, because it is not a large
step from there to say that some are endowed with more of this
divine spark than others, and so are qualified to be its mediators: philosopher kings and various rival teachers – perhaps
the rival factions alluded to in 1 Corinthians 1 among them, if it
is true that the divisions within that church were caused by a
variety of groups effectively claiming to represent different
schools of wisdom. Here, Christianity and Hellenism find
their sharpest disagreement, for wisdom as esoteric or superior

knowledge is not claimable by the Christian. Indeed, all forms of gnosticism that endow some beings with superior wisdom or spiritual virtuosity are excluded for a Christian theology, whatever has often been the case in practice.[8]

Greeks, then, tended to see wisdom as something at least potentially written into the human soul. That, especially if it is well endowed with the capacity for recollection, is intrinsically qualified to share in the wisdom written into the heavens, because something of its eternity remains with it while it is encased in the earthly tomb that is the body. In contrast to this, the Bible sees the human being as created: created, indeed, through the mediation of the divine wisdom, but created nonetheless. Such wisdom as does fall to the human being accordingly comes only as gift, indeed, a gift to be lost, as the case of Solomon too well illustrates. Those who reject their covenant responsibilities, the Nabals of this world, fall into folly and worse.[9] Wisdom is to be found in fear of the Lord, not a direct line to the divine realm of platonic recollection. There is, then, in this context, an absolute diastasis between the classical ideal of the intrinsic divinity of the mind and the attribution of creatureliness to the whole of the human being. That is one of the many things Kierkegaard argues in the *Philosophical Fragments*. Between him and his Platonic and Hegelian opponents lies an absolute gulf between a faith mediated by recollection and one dependent upon historical particularity. And so we approach the matter of Christology.

Christ

It is a commonplace that the Christologies of the New Testament writers are marked by a pre-existing tradition of wisdom speculation. Indeed the parallels between the structure of John 1.1ff and some of the earlier characterizations of the

---

[8] A colleague once went to the enthronement (*sic*) of a bishop, and made the observation that while all the words of the service denied that a superior spiritual status was being conferred, all the actions affirmed it. Christian ecclesiology has never broken free from neoplatonic hierarchy.

[9] 'Let not my lord regard this ill-natured fellow, Nabal; for as his name is, so is he; Nabal is his name, and folly is with him', 1 Sam. 25.25.

mediating work of the divine wisdom are manifest: 'Without him was not anything made that was made . . .' (John 1.3); 'When he established the heavens, I was there . . .' (Prov. 8.27). Yet there is only one explicit characterization of Jesus Christ as divine wisdom, and it is that of Paul's first letter to Corinth. This, significantly, takes its shape not from its drawing on other traditions, but from repudiating them:

> For Jews demand signs and Greeks seek wisdom, but we preach Christ crucified, a stumbling block to Jews and folly to Gentiles . . . but to those who are called, both Jews and Greeks, Christ the power of God and the wisdom of God . . . (1 Cor. 1.22, 24)

This raises the question: if we wish to speak not only as scholars of the Bible but as those who believe that it has something to say to the human condition, we must enquire what Paul's opposing of the Church's Christology to that of the religious interpretations of the world around might imply. Clearly, there is no absolute contradiction. That he uses the same word implies a measure of continuity with contemporary usage. This Jesus *is* wisdom, for Greeks too, though only on certain terms. Whatever we may wish to make of other aspects of Barth's programme, here Paul is a 'Barthian' in his understanding of language, in wishing to commandeer a concept in current employment for a new and specific use: to say that, whatever the world thinks wisdom, this is the real thing.

This wisdom is primarily neither a way of fitting human life into the order of creation – though that is its outcome, as we shall see – nor a focus of a general continuity between the mind and the world. It is, rather, a form of divine action in which the relation between creator and creation is realized in a highly particular way. Only after we have probed something of the character of this form of action shall we be ready to move to the passages which apparently, though not so explicitly as here, call upon the traditions of divine wisdom in their attempt to elicit something of the fullness of the reality of Christ.

There are two sides to the divine action characterized in this way. First, as action it is primarily saving, and that includes electing, action. ('God chose what is foolish in the world to shame the wise . . .' v. 27.) This is focused on the proclamation of the cross by the apostle, but the implication is clear that the saving action derives from the historic cross: 'Christ the power of God and the wisdom of God' (v. 24). Moreover, if it is not explicitly said to convey wisdom to the saved, the implication is there: 'Christ Jesus, whom God made our wisdom, our righteousness and sanctification and redemption' (v. 30). We may not be made wise, but Christ is made our wisdom, which is equated, glossed perhaps, with salvation described under three heads, apparently concerning divine action in our past, our present and our future. Christ is our wisdom *as* 'our righteousness and sanctification and redemption'. But, second, this divine action takes the form not only of human action, but of action of the most lowly kind. Indeed, there is the source of the offence to the Greek: only by a radical transformation of meaning can this action be motivated by anything that is recognizably *phronesis*. It is poles apart from Aristotle's ideal of the great-hearted man – man as hero – or the Stoic wisdom of 'apathy'. Yet it is an act of power, indeed, the claim goes, more truly an act of power than what the world could possibly think wise and effective action, 'exercised', to repeat Aristotle's words, 'for the attainment of truth in things that are humanly good and bad'.

For effective is precisely what it is claimed to be. What is presented is not the action of a suffering God, but of a powerful God mediating his action through that of a suffering man. This is borne out by something Paul says in a later chapter that we ought in any case to notice. The one who suffers the cross is also the 'one Lord Jesus Christ, through whom are all things and through whom we exist' (1 Cor. 8.6). We can understand the fuller cosmic Christologies of the later New Testament writings only through the focus provided here. The crucified *is* the one through whom the world was made and is upheld, a view of things taught in similar form by the Letter to the Hebrews. This means that we need to look more closely at the conception of divine action which is implied.

God

'[I]t is part of the concept of wisdom that wisdom takes time to achieve':[10] so Raymond Gaita in his account of human wisdom.

[10] Gaita, 'Response', p. 222.

That is certainly the case with what we call the economy of salvation: that human salvation is worked out by God's action through time, the time of Israel and Jesus Christ. I want to suggest, however, that this might be extended to cover all of what we mean by divine action. Perceptively Karl Barth paired the wisdom and the patience of God in his treatment of the divine perfections, in interesting parallel with Gaita's account of human wisdom:

> We define God's patience as His will, deep-rooted in His essence . . ., to allow to another . . . space and time for the development of its own existence, thus conceding to this existence a reality side by side with His own . . .[11]

The necessary relation of such a concept with the wisdom of God is demonstrated by the fact that:

> The Word of God, however, as the foundation of His patience is neither fortuitous nor capricious . . . Why is it that God is gracious and merciful? . . . The answer is that God is wise. . . . And this is not something dark in itself, but intrinsically illuminating, intelligible and purposeful. The recognition of it does not mean that we are plunged into darkness but, on the contrary, that we are delivered from the darkness of ignorance and brought into the light of a reason hitherto concealed from us . . .[12]

Here Barth might be expounding some of the implications of Paul's 'the foolishness of God is wiser than men', though that is one verse to which he does not make direct reference. The wisdom of God is foolishness in the eyes of the world, because we do not expect God, let alone human agents, to behave in that way.

And that brings us to the central systematic question involved here, the relation of God to time. As we have seen, one philosopher at least understands it to be the essence of wisdom for it to take time to learn. That is not to suggest that God takes time to achieve wisdom – after all, is not his wisdom mediator of

---

[11] Karl Barth, *Church Dogmatics*, eds G. W. Bromiley and T. F. Torrance (Edinburgh: T&T Clark, 1957–1975), vol. 2/1, pp. 409f.

[12] Barth, *Church Dogmatics*, 2/1, pp. 424f.

the creation from the very beginning? – but that it is part of his wisdom in action that it allows, or, better, enables, things to take their course. There is thus a line to be drawn from – let us say chapter 8 – of the book of Genesis to the opening chapters of the First Letter to the Corinthians. It is part of the patient wisdom of God that the tale of disaster which attended the Fall is answered in two ways: with the re-establishment of the creation covenant at the end of the story of Noah and with the call of one man, Abraham, to be the vehicle by whom, in course of time, a covenant of redemption was to be made with all the nations of the earth.

It is therefore of the essence of divine wisdom that, like the human wisdom called to be its image and likeness, it takes account of all the circumstances. Among those circumstances in this case is the human condition not only in its lostness after the Fall – however that is to be understood – but also in its general createdness – its having its being in space and time. The latter is particularly important here. Whatever some theologians and philosophers have sometimes tended to suggest, Origen, Tillich and sundry existentialists among them, our being in time is not a defect of being, but part of its goodness. If we listen to those who belong to a rather different tradition from those I have mentioned, beginning with Irenaeus, we shall learn that human life is eschatological *in its structuring*: it is created with a view to an end that more than replicated its beginning, because it is given *to be perfected.* That is to say, it reaches its perfection only at its end, and so needs time to become what it truly is. I am not suggesting, with the early Pannenberg,[13] that the present is created from the future, but that it is created from the past and oriented to a future perfection. It is, by its very nature, directed to a completion that *takes time.* And so divine action centred in the death of Jesus is action which is fully appropriate both to human fallenness and to its need of time in order to be itself. For the cross is where God engages with the human condition as it actually is, respecting both its temporal structures and the nature of those who are in need of being redirected to their proper course. Whatever may be the case with ours, God's

[13] Wolfhart Pannenberg, 'The God of Hope', *Basic Questions in Theology* 2 (London: SCM Press, 1971), pp. 234–49 (p. 243).

action is true *phronesis*, 'exercised for the attainment of truth in things that are humanly good and bad'.

The notion of God's patient action in time should be understood to hold good for all of what is called the divine economy, the whole spread of God's activity in and toward the world, summed up as it is in the traditional pairing of creation and redemption. God's action in and towards the world takes the form of *both* creating what is *and* redeeming what has failed to become what it is called to be. Clearly, on this account, what is called redemption takes time, and the divine action which brings it about is extended in time. But what of creating action? It has been argued by Paul Helm that

from the Creator's standpoint his creation is a whole; it is not a creation in time, but with time. From the standpoint of an intelligent creature the universe is co-eternal with God, for there is no time when the universe is not. For such an agent the universe unfolds as a temporal sequence, with a past, a present and a future.[14]

In this, Helm is working with a strong doctrine of the timelessness of God: God is in every respect timeless; any divine act will therefore be timeless; therefore, from God's point of view the universe is timeless. God may create it with time, but in no way is his action of creation to be conceived as temporal. The conception comes from Augustine – ultimately, perhaps from Philo – whose embarrassment with the Genesis account of six days, combined with his Platonism, caused him repeatedly to assert that God creates the whole world instantaneously, because it would be in some way a slur on God's omnipotence to suggest anything else.

This involves two mistakes, which have had serious consequences. The first is that it introduces a divorce between God's creating action, which is timeless, and his saving and redeeming action, which takes time. We shall return to that later. The second is that it perpetrates such a violation of the Genesis text that one is tempted to a sneaking sympathy for the so-called creationists, who at least have the merit of taking

[14] Paul Helm, 'Eternal Creation. The Doctrine of the Two Standpoints', *The Doctrine of Creation: Essays in Dogmatics, History and Philosophy*, ed. Colin E. Gunton (Edinburgh: T&T Clark, 1997).

the text seriously. But we do not have to pay that price. We are not faced with a choice between literalism and the kind of Platonizing allegory that turns the days into stages of the spiritual life, as in Augustine. Basil of Caesarea is more balanced when he says that, when Scripture says 'one day' it means that it wishes to establish the world's relation to eternity, and is depicting 'distinctions between various states and modes of action' – that is to say, different ways in which God acts towards the world.[15]

The relevance of this is in part that the Platonizing of the doctrine over the centuries has not only made such temporal processes as evolution more difficult to reconcile with the doctrine of creation, but it has also prevented theology from saying that there is a sense in which, to use a rather anthropomorphic form of words, God takes his time, that is to say, allows us to understand that creation is not to be understood as an instantaneous act, but as extended in our time. The most disastrous consequence of the Platonizing of the text is that it excludes a proper conception of the mediation of creation to emerge. This leads to an inadequate understanding of transcendence, so that Aquinas – to cite one influential example – can say that God does not allow the creation to act ministerially, but creates the whole by the word alone.[16] Creation by word, or simple fiat, is played against the other models of God's relation to the world found in Genesis and elsewhere, including, significantly for our theme, the wisdom literature. 'When he marked out the foundations of the earth, then I was beside him, like a master workman . . .' (Prov. 8. 29f.). Contrast Augustine's instantaneous creation by word with Basil's more relational view: 'He who gave the order at the same time gifted it (the earth) with the grace and power to bring forth' (8. 1). To deny that is to falsify what the text does have to tell us about the nature of God's action in creating. According to Francis Watson's exegesis of Genesis 1, 'the speech–act model occurs unambiguously on only three occasions in this chapter,'[17] and therefore requires

---

[15] Basil, *Hexaemeron*, 2. 8; Basil of Caesarea, *Homilies on the Hexaemeron*; The Fathers of the Church, vol. 46, tr. A. C. Way (Washington, DC: Catholic University of America Press, 1968).

[16] Thomas Aquinas, *Summa Theologiae* ed. and tr. J Cunningham (London: Eyre and Spottiswoode, 1963–1975), I. 45. 5.

[17] Francis Watson, *Text, Church and World* (Edinburgh: T&T Clark, 1994), p. 140.

supplementation. The second model for divine action is what he calls the 'fabrication model', where the objects of creation do not immediately spring into being but have to be constructed.[18] It is not absolutely distinct from the first model, and is often, both here and in the Psalms, used in conjunction with it, and with a third, which he calls the mediation model:

> God creates immediately by command and by fabrication, but he also and simultaneously creates mediately in employing one of his creatures as the womb out of which the others proceed . . . 'Let the earth put forth . . .'
> The creation narrative thus makes use of three interconnected but distinct models in order to represent the act of divine creation. Each has a different role, but the full meaning of each emerges only in combination with the others.[19]

Whatever else we are to make of Genesis 1, we must realize that it is consistent with a conception of the wisdom of God as shaping his creating activity to the form of that which is shaped, and it is of the essence of this that it is *within* time as well as over-against it. It is therefore a function of the wisdom of God that he allows the world time to become that which it is called and created to be. That is the reason why the past tense for creation cannot be rigidly distinguished from the present, creation from providence, even though some distinction remains necessary. 'The Lord by wisdom founded the earth . . . by his knowledge the deeps broke forth, and the clouds drop down the dew' (Prov. 3. 19–20).

This returns us to the first of the two mistakes in the Augustinian account, what I above called a divorce between God's timeless creating action and his temporal saving and redeeming action. It is at the root of the much-documented and lamented breach in the Western theological tradition between the orders of creation and redemption. One revealing symptom in our context is the almost complete lack of substantive christological structuring in the medieval tradition of creation theology, so that William of Ockham can even cite John 1.1ff. without reference to the part played in creation by the eternal Word.

---

[18] Watson, *Text, Church and World*, p. 141.
[19] Watson, *Text, Church and World*, pp. 142–3.

Creation for Ockham is a unitary act,[20] and this is indicative of another symptom of the Western failure, what Rahner has famously identified as the breach between the loci 'On the one God' and 'On the triune God' in the dogmatic tradition. It is the one God who creates, the triune who redeems, and while to put it in this way is something of a caricature, there is a failure of Christology to be discerned in this area. Christology is simply not determinative enough of the doctrine of creation in the West, and that is why we need the uniquely integrating focus provided by the notion of Christ as the wisdom of God.

And so we come to the links between the Wisdom literature and such passages as 1 Corinthians 8.6, Hebrews 1, Colossians 1 and John 1. To say that Jesus Christ is the mediator of creation is to say, among other things, that God's being is in some way oriented to the world of time and space that he takes to himself in the incarnation. That is why we can and must read christologically passages like that from Proverbs which speak of the ministerial action of wisdom in the creation and upholding of the world. The outcome is that in the concept of wisdom we have a way of integrating while distinguishing two forms of the one God's action towards and in the world. There must be two forms, and not, as in the programmes of such as Matthew Fox, a reduction of all divine action to creation. To argue for an order of redemption alongside of, and indeed, supervening on, the order of creation, is not to belittle the creation, but to affirm its importance. There is nothing intrinsically fallen about time in itself; there we can agree with the exponents of 'creation spirituality'. Creation's temporality is its glory: it is a universe ordered in both space and time. It is not time that is the problem, but the fact that those who live in it find themselves beset by sin, suffering and evil. Creation spirituality simply cannot encompass the weight of evil afflicting the created order. The problem with time is what happens in it, and it is serious enough to require that the divine wisdom meet it in the act of the incarnate Lord's death upon the cross.

For an account of the two sides of our life in time I cite Douglas Farrow on Irenaeus:

---

[20] *Quodlibetal Questions* 2, Q4. Art. 2. John 1.3 means that God made all other things through himself (*omnia alia a Deo per ipsum facta sunt*), *Opera Theologica* vol. 9, p. 215.

The love for God which is the life of man cannot emerge *ex nihilo* in full bloom; it requires to grow with experience. But that in turn is what makes the fall, however unsurprising such a devastating affair. In the fall man is 'turned backwards'. He does not grow up in the love of God as he is intended to. The course of his time, his so-called progress, is set in the wrong direction.[21]

We are created for a life in time – what we could, I suppose, call God's original blessing. But supervening upon that blessing is the human rejection of that grace, so that only through the wisdom of the cross can those who are perishing be redeemed.

To recapitulate the argument of this long section. The problem with all views of creation as an eternal act, rather than the act of the eternal God both towards and in time, is that they threaten to undermine the goodness of the intrinsic temporality of creation. In so threatening, they undermine the christological link between creation and redemption. It is an implication of the patient wisdom of God that not only does he will a world that is very good in its temporality, but that he also continues to act in and toward it in a way appropriate to its structure. The loving creation of something to be in and through time implies a continuing concern with that which is created. Wisdom is a function of the love of God in all its manifest variety of action in and towards the world, summed up as that is in abstractions designed to summarize its variety in unity, like creation, providence and redemption.

Conclusion

In conclusion, the following summary claims can be made:

1. The modern Western world has for the most part lost its hold on a concept of wisdom, although such as it maintains can be seen to have two, and sometimes overlapping, historical roots, in the Bible and in Greece.

---

[21] Douglas Farrow, 'St Irenaeus of Lyons. The Church and the World', *Pro Ecclesia* 4 (1995), pp. 333–55 (p. 348).

2. Despite their elements in common, there is a fundamental disagreement at the heart of the two traditions, which comes to a head in Paul's clear distinction between the crucified Christ as the wisdom of God and all other human systems of wisdom.

3. If wisdom, as is suggested in different ways by both Old Testament and Greece, is that human habitation of the world which integrates its various dimensions – the true, the good and the beautiful – then what we make of it will be rooted in what we think the world to be. That is to say, it will be rooted in our apprehension of what we make of the doctrine of creation, or its equivalent.

4. To say that the crucified Christ is the wisdom of God is to say that he is the key to the meaning of the whole of the created order, and therefore the source of true wisdom, wherever that is to be found.

5. It follows from all this that the wisdom of God in salvation and redemption is such that it allows not only for the temporality of things, the fact that 'things by season seasoned are/To their right praise and true perfection,'[22] but for the form of their fallenness also. If there is to be true redemption for a temporal but fallen world, it must consist in enabling things to come to their due perfection in and through the process of time: by 'redeeming the time'. It is that obscure but suggestive expression that enables us to return, finally, to that with which we started: the notion of right human thought and action in the world.

6. Because Jesus Christ is the wisdom of God, he is not only the action of God which takes into account the particular needs of the occasion to which it is directed, but also a form of that right human being which realizes the truth of being. He is, to repeat the words of Paul, our wisdom because he is our 'righteousness and sanctification and redemption'; that is to say, he is the means by which human failure to achieve the end for which the human race was created – its movement backwards – is reversed into a movement towards proper perfection. We are wise, therefore, when our being is conformed to that of his (Phil. 2). To be wise is not to exercise

---

[22] William Shakespeare, *The Merchant of Venice* 5. i. 108–9.

our inbuilt continuity with divine and timeless Platonic wisdom, but to be incorporate in him who is the one personal mediator between all divine and all created being.

9

The Spirit and Jesus: (1) Martin Kähler Revisited. Variations on Hebrews 4.15[1]

Humanity and History

'. . . the same of one substance with us as touching the manhood, like us in all things apart from sin.' Chalcedon's lapidary summary of the doctrine of the humanity of Christ, echoing as it does the Epistle to the Hebrews, 'tempted in every way, just as we are – yet was without sin' (4.15), can serve as a summary of one side of the New Testament's portrayal of the saviour. More than that, it serves as a test for what any church or theologian makes of the story of the earthly Jesus and its outcome. Martin Kähler, whom we shall be using as a case study, himself recognizes the importance of this, and indeed gives a list of other biblical parallels, particularly in Hebrews: 'for this reason he had to be made like his brothers in every way, in order that he might become a merciful and faithful high priest. . . . Because he himself suffered when he was tempted, he is able to help those who are being tempted' (2.17–8).

Of Jesus' humanity according to the Gospels and Epistles there can be no doubt, especially if we bear in mind that none of his acts before the resurrection is without parallel among Israel's prophets, priests and kings. To some of them, too, are attributed the kind of acts of authority, healing and power that we see Jesus performing in the power of the Spirit. Even the multiplication of the loaves and fish has its antecedents, in, for example the ministry of Elijah to the widow of Zarephath,

[1] Previously published in *Ex Auditu* 14 (1998), pp. 21–30.

where 'the jar of flour was not used up and the jug of oil did not run dry, in keeping with the word of the Lord spoken by Elijah' (1 Kings 17.16). This also is, according to the biblical view of things, a fully and authentically human act, albeit done in the power of God. And there lies the topic for today: how are we to understand Jesus' earthly career as a constitutive part of the gospel of divine grace?

The representatives of what for the sake of convenience I shall call the modern world view have had, to say the least, a number of problems with what can be called, with equal summary imprecision, the classical christological tradition. We have heard them so often that I shall simply extract those features which bear upon our theme. They centre on the question of the divinity of Christ, of whether in particular one described as the Gospels describe him can justifiably be granted divine status. In other words, can one so manifestly human be also divine? But there are problems about the humanity as well. The theological problem, and it is a genuine one, concerns whether the tradition has given adequate weight to its dogmatic claims of 'the same of one substance with us as touching the manhood'. It is now such a commonplace to accuse the tradition of failure here that we must beware of overdoing it. After all, do we not see in the mystery plays and late-medieval and Renaissance painting much realistic depiction of the saviour's humanity, and especially of his sufferings; do we not read in the Christology of Anselm, the inspiration of much of that painting, of the humble obedience of the one who went to the cross for our sins? Here, however, the problem is exacerbated rather than solved for the typical early modern critic of the faith. Apparently we have a God who unjustly compels his Son to undergo death for the sake of the world. Although Anselm had an answer to the charge – that true freedom consists in doing that which reason demands – it does not satisfy the typical modern.

The second objection to traditional Christology shows us why. The enlightened prefer their representatives to be successful rather than the opposite, a tendency well illustrated by John Locke's attempted defence of Christianity and its outcome. Building on a long tradition of defending the Christian faith in terms of its success – what Kierkegaard called world-historical boasting – Locke appealed, among other things, to Jesus' performance of miracles as signs of his divine calling.[2] Thus he founded a long tradition of enlightened defence of the faith, but only by means of a dogmatic transposition whose significance can scarcely be exaggerated. Such signs as the virgin birth and Jesus' miraculous acts are now called in service of his divinity rather than being seen as the locus of or functions of his humanity. In effect, a crude theology of interventionism locates the miracles outside what might be called the everyday human life of Jesus. This was a shift whose nemesis was near, as we all know too well. Hume brought to bear the assumptions of that very mechanistic philosophy to which it was hoped the miraculous would offer an exception. But for mechanism there are finally no exceptions, and once the history of Jesus is interpreted in terms of an impersonal cosmology, it is in effect deprived of its character as history. History is subsumed under nature. The nineteenth-century liberals tried to carve out a place for history by shifting interest from the outer events to Jesus' inner life or moral teaching, but the theological displacement is the same. Almost everything hangs on Jesus' human success; the cross becomes an offence to be avoided, the resurrection having already been effectively ruled out of court.

This shows, as if it needed to be shown, that our third theological problem is the question about the nature of history. No human figure is interpretable without employing, implying or assuming a philosophy or theology of history. For recent thought, there are, in general, two possible ways of construing this: one's philosophy of history is either empiricist – that is to say, quixotically attempting to deliver the facts and nothing more – or idealist, according to which the onus is on the intellectual construction of the historian, who imposes some pattern upon the material to hand. There have been attempts to evade or transcend the dilemma, notably that of Hegel and the Marxists, who provide object lessons for us all. One construes divine action in largely immanent terms: God is real, but is identical or virtually identical with history, which has a meaning but not a Lord. The others more thoroughly displace divine action by that of history, which effectively becomes the deity. The outcome is a paradox. God is abolished to make room for human

---

[2] John Locke, *The Reasonableness of Christianity* (1695, various editions).

freedom, but a more severe master emerges from the action. History ceases to be the place of genuinely human action, because there is no space for the very human freedom which modernity is so desperate to establish. Only from the point of view of the eternal creator of the ends of the earth can the realm of history be envisaged without detracting from its character as truly historical: that is, truly spatio-temporal happening to which genuinely human action is intrinsic.

In its origins the conception of history as the realm of human action had some such end in view, and a brief observation about these may help us on our way. For Herodotus, the great struggle between Persia and Greece, involving as it does large tracts of history of the ancient world, is significant both humanly and, in a manner of speaking, divinely. He has his own two-nature doctrine of history, as the place of human action and divine overruling. It is not the Bible's view of history or of God. Behind the titanic struggle he describes is divine and impersonal fate, jealous of human glory and bringing it relentlessly to the dust. Yet there is a real distinction between divine action and human history. The contrast between Herodotus and the Bible makes clear the issue that is often confused in modern theologies of history with their often hybrid combinations of Hebrew and Greek. What, finally, makes things go the way they do, impersonal fate or providential divine action? And what part, if any, is granted to genuinely human action in the things that take place? Indeed, what do we understand genuinely human action to be? Martin Kähler's famous critique of the nineteenth-century quest for the historical Jesus takes us, I believe, half way to a christological answer to the question.[3]

Kähler on the Humanity of Christ

And so we come to Martin Kähler, who should not be judged for the iniquities of those who have misused him – at least, not for

---

[3] Martin Kähler, *The So-called Historical Jesus and the Historic Biblical Christ* tr. and ed., with an Introduction, by Carl E. Braaten (Philadelphia: Fortress Press, 1964). Subsequent references to this book will appear in parenthesis in the main text.

all of them. Notable are those of his pupil, Paul Tillich, whose extension of the principle of justification by faith to the intellectual sphere may indeed owe something to Kähler. But the debt does not extend as far as Tillich's cavalier treatment of the humanity of Christ, according to which, 'He who is the bearer of the final revelation must surrender his finitude – not only his life but also his finite power and knowledge and perfection.'[4] Tillich is aware of the pitfalls of nineteenth-century Christology, and in his own way seeks to avoid a Christology of success. But his much-quoted expression, 'He proves and confirms his character as the Christ in the sacrifice of himself as Jesus to himself as the Christ'[5] could imply, and has often been taken to imply, the most radical rejection of Jesus' humanity, who becomes, in a Euchtychian way, little more than the bearer of the divine.

It may be that it is the mediation of Kähler through Tillich that has led to his being misunderstood. In beginning his recent study of *The Historical Christ and the Jesus of Faith*, Stephen Evans grants him but one dismissive footnote as being one of those theologians who have attempted to draw a distinction, which he wishes to subvert, between 'the historical Jesus' and 'the Christ of faith'.[6] Despite the fact that Evans's title represents an inversion of Kähler's, the latter's important book is not otherwise treated in this study, perhaps because the author rightly has in his sights the simplistic theology of history to be found in such works as Van Harvey's *The Historian and the Believer*,[7] as well as the antics of the Jesus Seminar. Evans rightly argues that the narrowing of the concept of history to exclude such conceptions as incarnation and the miraculous simply derives from a priori prejudice, and he develops a strong case for understanding what he summarizes as the 'incarnational narrative' as properly describable as historical.[8] What Evans seeks is a view of

[4] Paul Tillich, *Systematic Theology* (London: Nisbet, 1968), vol. 1, p. 148.

[5] Tillich, *Systematic Theology*, vol. 2, p. 142.

[6] Stephen Evans, *The Historical Christ and the Jesus of Faith. The Incarnational Narrative as History* (Oxford: Clarendon Press, 1996), p. vi.

[7] Van A. Harvey, *The Historian and the Believer* (London: SCM Press, 1967).

[8] Evans, *The Historical Christ*, especially chapter 1. For a wonderful assault on the philosophical assumptions of some contemporary biblical criticism, see Alvin Plantinga, 'Two (or more) Kinds of Scripture Scholarship', *Modern Theology* 14 (1998), pp. 243–78.

history which concedes that the gospel picture of Jesus can
rightly be so described.

However, that there is more in common between Kähler and
Evans than first meets the eye is suggested by the fact that the
former had opponents similar to those of the latter. Kähler's
intention, he says explicitly, is to avoid both historicism and
dogmatism. He even accepts modernist criticisms of the old
credal formulae. What he objects to is that attempts to fill out
'the pallid outline' of the christological dogma by employing
the biblical portrait of Christ have in process of time come to be
displaced by exercises in human creativity (pp. 43–4). His first
concern therefore is to provide a critique of the Life of Jesus
movement, and in particular its wild speculation which offends
against what Kähler holds to be 'the cardinal virtue of genuine
historical research', its modesty. A large part of his case is that
there are features of the biblical portrait of Jesus that cannot be
dealt with by secular historiography. Salient among them is his
sinlessness, which entails that the distinction between Jesus and
ourselves is not one of degree but of kind.

Kähler is surely right to hold that to ascribe sinlessness to
Jesus is completely different from either idealizing him or
attempting to understand him by analogy with other human
beings:

> All this is a miracle which cannot be explained merely in
> terms of an innocent disposition. It is conceivable only
> because this infant entered upon his earthly existence with a
> prior endowment quite different from our own, because in all
> the stages of his inner life an absolutely independent will was
> expressing itself, because God's grace and truth became
> incarnate in him. (pp. 53f.)

Notice that Kähler is rooting Jesus' sinlessness in the fact that
his life was the expression of 'an absolutely independent will', a
feature we shall need to discuss below. He concludes that: 'The
Gospels confront each of us with an Either/Or. The question is
whether the historian will humble himself before the unique
sinless Person . . .' (p. 55). It is important here to note that our
author is dealing with that in which Jesus is different from
us, as 'the source from which the outpouring of the purifying
Spirit is to proceed . . .' (p. 57). Even here, however, he is aware
of the dogmatic pitfalls, '[t]hat he was like us is, of course,

incomparably significant for us' (pp. 58–9). Yet although the character of the likeness is 'self-evident', Scripture, he claims, makes no attempt to demonstrate it. The Bible is mainly interested in Jesus' difference from us, for therein lies our fulfilment. Beyond all the likenesses that we may discern, 'there is something unique in the way he did things, for there has never been a man like him' (p. 59).

When he moves from the incarnation to the resurrection, Kähler anticipates some of the criticisms made, notably by Hans Frei, of the eighteenth- and nineteenth-century hermeneutical enterprise.[9] 'The risen Lord is not the historical Jesus behind the gospels, but the Christ of the apostolic preaching, of the whole New Testament' (p. 65). Our author is accordingly not playing the Christ of faith against the Jesus of history in the way Bultmann was later to do, but asking us to revise our understanding of who the Jesus of history is. He does, indeed, give hostages to fortune: 'this real Christ is the Christ who is preached' (p. 66). Yet the gulf that separates him from Bultmann is shown in the fact that it is Jesus of whom he is speaking – 'the Jesus whom the eyes of faith behold at every step he takes and every syllable he utters . . .' (p. 66). In a footnote he defends himself against misunderstanding: 'I am here referring to the portrayal of Jesus in the Gospels, interpreted of course from the viewpoint of the faith one encounters there as well as in the rest of the New Testament' (p. 67). In doing this, he turns the tables on the historians, suggesting that the proper function of historical method is the more modest one of the handmaid rather than the queen, of protecting the gospel from later embellishments of the biblical picture.

Kähler's project is to restore a balance which had been lost as a result of the rejection of dogmatics in the name of history. But he is not playing dogmatics against history, as is sometimes suggested. For him, the function of dogmatics is not to distort the history by ignoring it, but to mediate 'the plain Christian faith, to set limits to the learned pontificating of the historians' (p. 73). The reason is that there is something here that must first be received rather than established by independent intellectual

---

[9] Hans Frei, *The Eclipse of Biblical Narrative* (New Haven and London: Yale University Press, 1974).

struggle. All that we need for an understanding of Jesus is, after all, to be found in the pages of Scripture. '[A]ll the biblical portrayals evoke the undeniable impression of the fullest reality, so that one might venture to predict how he might have acted in this or that situation . . . This is why to commune with Jesus one needs nothing more than the biblical presentation' (p. 78). I repeat: Kähler is here speaking of the earthly Jesus, not a dogmatic abstraction. He continues to hold two themes in harness: the uniqueness of the one here presented, and the sheer reality of the portrayal. He is as concerned as anyone with the historical authenticity of the Bible, yet on its own terms. Let us hear him at length in a crucial passage:

> Carlyle had good reason for speaking of the inexorable truth of the biblical portrayals, for all of these portrayals are of people like ourselves. But what about the biblical picture of Jesus? That it seems so familiar to us now is an understandable delusion. We know this picture from childhood . . . But if we paused to reflect and look around, then he would surely seem very strange to us in his noble sublimity. Yet he seems as lifelike and real as if we had seen him with our own eyes. How could such a realistic picture of the sinless One be a poetic creation? Poetry has only sinful men within its purview . . . The biblical picture of Christ, so lifelike and unique beyond imagination, is not a poetic idealization originating in the human mind. The reality of Christ himself has left its ineffaceable impress upon this picture. (p. 79)

Make of that what you will, it is not written by one who rejects a historical Jesus; rather, Kähler rejects a narrow way of conceiving that reality. This history is the reality of one whose human life is recognizably such, but uniquely different from ourselves. Kähler is right that if *Historie* means only that etiolated conception of history represented by the Jesus Seminar, then we need another concept for it. What is at stake is the meaning of history, and of God's ordering of it.

The discussion of Kähler today tends to centre on his view, later taken up in radical form by Bultmann, that the real Christ is the preached Christ. Pannenberg, for example, lights upon this as the Achilles' heel of his book. 'It is false to say that the preached Christ is the real Christ. One can and must get back to Jesus himself from the witness of the apostles by trying to recognize, and thus making allowance for, the relation of New Testament texts to their respective situations.'[10] One consideration for Pannenberg here, I think, is to reject the use of Kähler in order to evade the challenge presented by Bultmann's historical septicism. Yet it is surely clear that Bultmann and Kähler inhabit different worlds. The expression 'the real Christ is the preached Christ' is not used by Kähler in a Bultmannian sense. The preached Christ means the one who is proclaimed as a living historical reality, not one whose reality is in some way realized only in the preaching.

The crucial question to our author is rather different. Does he so stress the difference of Jesus from others that he deprives him of a true humanity? When he claims that, 'No man has ever spoken or acted thus . . .', he is indeed only repeating what the New Testament says. Scripture does emphasize Jesus' humanity, 'but hardly ever without adding expressions like "without sin," "by grace," "in humility and perfect obedience," etc.' (p. 59). Here, once again, he is right. Only the shallowest theology will hold that Jesus' utter uniqueness in this respect is to make him other than fully human. There is of course a theological point to be made: that the sinless is more truly human than others of us, whose sin, by virtue of the fact that it is sin, represents a lessening of our humanity. There is, then, some truth in the rhetorical question Kähler asks: 'Which is the more important for us, that wherein Jesus is like us, or that wherein he was and is totally different from us?' (p. 58). But only some, for both aspects have claim to centrality: that the unassumed is the unhealed – for salvation depends upon the Lord's total identification with our human condition – and that there is a radical difference of some kind.

Kähler, by locating Jesus' uniqueness so centrally in his sinlessness – important as that is – has thrown the matter out of balance. To put the same enquiry another way, we can ask whether the incarnation and Jesus' sinlessness are equivalent. Is it Jesus' sinlessness that makes him different in kind from us? And so we return to the place where we began, with the Letter to the Hebrews, 'tempted in every way, just as we are – yet was

[10] Wolfhart Pannenberg, *Jesus – God and Man*, tr. L. Wilkins and D. Priebe (London: SCM Press, 1968), p. 23.

without sin' (4. 15). We might say that Kähler has made much of
the second half of that verse, but less of the first. It is indeed,
central to his enterprise to do so. But can there be an adequate
Christology without far more attention being given to that side:
to what we might call the ordinariness of the Jesus of the
Gospels? Can we have our cake and eat it? A saviour whose
exceptionableness is that of a man who is in some ways not
exceptional, for that is what the first half of the verse – 'in every
way, just as we are' – implies? An answer to that question
requires a more detailed study of what it is that makes Jesus truly
human.

Marks of the Human

The following have some claim to be the chief marks of an
adequate treatment of the humanity of Jesus Christ. It is noteworthy that they are aspects of the story in which Martin Kähler
shows little interest, partly, perhaps, because they were not
germane to his thesis to establish the saving uniqueness of
Jesus, but also because he appears to have shared a traditional
weakness of dogmatic Christology: simply to fail to do justice
to the details of the story which our verse from Hebrews
summarizes.

1. In the light of the strictures on modernist Christology
made in the first section, we must begin by saying that a full
doctrine of the humanity of Christ will require us to construe as
fully a part of his human history those episodes which are sometimes taken to indicate his divinity, in particular the conception
and birth, the miracles and the resurrection. Let us begin with
what Barth, not in every way helpfully, perhaps, called the miracles at the beginning and end of Jesus' life. A large part of the
significance of the narratives of Jesus' birth derives not only
from the fact that here we have a miraculous new divine initiative of salvation but that this is realized through one who is fully
and authentically human flesh and blood. A real human being
is shaped from the flesh of the Virgin by the Father's creator
Spirit. As Irving puts it, 'He submits Himself unto His Father to
be made flesh; His Father sendeth the Holy Spirit to prepare
Him a body . . . and thus, by creative act of Father, Son and Holy
Ghost, not by ordinary generation, Christ is constituted a Divine

and human nature in one person.'[11] Yet as Irving was to uphold, at the expense of much suffering, this was a flesh that was truly liable to the assaults of the enemy, not one automatically predetermined to innocence.

Similar points hold with the resurrection. It is indeed the case that the resurrection is crucial to the truth of Christianity. If it did not happen as, in some recognizable sense, a historical event, then our faith is indeed in vain, as the Apostle held. But the tendency to hang everything on its character as miracle can take our attention away from the fact that its dogmatic significance is tied up as much with Jesus' humanity as with his divinity. As the first-born from the dead, he represents as human the destiny of those who will later die in him, as the extended parallel between him and the believer in 1 Corinthians 15 makes clear. Flesh and blood may not be able to inherit the Kingdom, but it is flesh and blood which die, decay and are raised to eternal life. It is becoming an increasingly frequent dogmatic claim that the resurrection of Jesus as much as his birth should be understood trinitarianly: as the Father raising the Son through the mediation of the Holy Spirit. The significance of this will be made clearer as the argument proceeds, but the central point is that the Spirit, as the Lord and giver of life, has here to be understood in terms of God's enabling the creation to become that which it was created to be. The two defining miracles are thus not simply miracles, but point to the fact that it is through this particular, truly human, life, that the 'creation itself is liberated from its bondage to decay and brought into the glorious freedom of the children of God' (Rom. 8. 21).

2. The second mark of Jesus' humanity is that it is only through the agency of that same Spirit that authority is granted to him to speak the word of truth and renew the face of the earth by reclaiming it for its King. This is well illustrated by Mark's account of the ministry of Jesus in the episodes leading up to Peter's confession at Caesarea Philippi. Jesus' healings according to Mark are sometimes by word alone and sometimes through physical interaction with the material world (compare here the different forms of God's creating action in Genesis 1).

[11] G. Carlyle, ed., *The Collected Writings of Edward Irving in Five Volumes*, vol. 5, (London: Alexander Strachan, 1865), p. 159, see also pp. 160f.

That Jesus is the lord of creation come to reclaim his own is frequently made clear. The storm is stilled almost by an act of exorcism, so that the wondering question is asked: 'Who is this? Even the wind and the waves obey him!' (Mark 4. 41). But this portrayal of Jesus as the lord of creation is not at the expense of an equal emphasis that this is the work of a truly human agent, not a worker of 'magic'. 'He could not do any miracles there, except lay his hands on a few . . .' (6. 5). Thus the rule of God is mediated by the words and actions of a genuinely human agent: the 'hand of God' (Irenaeus), who is God humanly at work reclaiming the world from its bondage to vanity. It is in this light, I believe, that we should understand the 'staged' nature of some of the healings. The fact that the blind man first sees, 'people; they look like trees walking around' is physiologically credible: people do have to learn to see, so that Jesus' healings are accommodated to the condition of those in need of healing. Once again, we cannot escape an emphasis on the Lord's embodiment; that his living of the human life is in that respect identical to ours. After all, all embodiments are particular and unique; the fact that this one took the form that it did does not remove its genuine humanity, unless other considerations are deemed to do so.

3. To step back a little in the Gospel narrative, we come to the third requirement for a proper treatment of the humanity of Jesus, and that is the granting – with our text from Hebrews and Chalcedon – of a definitive place to his being tempted – a feature which for Luke is made part of the whole story, for temptation is renewed and completed in Gethsemane, making the whole of the ministry the locus of the testing. ('When the devil had finished all this tempting, he left him until an opportune time', Luke 4. 13.) That is to say, it is intrinsic to the humanity of Jesus that he endures the assaults of evil and the evil one without succumbing to them: that is, without their having the disrupting and alienating effect on his relation to God and the world that they do for fallen humankind. One cannot, as Tillich insisted, be fully involved in human society and history without sharing in their ambiguities. But crucial for the teaching of the saving significance of Jesus' humanity – something on which Tillich was much weaker – is the fact that Jesus' relation to the Father was not that of others; that where all others fail, he remained true and 'by the power of the eternal Spirit offered

himself unblemished to God . . .' (Heb. 9.14). Like the verse from Luke, this, too, makes a point that the two episodes of temptation frame the whole life of Jesus, pointing forward to his death and defining its character.

4. The fourth requirement is the articulation of a full continuity of this man with the prophets, priests and kings of Israel. All human beings are particular, taking the shape of their lives from the contingency of their earthly beginning, middle and ending. To idealize Jesus, as the modern world so easily does, is to deprive him of his contingency as rooted in and emerging from the people of Israel. The neglect of that, as we know all too well, is one of the great offences of modern theological history; while the sheer inadequacy of modernity's attempt to do justice to Jesus' Jewishness is signalled by the fact that this is the very feature that is lost as the result of its idealizing activities. It was particularly true of the nineteenth-century lives – beginning egregiously with Schleiermacher's attempt to minimize the theological significance of Jesus' Jewishness – that this feature tended to be lost as the result of idealizing. Similarly, in opposition to Tillich we must emphasize that it is not by surrender of his Jewish particularity and finitude but by its mediating function that Jesus' life has its theological significance.

5. There can be no adequate theology of the humanity of Christ without due weight being given to his ascension, which establishes the continuity of the Kingdom re-established in the ministry of Jesus with that affirmed in 1 Corinthians 15. The earthly Jesus is the one who rules at the right hand of the Father until all his enemies have been conquered. Here it becomes possible to produce a counter-definition to that propounded by Martin Kähler. The real Christ may indeed be the preached Christ, the one to be found within, not behind, the words of the text. But he is also the ascended Lord, at the right hand of the Father and as such one who is *quodam modo praesens, quodam modo absens* to and from the Church and the world. This gives the notion of the preached Christ a reference to reality which enables other features of his presence-in-absence to be included. The ascended Jesus is the Jesus made present by the Holy Spirit in the sacraments, the communion of the people of God and wherever the Kingdom is realized in the world.

6. The question of mediation raised by the last point is also the question of pneumatology. It is noteworthy how repeatedly

the Holy Spirit becomes part of the story at crises of Jesus' ministry. We have seen how for Irving it is by the Spirit that God the Father shapes a body for his Son in the womb of Mary, and how for parts of the tradition it is by his Spirit that the Father raises the Son from the tomb. In between, the Spirit maintains the relation between the incarnate Jesus and the Father whose will he is sent to do. We can repeat here the allusion to that crucial episode for our theme, the temptation. In all three Synoptic accounts, the Spirit leads Jesus out into the wilderness to be tempted. If, to return to the Christology of Hebrews, it is through the Spirit that Jesus offers a perfect sacrifice to the Father as at once priest and victim, it follows – it is implied in a strong sense – that the whole of Jesus' authentically human life is made what it uniquely is through the action of the Spirit.

Together, these six points introduce an important theological principle, which will feature prominently in the next section of the chapter. In relation to the created order, and particularly in relation to the human creature, 'macrocosm' of the creation,[12] it is the Spirit's function, through God the Son, to enable the creation to become that which it was created to be. (It is thus an essentially eschatological mode of activity.) In so far as human beings are enabled by the Spirit to be obedient to the Father who gave his Son for the salvation of the world, they become and achieve that which they are called to be and do. It is that aspect which is absent from Kähler's account. Jesus' human uniqueness, that sinlessness of which he made so much, surely consists not so much in that to which our author refers

> because this infant entered upon his earthly existence with a prior endowment quite different from our own, because in all the stages of his inner life an absolutely independent will was expressing itself, because God's grace and truth became incarnate in him

---

[12] '[T]he more correct way would be to consider man as a macrocosm, because he is called to comprehend the whole world within himself . . . The idea that man is called to become a world writ large had a more precise expression, however, in the term "macro-anthropos".' Dumitru Staniloae, cited by Andrew Louth, 'Review Essay: the Orthodox Dogmatic Theology of Dumitru Staniloae', *Modern Theology* 13 (1997), pp. 252–67 (p. 259).

but in the fact that the incarnate one was maintained in truth by the Spirit, uniquely. The two, to be sure, are not necessarily antithetical. The point is that unless the second of them, the relation to God the Father maintained by the Spirit, is also stressed, the Lord may no longer appear to be truly subject to the same conditions as ourselves, but made perfect in quite another way.

Historic History

We return to the matter of the theology of history by taking up another of Kähler's points. Notice that when he says that, 'No man has ever spoken or acted thus . . .', he is not saying that no one has ever said the same things Jesus said, ever done the things that he did. As I have already noted, none of Jesus' acts is, on its own, unparalleled. We can even give Troeltsch his due. Paul notes that people are even, exceptionally, willing to give up their lives for others (Rom. 5.7). What is crucial here is the unique conjunction and configuration of finite historical events that gives them their particular and saving significance. This can be illustrated with a secular, or almost secular, parallel, which in its own way illustrates the working of the Holy Spirit, at least if we are able to grant that wherever there is beauty, truth or goodness it is in some way the work of the Spirit who perfects God's good creation.

A famous study of Coleridge's poetry explores, in immense and detailed depth, the sources of 'The Rime of the Ancient Mariner'.[13] It shows that there is no word, no image, no idea in that unique poem that is not to be found elsewhere in the huge range of sources studied by that self-described 'library cormorant'. The inspired character of the poem is to be found in the unique integration and combination of his sources that Coleridge achieved. The new creation is a unique reorganization of components of the old. Similarly, it matters not whether things Jesus said, did and suffered are, variously and individually, said, achieved and suffered by others. In a certain sense,

---

[13] J. Livingston Lowes, *The Road to Xanadu* (Boston and New York: Houghton Mifflin, 1927).

even miracles belong among the 'ordinary' in the sense that it is not only the incarnate Son but others of God's servants who are enabled to perform them. What is unique is that through this particular combination of finite historical particulars God achieved the salvation of his world. God's lordship over history is realized by enabling ordinary historical events to come together in an ordinary/extraordinary human being who was and did what he was and did through the power of the Spirit. What does this imply for our theology of history? It is not enough to say that revelation is not a predicate of history but history a predicate of revelation. If the much-quoted Barthian slogan means that God determines the meaning of history, it is right, as is Kähler's equivalent conception. But if we are to guarantee to history its own proper – 'secular' – reality, more has to be said. And here it has become easier for us than it was for Kähler and Barth. One of the convictions being increasingly borne upon us is that modernity is not as different as was once supposed, and is certainly no more 'objective' in its judgements than other eras. Already in 1896 Martin Kähler was aware that Whig history is not necessarily history unvarnished, and, indeed, that such does not and cannot exist,[14] and the case has been reinforced by Stephen Evans. Can we then continue to employ such expressions as 'the standards of contemporary his-torical science', 'biography in the modern sense', and contrast them with the supposedly unscientific standards of earlier eras as if that decided the matter? The question of what history is, remains an open, if highly contested, question, and it is the calling of the Christian theologian to enter the contest on behalf of a fully theological conception of things.

What then is it, according to the account attempted above, that makes the historic Jesus Christ significant for history in the way that Scripture holds? First, it is the case that God achieves his purposes for the world through history that is, through the call and empowerment of particular human beings and peoples. Abraham and Cyrus, Israel and Babylon, the Church and Rome (the 'Babylon' of the book of Revelation), all in

---

[14] 'Disguised as history, the historian's theory passes imperceptibly into our thoughts and convictions as an authentic piece of reality, as a law emanating therefrom' (p. 56).

different ways serve the providential purposes of the eternal creator, while yet retaining their autonomous or independent[15] human reality. Second, the centre of history and of God's ordering of it, the axis on which all action and meaning turns, is the history we are considering in this chapter the life, death, resurrection and ascension of Jesus of Nazareth, all understood as the history of a – the – truly human person. Why should this be so? To answer that, I shall sketch in some theses about the nature of history.

1. History is that which happens to, and within, the universe established 'in the beginning' by God's creating action. It is misleading to say, as has been said, that reality is history, but it is reasonable to hold that created reality has a history beginning at creation and destined to end when Christ submits all things to the Father. A firm distinction must here be maintained between the creation – meaning the universe which God has established – and history – meaning that which happens within that universe. As Oliver O'Donovan has argued, only so can we ground history's meaning as history:

> That which most distinguishes the concept of creation is that it is complete. Creation is the given totality of order which forms the presupposition of historical existence. . . . Because created order is given, because it is secure, we dare to be certain that God will vindicate it in history.[16]

It is, in this context, more illuminating to suggest not that reality is history, but that history in one of its central senses refers to that intentional and purposive activity performed by the human species, those created male and female in the image of God, within the created order established by divine action.

2. All historical action therefore takes place within some relation to God. There are varying forms of relation between human agents and God, arising from both the diversity of the

[15] None of these words adequately expresses the reality of the fact that the human relation to God is what establishes our distinctive humanity, which is neither left to itself not mechanically determined. The best word is perhaps the German selbständig.

[16] Oliver O'Donovan, *Resurrection and Moral Order. An Outline for Evangelical Ethics* (Leicester: InterVarsity Press and Grand Rapids, MN: Eerdmans, 1986), pp. 60–1.

creation and the human sin that generates a double history. On the one hand, there are those things which take place according to God's will; and, on the other, those things according to God's permission but against God's will and destined to be reversed by the redemption achieved on the cross. History on this account is the realm of human activity willed and permitted by God between the creation and the end of the age. It seems to be the case that actions according to God's permission are free because to permit something leaves it to the agent whether a thing is done or not, while the same does not hold for those performed by God's will, which appears to leave no choice. However, as often, appearances are deceptive, and there is a case for saying the opposite. On a biblical view, it is more nearly the case that those human actions performed merely by God's permission are those which disrupt the purposes of creation and impede its perfecting. These are the bearers of those dark forces released by the breaking of the seals of Revelation 6, the acts of God's 'left hand' by which the results of sin are allowed to have their day, but no more. By contrast, actions which take place according to the will of God have their model and basis in the life of Jesus, who 'by the power of the eternal Spirit offered himself unblemished to God . . .' (Heb. 9.14). Every human action is either the one or the other: the fruit of obedience or of disobedience. History is, at one level, the sum of those actions. As we have seen, Jesus is the particular human being that he is by virtue of his relation, as the incarnate Son, to the Father mediated by the Spirit. That which Jesus does in obedience to the Spirit of his Father he does freely, because that is the way by which he is empowered to fulfil the particular righteousness laid upon him. By analogy, this is the case with all human actions.

In sum, history is the realm of human action in relation to God, other human beings and what we call the non-human world. All those human actions which are not constrained by either external or internal compulsion – of being forced by violence, sickness or forms of moral slavery sometimes known as 'the demonic' – are authentically human in the weak sense that they are the work of created, finite agents. They are not all authentically human in the strong sense that they conform to the pattern of Jesus' life, obedient in all things to the guidance of the Spirit. What they have in common is that, being finite, they take place in the created world which is given, and maintained in, its distinctive reality by God. When we ask how God can determine human wills without compelling them, we can understand from the life of Jesus that he does it through the Spirit, whose bidding can – in some cases[17] – be disobeyed, as must conceivably be the case if Jesus' temptations were real ones.[18] The Holy Spirit is, as we have seen, the one who, through Christ, enables the creation to be itself by bringing it into proper relation to God the Father. That is to say, the Spirit's historical action is to come into personal relation with human agents, liberating them to be themselves and empowering anticipations of the eschatological reconciliation of all things.

3. History is at another level what God makes of those human actions. Here again the paradigm is found in what happened to and with the earthly Jesus: 'this man was handed over to you by God's set purpose and foreknowledge; and you, with the help of wicked men, put him to death by nailing him to the cross' (Acts 2.23). The mystery of history is the mystery of how human actions, even, and in this case especially, the most wicked, are used in such a way that their effect is the reverse of that intended. This ordering of history by God is not, however, at the expense of human freedom and responsibility, although it involves the overcoming (eschatologically and sometimes in anticipation of that) of those actions which would pervert the predestined course of history. 'The Son of Man will go just as it is written about him. But woe to that man who betrays the Son of Man' (Mark 14.21).

Once again, Christology and pneumatology are the key. For Irenaeus, as is well known, the Son and the Spirit are conceived as the two hands of God, the persons mediating God the

---

[17] I say in some cases, because we have in Scripture a number of cases when disobeying the heavenly vision is in effect impossible. That there is no absolute freedom to disobey is clear in the case of the conversion of Paul, and of others who have found that in the end they had, effectively, no choice, being set free despite themselves.

[18] Here something should be said about the traditional dispute about whether Jesus 'could have' sinned. 'He could not have sinned' appears to suggest that Jesus' temptations were unreal; 'He was able not to sin' that Pelagianism is justified. I owe to Thomas Smail the suggestion of a third way: 'He was enabled – by the Spirit – not to sin.'

Father's action in the world. What I have attempted in this chapter is a theology of recapitulation after that of the great theologian. In the earthly Jesus we meet the Son of God become man in order to remake the history that in Adam failed; indeed, to re-establish the history of creation after its subjection to vanity. In the earthly, bodily, existence of this man, the history of creation and redemption come together. His triumphant living out of human life becomes the basis of the promised redemption of all things, a recapitulation continued in the life of the Church, under promise.

All this gives us a clue as to who and what is the one described by Stephen Evans as 'the historical Christ and the Jesus of faith', by Kähler as the 'geschichtliche, biblische Christus'. He is, we might say in summary conclusion, the one whose authentically human actions – authentic in a strong sense, because obedient through the Spirit to the will of his Father – are the action by which God returns history to its proper telos, the praise of its creator, pulling it back from its journey to disaster. He is the one in whom the creator and the creation come together, as the story told by the Letter to the Hebrews shows so clearly: that the Son through whom God made and upheld the world, offers, triumphantly through testing and temptation and by the eternal Spirit, the sacrifice of praise and obedience that is the human calling.

10

The Spirit and Jesus: (2) 'One Mediator . . . the Man Jesus Christ'. Reconciliation, Mediation and Life in Community[1]

The Question of Mediation

The question of mediation is a central one for all theology. If God is God, and not the world, and if we are still to know him, then some form of mediation, some way of getting from here to there, is required. Traditionally, there have been two often competing routes to God. The first begins with us, and seeks to move upwards from the earth to the heavenly realm – the way of ascent – or, as in some modern theories, inwards to the God found within. This is the way sometimes polemically described as 'religion', as the human quest to reach God by our own bootstraps. The other begins with God, who 'descends' into our world to make himself known. The matter, however, is far more complicated than a choice, or compromise, between two approaches, for a second question is intimately bound up with the first. Different means of mediation bring in their train widely different concepts of what it is to know God.

Let me illustrate both sides of the question. Between Irenaeus and the Gnostics in their dispute around the end of the second century AD were immense differences about both mediation and the content of what was conceived to be mediated. The Gnostics posited a realm of intermediate beings between the high God and the material world in which human beings were

---

[1] The Dr J. Campbell Wadsworth Memorial Lecture, McGill University, Montreal, 10 April 2001. Previously published in *Pro Ecclesia* 11 (2002), pp. 146–58.

164

incarcerated. These angelic beings were midway between God and the world: they could, at least in theory, mediate because they were intermediate, with a foot in both camps, so to speak. They were divine, but not so divine as the high God. The religion of the Gnostics was therefore one of ascent: out of this physical and material world, the source of error and corruption, into the higher spiritual realm beyond *via* the beings who belonged in some realm that was in different respects both and neither of these. Their ethic, as is well known, was consequent upon this, and took contradictory forms, of either a renunciation or a self-indulgent acceptance of the pleasures of the flesh – the latter being very much the condition of our modern world, except that it is not too confident that there is anywhere to ascend to. That we are here in the realm of matters which are of far broader import than merely Christian concern is evident enough from the fact that the likeness between the ancient and modern worlds is significant despite the attempted modern restriction of meaning to the immanent. Our civilization may seek to live by this world alone, but it is gnostic in being unable to be at home in it, let alone in a world transcending it.

By contrast, Irenaeus' concept of mediation was firmly christological and trinitarian. At the centre was the human career of the man Jesus, who recapitulated the career of Adam, going over the sorry story of human sin but this time emerging triumphant. This affirmed against the Gnostics the importance of human life in the world, giving both liberty to enjoy it rightly, and seriousness in the life of discipleship. But it was not restricted to the story of a man, however good. The human career of Jesus was also an act of divine mediation. What he achieved was the work of the Father in overcoming sin, death and the devil. This is because he is also and at the same time the eternal Son of God. The God who created by his two hands, the Son and the Spirit, was able and free to mediate his action within the world, and shown to be that kind of God by what Jesus did and what was done through him. The Son and the Spirit are God himself in action: that is to say, they mediate God the Father's action in the world, both in creation and in what we call redemption. Thus the first great battle against heresy was essentially about mediation: the mediation of God's action in and toward the world, and consequently of our action in it also, for, as we have seen, the two are inextricably bound up with one another.

Irenaeus' central concept was, as we have seen, 'recapitulation' rather than mediation. In using it, he took a biblical term, one used rarely in Scripture itself, and adapted it to achieve a much broader and more comprehensive purpose than the original, which he took from the Letter to the Ephesians. That is the way of all theology: a word, sometimes biblical, sometimes not, is used to characterize a major and perhaps universal dimension of the biblical account of God's creating and saving work – to recapitulate aspects of the work of God, we might say, if it does not complicate matters too much – in order to bring a range of similar acts, phenomena or events under a single head. Let me give an example. In Genesis 1.26 it is said that 'God created man in his own image . . . male and female he created them.' The word 'image' is subsequently used rather rarely in Scripture, indeed in the New Testament mostly of Christ rather than of human beings in general. And yet for better or worse it has become a central theological concept to express what is distinctive about our human species. And notice how economically and comprehensively the Genesis text enables the purpose to be achieved. The singular – man – is used to speak of the fact that there is one species. Human beings are a unity despite our corrupting of it with our various forms of divisive behaviour. The plural – male and female – is used of our plurality, the fact that we are made in two sexes, to live in reconciled relation with one another under God. Thus, in a single concept are encapsulated so many features of our life: our relation to God, our human unity, the richness and manifoldness of our life and of our relations to one another. That economy and comprehensibility is what justifies a theological term, so long as it gets things right, to be sure. It aids understanding not by forcing variety into a false unity, but by showing how a whole range of things belongs in a measure of unity.

Similarly, the concept of the mediator appears fairly rarely in the pages of Scripture. Literally, it means the one in the middle, the 'middle man' as we sometimes say in the language of commerce. As I have already hinted in the reference to Gnosticism, there are various ways we might understand this, because 'middle' can be taken to mean either one who is midway between the creator and the creation, as famously happened in another early heresy, Arianism, or one who mediates because he is truly both divine and human.[2] Let me look briefly at two biblical uses of the word before moving to examine some theological developments of it.

Crucial is 1 Timothy 2.5. Let me give two translations, the one a modern bowdlerized version, which obscures the meaning, the other a literal one. 'For "there is one God, and one mediator between God and people, a person, Christ Jesus, who gave himself as a ransom for all." '[3] There are two problems with the translation of *anthropos* as 'a person', which is systematically misleading. First, persons can be both divine and human, whereas here the stress is on Jesus' humanity; while, second, to speak of the person of Jesus Christ is to speak of him as the incarnate Son, as both divine and human. Literally the text might read: 'For there is one God, also one mediator between God and men, the man Christ Jesus, who gave himself as a ransom for all.' The juxtaposed 'men', 'man' make it quite clear what the other translation does not: the community of being between Jesus and ourselves. (The REB sensibly keeps the continuity between Jesus and ourselves, indeed stressing it: 'mediator between God and *man*, Christ Jesus, himself *man*, who sacrificed himself to win freedom for all *man*kind', turning the literal 'men' into 'man' to ensure that the wrong construction is not given to 'men'.) The link drawn between God and Jesus, as well as the theology of the letters to Timothy and Titus in general, shows that the author is not intending to say that Jesus is *only* a man, but with that we are not at the moment concerned.

Our other source of the expression 'mediator' is the Letter to the Hebrews (8.6, 9.15, 12.24), according to which Jesus is the mediator of a 'better' covenant – than that mediated by Moses – or a 'new' covenant. The author's general intention is

---

[2] The major crisis in Christianity's struggles over mediation was centred on the challenge of Arianism. Whatever Arius actually taught, and there has been recent scholarly dispute about that, Arianism as a phenomenon is a more sophisticated version of what Irenaeus faced. There is not now a realm of intermediate angelic beings, but God the Son performs the same function. Here once again the assumption is of the inappropriateness or incapacity for God to involve himself in the physical world.

[3] William Mounce, *Pastoral Epistles. Word Biblical Commentary* vol. 46 (Nashville: Thomas Nelson, 2000), p. 87.

to contrast the covenants and institutions of the Old and New Testaments, not to abolish or even belittle the former but to stress the utter superiority of Christ. If it is possible to mistake the Christology of First Timothy, there is no room for doubt here. The one of whom he speaks is the divine mediator of creation and providence before he is mediator of the new covenant. The Son is the one 'through whom [God] made the universe'; 'he sustains all things by his powerful word' (Heb. 1.2, 3). It is a staggering claim. This is the one who, taught obedience by what happened to him, lived a fully human life, tempted as we are, although without sin, and offered his life, perfected, to God the Father through the eternal Spirit. It is as such that he has become both a means of approach to God and an intercessor on behalf of those whose flesh he *bears*, and note the present tense. For the Letter to the Hebrews, as for 1 Timothy, there *is* one mediator, not *was*, who *has* achieved reconciliation and now *is* its mediator.

Let me make one point clear at this stage. According to our two authorities, mediation is the means by which the broken human relationship with God is mended. I showed that for Hebrews there appears also a concept of the mediation of creation, though the word 'mediator' is not there used. Because of that silence, it is right to begin where the New Testament begins, with mediation referring to the specific act of renewing a broken relationship. From God's side, the relationship with the world is unbreakable, so long as the world remains. But, given the breach of the relationship from the human side, a new form of mediation is required to deal with the new and dangerous situation. It requires that the one through whom God created the world is now mediator of reconciliation, which therefore takes centre stage in an account of what mediation is. In that light, and leaving on one side for the time being the notion of the mediation of creation, let us examine some figures from our Western history who have determined the shape of our thinking about this matter.

Some Historical Treatments of the Mediator

First, Anselm of Canterbury, whose vision is a far broader one than his critics have often made out. His great book, *Why the*

God-Man, is effectively a study in mediation. Why, he asks, do we need one who is both God and man if God's purposes for his world are not to be thwarted? It is because sin is not for him merely a moral fault; it is something gone wrong with our relation to God which upsets the whole balance of the universe. Human failure to fulfil God's just requirements sets all of reality out of kilter, and threatens God's gracious purposes for his world. The situation is so grave that it is outside human resource; and yet it is human fault and responsibility that have made it as it is. God, is, so to speak, faced with a dilemma: if he acts according to abstract justice, he will be bound to wind up the whole business. But in that case he will have failed. What is needed is one who is – though Anselm does not use the word – a mediator: while only man ought to do what is needed, only God is able to do it.[4] Therefore salvation can be achieved only by one who is both God and man. The weaknesses of Anselm's thesis are much rehearsed, and I will mention only that relevant to our enquiry. While it does not quite reduce the relationship between God and man to a merely legal one, it does tend to concern itself with forgiveness at the expense of new life in the gospel. To be sure, that is not Anselm's concern in his book, which has a more restricted aim in mind, and therefore he should not be criticized for failing to do what he did not intend to. Yet it did bequeath a rather thin account of the human condition, before and after reconciliation. As T. F. Torrance has suggested, the Western tradition of soteriological thinking has tended to conceive relations between creator and creation in too external a manner, salvation appearing to be a judicial transaction consisting in the transfer of penalty.[5] In the light of Irenaeus' engagement with the Gnostics, we must also therefore ask about the absence of a reference to the wider created world in the context of the mediation of reconciliation. Yet Anselm's point remains. When the creation has gone astray, only God can save it; but if he is to save it truly, it must be not through some external act, but as one of us.

---

[4] Anselm of Canterbury, *Why the God-Man?*, II.6. ET in *Anselm of Canterbury*, eds J. Hopkins and H. Richardson (London; SCM Press; New York: Mellen, 1974).

[5] Thomas F. Torrance, *The Mediation of Christ* (Exeter: Paternoster Press, 1983), p. 50.

It is to Calvin that we owe the most explicit account of Christ as mediator, and to that we now turn. Although he belongs in the tradition of the great Archbishop of Canterbury, the Reformer is centrally concerned, as Anselm was not, with mediatorial divine action in the present. Let us look at some of the highlights of his beautifully clear account.[6] Although Calvin, like his great teacher Paul, does speak in terms of the legal relation between God and man, his vision is far broader than that, as his language shows. His first image takes us away from the rather external language of Anselmian satisfaction theology to that of a renewal of the relationship with God. In the first section of the chapter in which he deals explicitly with mediation, Calvin writes that because of our estrangement from God, no one, unless he belonged to God, could serve as intermediary, or go-between, we might say. So, it was necessary for the Son of God to become 'Immanuel', God with us, and in such a way that 'his divinity and our human nature might by mutual connection grow together'.[7] Note the stress on growth in mutuality. Calvin is a theologian of union with Christ, and his theology of mediation serves that.

In the third section of his chapter, Calvin has recourse to Anselmian language. Who but true man, he asks, could 'present our flesh as the price of satisfaction to God's righteous judgement, to pay the penalty which we had deserved'?[8] But the question with which he prefaces this section shows that he is not concerned with balancing the accounts, so much as with life. Who but the life could swallow up death?[9] For all the things which we might want to put differently, Calvin is fundamentally concerned in his treatment of salvation with life, with the indulgent Father who gives us himself in his Son. And he is insistent that the mediation requires that Christ be both human and divine. 'Those who despoil Christ of either his divinity or his humanity diminish his majesty and glory, or obscure his goodness' – and notice the proper juxtaposition of glory and

[6] John Calvin, *Institutes of the Christian Religion*, ed. J. T. McNeill, tr. and indexed F. L. Battles (Philadelphia: Westminster Press, 1960), II.xii.1 (pp. 464–74).
[7] Calvin, *Institutes* II.xii.1.
[8] Calvin, *Institutes* II.xii.3.
[9] Calvin, *Institutes* II.xii.2.

goodness; or, on the other hand, they weaken and overthrow faith in divine salvation.[10] For Calvin, the doctrine of mediation is designed to show that who Jesus is and what he does – what we call his person and his work – are inextricable. He does what he does – restores us to fellowship with God – because of who he is as both God and man, God with and for us – though also in one respect against us, as Barth would rightly remind us – in Jesus Christ.

And that takes me to another point that makes possible an enrichment of the concept of mediation with which we are working. There has long been much discussion about what is taking place on the cross and how best to describe it. Is it to be described as what we call penal substitution, an idea with which many moderns – and, it must be not be forgotten, many ancients also – are uncomfortable? That Christ bears the penalty for sin seems to me part of the message of Scripture. Yet we have seen that Calvin is far broader than this, and certainly does not limit the meaning of the cross to a question of penalty. Referring to Paul's statement that 'by Christ's death in his body of flesh and blood God has reconciled you to himself', Christoph Schwöbel makes the following point:

> There is no indication that the humanity and the divinity of Christ must be distinguished in the act of reconciliation. If we want to talk about substitution in this context, it is not penal substitution but mediatorial substitution.[11]

That is surely the point. Jesus' life and death are there not to perform some external substitution, but yet to take our place in such a way that we are truly brought to God. Here again we can do no better that to cite some words from the earliest days of Christian theology:

> In whom could we, lawless and impious as we were, be made righteous except in the Son of God alone? O sweetest exchange! O unfathomable work of God! . . . The sinfulness

---

[10] Calvin, *Institutes* II.xii.2.

[11] Christoph Schwœbel, 'From Biblical Observations to Dogmatic Reconstruction', *The Theology of Reconciliation*, ed. Colin E. Gunton (Edinburgh: T&T Clark, 2003), pp. 13–38.

of many is hidden in the Righteous One, while the righteousness of the One justifies the many that are sinners.[12]

In sum, then, for Calvin the suffering of the mediator under God's judgement serves reconciliation and life. But beyond the images we have reviewed there is another on which he draws, and it is perhaps even more important if we are to understand the nature of mediation. It is that taken from the Letter to the Hebrews, of Jesus as our great high priest, the mediator of the new covenant. The doctrine of the eternal priesthood of Jesus serves to guarantee the internal relation of the believer to Christ against suggestions of some merely external legal transaction. The aim of Christ's priesthood is to bring us to God, and in a particular way:

> [S]ince Christ holds out His hand to us we have no need to look for a mediator far off: that there is no reason for us to fear the majesty of Christ, since He is our Brother; and that we must not be afraid that He is unaware of our ills and not touched by any feeling of humanity to bring us help, since He has taken our infirmities on Himself so as to be better able to help us.[13]

Calvin takes from the Letter to the Hebrews an immense stress on the humanity of the mediator, the humanity which is needed if we are to be reconciled to God: 'if He had been chosen from among the angels or from anywhere else, we could not have been united with God through Him because He would not reach down to us'.[14]

It is clear that Calvin's primary conception of mediation is that of Jesus as the mediator of salvation, by which he clearly means a reconciled relation to God. It is access to God the Father as love in which Calvin is chiefly interested, and his polemics against Catholicism derived from the fact that he

---

[12] *The Letter to Diognetus* 9.4f.

[13] John Calvin, *The Epistle of Paul the Apostle to the Hebrews and the First and Second Epistles of St Peter*, tr. W. B. Johnston (Grand Rapids: Eerdmans, 1963), p. 55.

[14] John Calvin, *Commentaries on the Epistle of Paul the Apostle to the Hebrews*, tr. J. Dwen (Edinburgh: Calvin Translation Society, 1853), p. 59. So also p. 98, on Heb. 7.17, where Calvin treats Christ's eternal priesthood, another theme that he takes from Anselm.

believed his opponents to have interposed other mediators than Christ. However – and this will take me to a further development of the theme – Calvin's thought is by no means limited to that. As Barbara Pitkin points out in her recent study of Calvin, 'Calvin also extends the term to the eternal Son who, even prior to the incarnation, was the only channel between God and fallen and even unfallen humanity.'[15] She refers to his reply to 'Servetus's view that God was not revealed to Abraham and the other patriarchs but that they worshipped only an angel'. The angel was, rather, 'God's word, who already at that time, as a sort of foretaste, began to fulfil the office of Mediator'.[16] The year after the publication of the *Institutes,* Calvin is even more explicit in his reply to Stancaro:

> [T]he name of Mediator applies to Christ not only because he took on flesh or because he took on the office of reconciling the human race with God. But already from the beginning of creation he was truly Mediator because he was always the Head of the Church and held primacy even over the angels . . .[17]

The Word mediates God's love and judgement to his people even before the historic incarnation and life of Jesus.

Mediation in Broader Perspective

The first reason why we cannot limit mediation to our Christian era is that Christ is head of a Church which includes at least Israel also. But can we limit the conception so, even when it is extended to the angels and archangels? Must we not understand the mediation of Jesus not simply of personal beings, but of all God's creation? Shall we even understand the mediation of reconciliation unless we see it in the context of the mediation of that from and within which the personal has its being? Let us

---

[15] Barbara Pitkin, *What Pure Eyes Could See. Calvin's Doctrine of Faith in its Exegetical Context* (New York and Oxford: Oxford University Press, 1999), p. 150.

[16] Pitkin, *What Pure Eyes Could See,* p. 236 n. 78, citing Calvin, *Institutes* I.xiii.10.

[17] Cited by Pitkin, *What Pure Eyes Could See,* p. 151.

explore this question, for it is both difficult and important. It is difficult because we appear to be confusing two different concepts of mediation. The first, as we have seen, has to do centrally, though certainly not exclusively, with the divine Christ's humanity. As we saw above, Timothy, Hebrews and Calvin alike stress that aspect of things. But when we come to speak of the Son by whose agency God *mediated* the universe, are we speaking of the same kind of action? In what sense is Jesus Christ *identical* with the eternal Word? Clearly, Jesus has a beginning in time, in the respect that the Word became incarnate at a datable time and specifiable place. If we lose that, we lose everything. But what is known as the doctrine of Christ's pre-existence equally clearly implies – also and without threat to that – that he does not have a beginning in time.[18] As Douglas Farrow and, in a different and rather differently nuanced way, Robert Jenson, have both recently argued, without asserting an identity of Jesus and the eternal Son of some kind, we fall into doctrines which exclude Jesus from the Old Testament – and, correlatively, exclude the Old Testament from our theology.[19]

Much hangs on that. If we fail to hold together the mediation of salvation and that of creation, we risk a reversion to the very Gnostic, or near-Gnostic, equation of the person with the soul which has so dogged our tradition, and is near to the surface in Calvin. If Christ is mediator of salvation only, there is a twofold price to pay. We run the risk of breaking his link with Israel and of making his work salvation out of the world rather than along and with it. Calvin has, to be sure, the resources with which to deal with this problem. In his treatment of the three offices of Christ as prophet, priest and king he draws explicit links with the ways in which God's action was mediated to and in Israel. The offices are crucial to his account of how Jesus' work is mediated in the present. So it is, for example, with the kingly

---

[18] Unless we are to fall into the Arian trap of saying that there was when he was not. That, as has been implied by the argument so far, would subvert the kind of mediation with which we are concerned by depriving Christ of his full divinity.

[19] Douglas B. Farrow, *Ascension and Ecclesia. On the significance of the Doctrine of the Ascension for Ecclesiology and Christian Cosmology* (Edinburgh: T&T Clark, 1999); Robert W. Jenson, *Systematic Theology*, vol. 1, *The Triune God* (New York and Oxford: Oxford University Press, 1997), Part 2, ch. 8.

office: 'The Father has given all power to the Son that he may by the Son's hand govern, nourish and sustain us, keep us in his care, and help us.'[20] The climax is the priestly office, so important for this great expositor of the Letter to the Hebrews: 'as a pure and stainless Mediator he is by his holiness to reconcile us to God'.[21] It is this that gives point to his present work, his mediatorial substitution. 'Since he entered heaven in our flesh, as if in our name, it follows . . . that in a sense we already "sit with God in the heavenly places in him".'[22]

> [H]aving entered a sanctuary not made with hands, he appears before the Father's face as our constant advocate and intercessor . . . He so reconciles the Father's heart to us that by his intercession he prepares a way and access for us to the Father's throne. He fills with grace and kindness the throne that for miserable sinners would otherwise have been filled with dread.[23]

That, I believe, take us to the very heart of the Christian faith. If the preaching of the cross and its outcome is not at the centre of worship and life, we are no longer about the Father's work. Reconciliation with God through the work of Christ is that without which nothing else will work. Unfortunately, the term 'reconciliation' is today sloppily used as if there can be true reconciliation without the price paid by Christ on the cross and the consequent cost to those who live by it. We live in an era of cheap reconciliation, when the word comes to mouth too lightly and we assume that it is something we achieve. (In Bishopsgate in London there was once a notice fixed to a church bombed by the IRA. It informed the public that the church was being rebuilt as 'a centre for peace and reconciliation'. The form of words, however, raises serious questions. Is the church not already this? In that case, is it not being suggested that something is being added so that an 'ordinary' church becomes something more, that more being peace and reconciliation? And can we have peace and reconciliation without a prior

---

[20] Calvin, *Institutes* II. xv. 5.
[21] Calvin, *Institutes* II. xv. 6.
[22] Calvin, *Institutes* II. xvi. 16, (citing Eph. 2.6).
[23] Calvin, *Institutes* II. xvi. 16.

mediation through the cross of Jesus?) This is a reconciliation for which he paid the ultimate price, and he is the one source of reconciliation.

We return to Calvin. 'The Son of God, utterly clean of all fault, nevertheless took upon himself the shame and reproach of our iniquities, and in return clothed us with his purity.'[24] The matter of sin is an important one. T. F. Torrance rightly refers Jesus' mediation back to Israel's Day of Atonement as it is described in Leviticus 16. The second goat

> was to be brought forward so that the high priest could lay his hands upon its head and confess over it all the iniquities of Israel and all their acts of rebellion, whereupon it was to be sent away alive into the wilderness, carrying upon itself all the sins of Israel into some waste land.[25]

Compare Mark 1.12–13: 'At once, the Spirit drove him out into the wilderness, and there he remained for forty days, tempted by Satan.' The cost of the mediation of salvation by the man Jesus Christ was a life of constant trial and temptation, ending with the supreme gift of his life, for the sake of human sin, and theology should not forget it for a moment.

Yet the fact that the one in the wilderness is the mediator also of creation reminds us that we need to go further than that. The question through which we can approach what we need to say is this: Who is the person who comes to the Father through the mediation of Christ? If it is to be the whole person, body and soul – or, perhaps better, body and spirit – together, then we cannot escape asking about the way in which the human person is a part of the material creation, and with whose whole being Jesus' mediation is concerned. And I begin this next stage of the argument with another citation from T. F. Torrance. 'One of the most startling features about the Old Testament Scriptures is the way in which they represent the Word of God as becoming physically implicated with Israel in the very stuff of its earthy

---

[24] Calvin, *Institutes* II.xvi.6.

[25] Torrance, *The Mediation of Christ*, p. 45, cf. p. 46: '[Jesus] was driven by the Spirit like a scapegoat into a waste land where under the burden of our sin he became prey to the forces of darkness which sought to wrench him away from his mission as the Servant of the Lord.' Torrance refers also to Isaiah 53: 'he was cut off . . .'.

being and behaviour.'[26] From or with the assistance of Israel we need to learn at least three things.

The Nature of the Human Condition

As we have seen, Jesus' mediation is first of all directed to the human bondage resulting from sin, sometimes personified as slavery to the devil. This, however, is not a merely moral fault but one which permeates the whole of our humanity. It brings death in its train, death meaning here not just the dying of the body, but the dissolution of the whole person. To put it the other way round: human beings are made for eternal life, a form of being with God which confers what Irenaeus and his successors called incorruptibility. One of the many great-nesses of Irenaeus is that he proclaims, in a way that many later theologians failed to hear, the eschatological perfecting of our bodily humanity, and its transformation to life with God. Paul was his educator here with his doctrine of the resurrection of the flesh: 'For the trumpet shall sound, and the dead will rise imperishable, and we shall be changed' (1 Cor. 15.52).

That Jesus reconciles through his body of flesh and blood accordingly has implications for all of our humanity. And that is where the Old Testament serves as a corrective to many of the ways we are tempted to think of ourselves. Adam is of the earth; indeed, that is part of what the name means. He is made from the mud that Jesus was later to apply to blind eyes as part of the process of their healing.[27] Here I need do no more than review some of the the themes of Hans-Walter Wolff's study of biblical anthropology.[28] Wolff devotes a chapter each to three Hebrew words with which the Old Testament writers characterize the

---

[26] Torrance, *The Mediation of Christ*, p. 25.

[27] Eve from his side signifying, as is sometimes commented, complementarity rather than inferiority or superiority, because not from his head or feet. And these creatures are made distinctively what they are not by virtue of the fact that an immaterial soul is inserted into their bodies, but because God breathes into them the breath of life.

[28] H. W. Wolff, *The Anthropology of the Old Testament*, tr. Margaret Kohl (London: SCM Press, 1973), chs 2–4.

human condition. *Nepes*, often translated as 'soul' means first
of all throat – as in 'He satisfies the hungry throat' (Ps. 107.9)
– and so refers to 'needy man', the creature in need of sus-
tenance from God. At another level, *basar* meaning, materi-
ally, flesh – 'eating *basar* and drinking wine' (Isa. 22.13) – can
refer to the human body as a whole, as in the famous description of marriage, where man and woman become 'one flesh'
(Gen. 2.24). More generally, it refers to 'man in his infirmity',
both physical and ethical, characterized as he is by being
dependent at once on physical and divine support. '*Basar* is
really man as a being who is weak and incapable . . .' The
third word, *ruach*, 'spirit', refers in our context to 'man as he
is empowered'. It expresses not a permanent piece of equip-
ment, like the soul of Greek and some modern philosophy,
but something that can be given and taken away, something
always in the gift of the creator. 'That a man as *ruach* is living,
desires the good and acts as authorized being – none of this
proceeds from man himself.'[29] The picture, in sum, is of a
spiritual – material unity, a psycho-physical person whose
created reality depends at every turn on being upheld
and empowered by the Spirit of God. It is such a material –
spiritual being which must be understood by 'the man Jesus
Christ, the mediator'.

The Centrality of the Community

Here we must tread our way carefully between two extremes.
Much recent theology, particularly as the result of ecumenical
discussion, has rediscovered the centrality of the Church; it has
also sometimes over-inflated its role, as if the Church were itself
the mediator of salvation. God uses the Church as he uses Israel,
but it is only by overmatching their all too obvious limits and
weaknesses. In so far as the Church, in both worship and life, is
enabled to set forth Christ, thus far does it mediate the work of
the mediator. The other danger is to make the Church merely
instrumental, merely the means to something that is essentially
external to it. Perhaps Calvin is near to that danger when he

[29] Wolff, *The Anthropology of the Old Testament*, p. 39.

speaks of the Church as among the external means used by God for the sanctification of the believer. To be sure, the end is external to the Church in the sense that it is God's reconciliation of all things which the Church serves. But just as there is no salvation apart from the people called Israel, so there is none that does not take shape in concrete patterns of community. The saving work of Christ is mediated as God calls flesh and blood human beings to join together before the Word and sacraments. Mediation is thus a matter not of inward experience but of concrete human relationship 'in Christ'. And that takes us to the third consideration.

The Doctrine of the Holy Spirit

The Holy Spirit is the Lord and giver of life, both the life that we live and the eternal life that is promised at the resurrection. The fact that the Spirit is not just the giver of some internal feeling but is the Lord of all life, we learn from the book of Ezekiel above all. The Spirit's work, as chapter 37 makes clear, is eschatological, and it is this that enables us to bring together all our themes so far. First, the Spirit is the one who enabled Jesus to be the true human being, the one who as the second Adam – another Adam of flesh and blood – recapitulated our human life in the way it was meant to be. After his ascension Jesus becomes the mediator of the Father's Spirit to the Church, as we learn from Ephesians 4.7ff. especially. Here is the theme with which we began: that Jesus Christ descended to our condition that he might ascend to the Father's side in order to give to the Church the gifts of the Spirit that enables her truly to realize the communion of the last days. 'It was he who gave some to be prophets . . . so that the body of Christ might be built up until we reach unity in the faith and in the knowledge of the Son of God and become mature, attaining to the whole measure of the fullness of Christ.' As Wesley Carr pointed out in a paper written a quarter of a century ago, the New Testament expresses the work of the Spirit through two focuses: the Church and eschatology. The Church is the community of the end times, and made to be so by the Spirit. 'Christians hope to be one with Christ in the final resurrection and their experience in the Christian community is a partial and anticipatory experience of that end.'[30] '[T]he Spirit becomes for the believing community more the environment in which it lives than an object of its consciousness.'[31] Whether 'environment' is the right word to use must be doubtful. But the point remains: through the Spirit and in the Church the blessings of Jesus' reconciling death on the cross are mediated now, in anticipation of the time when Christ will offer us all, perfected, before the throne of his Father.

The final point therefore takes us back to the place where we began. There can indeed be mediation by ascent, but it is not that envisaged by all the forms of the so-called Christology from below. There is no ascent without the prior descent of the Son of God to our realm of sin and death, no Christology from below unless the man Jesus is confessed as the mediator of creation also. And that is possible only through the gift of the Spirit, not by any other means, lest we seek to penetrate the divine incognito, the Jewish flesh of Jesus, and by so doing deprive Jesus of his mediatorial humanity. 'In saying "He ascended" what does it [Ps. 68] mean but that he had also descended into the lower parts of the earth? He who descended is he who also ascended far above the heavens, that he might fill all things' (Eph. 4.9–10). The man, Jesus Christ, the mediator of salvation is first of all mediator of creation so that finally he might be eschatological mediator, recapitulating, summing up, all things in himself.

[30] Wesley Carr, 'Towards a Contemporary Theology of the Holy Spirit', *Scottish Journal of Theology*, 28 (1975), pp. 501–16 (p. 506).
	[31] Carr, 'Towards a Contemporary Theology', p. 508.

11

Atonement: The Sacrifice and the Sacrifices. From Metaphor to Transcendental?[1]

The Language of Sacrifice

We no longer slaughter animals ritually, and yet the word 'sacrifice' remains in our language as a pervasive metaphor. It does so often, though by no means always, in debased forms, as when we offer to sell an object 'at a sacrifice' or when parents speak of making sacrifices for their children. What does such frequent and sometimes debased usage indicate in an age when the actual practice of sacrifice has virtually disappeared? It can mean either of two things: that the usage is no more than the last trace of a once religious world view, doomed to final extinction in a 'secular' age; or it may mean the very opposite, that the usage points to an area of human experience that cannot be described except by means of such language because it is in some way basic to our human indwelling of reality. That modern usage is not simply a debased survival from an earlier age is implied by the fact that, as Frances Young has suggested, one can find in serious modern works of literature a real engagement with the notion of sacrifice.[2] It is this latter side of things that I wish to take up and develop. To speak of sacrifice is to enter a world of metaphor by means of which a range of human interaction with the world is encompassed. Further, I wish to argue that the notion derives from something deep in human

---

[1] First published in *Trinity, Incarnation, and Atonement. Philosophical and Theological Essays*, eds Ronald J. Feenstra and Cornelius Plantinga (Notre Dame, IN: Notre Dame University Press, 1989), pp. 210–29.

[2] Frances Young, *Sacrifice and the Death of Christ* (London: SCM Press, 1975).

nature, of such a kind that it appears to be rooted in a universal or near universal feature of our life on earth.

Such an argument, however, faces a number of initial difficulties. For many centuries the concept of sacrifice was a central feature of Christian theologies of the atonement, but in recent times the very notion of the atonement has come into question, as an article by Colin Grant has shown.[3] Scorn has been poured, particularly by Enlightenment thinkers and their successors, on the use of so apparently barbaric an institution to expound what may appear to be an essentially moral relation between God and his creatures. Indeed, the mainstream of the Enlightenment stood against almost everything for which the Christian doctrine of the atonement stands.[4] Morally, its direction was to deny the human need for divine grace, both theoretically, as in Locke's belief in the rational demonstrability of all ethical principles[5] and practically, as in Kant's view of the near omnipotence of practical reason. Further, what chiefly concerns the argument of this chapter, the Enlightenment's view of language and its capacity for truth effectively ruled out of court the way in which the truth of the atonement had been understood and expressed. That view can be summarized in Hobbes's categorization of metaphor among the abuses of language: 'when [men] use words metaphorically; that is, in other sense than that they are ordained for; and thereby deceive others'.[6] What could not be described in clear and distinct concepts could not be taken seriously.

While we need not pause long over the fact that Hobbes can express his objection to metaphor only by using one (that is, 'ordained'), we must give more consideration to the fact that

---

[3] Colin Grant, 'The Abandonment of Atonement', *King's Theological Review* 9 (1986), pp. 1–8.

[4] Shared with the Christian doctrine of the atonement is a pervasive concern with human freedom, so that the Enlightenment can in some ways be understood as attempting a secularization of Christian theology. Many indications of this are to be found in Kant's *Religion Within the Limits of Reason Alone*.

[5] John Locke, *An Essay Concerning Human Understanding*, 3.11.16.

[6] Thomas Hobbes, *Leviathan or the Matter, Form and Power of a Commonwealth, Ecclesiastical and Civil*, ed. Michael Oakeshott, introduced by Richard S. Peters (London: Collier-Macmillan, 1962), p. 34.

for a tradition of theology which had focused variously on metaphors taken from such cultural realities as the battlefield, the law court, and the altar such a theory of language was disastrous. To say that Christ died as a sacrifice for sin, or that his life, death, and resurrection were a victory over the forces of darkness, could be understood as at best a rhetorical way of saying what must be said otherwise in supposedly more rational language. And so it came about that various forms of exemplarism took the field, under the impulses provided by the rational criticism of traditional theologies by Kant, Schleiermacher and Hegel. To take one simple and rather crude example, owing something to Hegel, the doctrine of reconciliation could now be held to teach not that God and his erring creation were reconciled on the cross, but that the latter was a symbol of the reconciliation of the finite and infinite realms achievable by human cultural endeavour. In place of an act of God centred in a historic life and death, towards the otherwise helpless, the emphasis came to be upon those who by appropriate action could help themselves.

If that is something of a caricature, it nonetheless makes the point that the disappearance of a language makes it impossible to say what the language once purported to say. But if the disappearance of the theology was due to a false philosophy of language, may there not be some opportunity for repair when a more adequate philosophy is substituted? I believe that it is now established, though there is no space to review the arguments here, that metaphor is an intrinsic feature of all human language, and that such a claim makes no distinction between different fields of human thought and action. Metaphor is as necessary to the language of science as it is to that of poetry. Moreover – and here, of course, there is more room for argument – I would also claim that metaphor may be used realistically, in that it enables not simply a human response to reality, though that is part of the matter, but also dimensions of reality to come to human expression. That is to say, I would hold that metaphor is at the centre, and perhaps is the chief vehicle of, human rational relation with reality. Broadly, I want to advocate an interactionist view of the matter: that as the mind interacts with the world in a kind of reciprocity of asking questions and receiving answers, metaphor plays an essential part as the vehicle by which discoveries come to expression. To use Richard

Boyd's phrase, metaphor enables us to 'cut the world at its joints'.[7]

Within such a general theory of metaphor there will, to be sure, be wide varieties of usage. I am not trying to justify the theological by the scientific or literary, but rather to signal acceptance of recent arguments that, far from being a misuse of language, metaphor is at its heart. As has already been suggested, the Christian doctrine of the atonement operates with a number of central metaphors. As they emerged in New Testament characterizations of the meaning of Jesus, they operated as ways by which the early Church attempted linguistically to cut at its joints the world made real to it in the redemption found in Jesus. In the remainder of this chapter I wish to concentrate on one of those central metaphors and to use it in both illustration and defence of the view that through the metaphors of atonement we are able to understand something of what it is to claim that in Christ God was reconciling the world to himself.

Transcendental Explorations

There are, it must be conceded, some reasons why the old forms of the doctrine of the atonement deserved to come into disrepute. I need not rehearse them, for attacks on the way in which Calvinist doctrine in particular took shape in the centuries after Calvin have long been commonplace. There is, moreover, a tendency for statements of the doctrine in general to degenerate into rhetoric. Aulen's celebrated Christus Victor[8] is a case in point. Although it was not intended to be much more than a statement of the history of the doctrine, and claims little systematic development, and although it has undoubtedly served as an eye-opening corrective to the one-sided assertion of other versions of the doctrine, it does rather leave matters hanging in the air. Does it really concern us that Christ won on the

---

[7] Richard Boyd, 'Metaphor and Theory Change: What is "Metaphor" a Metaphor for?' in *Metaphor and Thought*, ed. A. Ortony (Cambridge: Cambridge University Press, 1979), p. 358. See also Janet Martin Soskice, *Metaphor and Religious Language* (Oxford: Oxford University Press, 1985).

[8] Gustaf Aulen, *Christus Victor. An Historical Study of the Three Main Types of the Idea of the Atonement*, tr. A. G. Hebert (London: SPCK, 1970).

cross a cosmic battle against the demonic, when we have the demons in our own times to overcome and do not necessarily see the connection between that battle and ours? But the point does not apply to the metaphor of victory alone. Does it, similarly, help us to be told that Christ bore the sins of the world on the cross, if we still have our own sins to bear? The crucial link that must be made is between the past historic event and life in the present, and mere statements of a past victory or sacrifice do not enable us to make it.

In order to make a link, I wish to develop the suggestion made in the opening words of the chapter, that the notion of sacrifice continues to be present in modern language and literature because it in some way reflects a basic human response to the world in which we live. It enables us to think and speak about certain aspects of our world that are important for life within it. The argument will proceed as follows: First, I shall outline some features of the way in which the metaphor of sacrifice has taken shape in Bible and tradition. The notion, it will be claimed, is not simply an outmoded picture; indeed it is not simply a picture at all, but a metaphorical way of saying about God, the world, and human life within it, what cannot otherwise be expressed. Second, an attempt will be made to show that sacrifice is not merely an important metaphor – one way of expressing the human relationship with God, creator and redeemer – but something even more fundamental: a notion without which we cannot make sense of our world. More positively, I want to suggest that the notion of sacrifice is not just a metaphor, but a transcendental, a transcendental that is given definitive shape theologically by the sacrifice of Jesus Christ.

What is meant in this context by 'transcendental'? To seek for a transcendental is to seek for those features of our language and experience by means of which reality at its most fundamental makes itself known to us: features that might be called 'necessary notes of being', 'the forms through which being displays itself'.[9] An essay by Norman Kretzmann gives an account of the medieval conception of the transcendentals: predicates like 'one', 'true', and 'good', which, like 'being', might be

---

[9] See Daniel W. Hardy, 'Created and Redeemed Sociality', in *On Being the Church*, eds C. E. Gunton and D. W Hardy (Edinburgh: T&T Clark, 1989).

supposed to qualify everything that is.[10] Under the influence of Kantian philosophy we have come to believe that such a quest is doomed, because at best there can be found only those concepts by means of which the mind structures its experience. According to that kind of doctrine there is no way by which we may discover whether the supposed concepts correspond to the way the world is apart from our conceiving. *A fortiori*, the quest for some 'objective' transcendental would seem to be even more absurd, a search for a chimera.

Undoubtedly, something has to be conceded to the Kantian view: our concepts are in part the product of the mind as it attempts to come to terms with the world. But, as recent studies of metaphor have claimed, there is a case for saying not only that the mind shapes concepts, but that it does so in ways that in some way answer to the world which it seeks to understand.[11] The quest for transcendentals in the post-Kantian world is similarly an enterprise that takes account of that interaction between mind and world neglected both by naive realism and by the kind of idealism generated by Kant. It will therefore necessarily take a different form from its medieval predecessors. In the first place, it will need to be more empirical in orientation, and to examine the shape which human life takes in interaction with the world as it enquires whether there are embodied in our thought and action universal or near universal features which lead us to ask the question about transcendentals. What we are looking for are, at the very least, expressions of the way in which the human race learns to inhabit the world. Kant's scepticism about the task is justified by the evidence that the history of metaphysical disputes is too confused for any naive version of the doctrine to succeed. But it would be wrong to concede his case that there is an absolute pluralism. Questions about existence in the world appear to emerge in similar form in many cultures. Thus, for example,

---

[10] Norman Kretzmann, 'Trinity and Transcendentals', in Feenstra and Plantinga, eds, *Trinity, Incarnation, and Atonement*, pp. 79–109.

[11] For one of the best descriptions of the development of scientific conceptuality up to the time of Kant, see T. F. Torrance, *Transformation and Convergence in the Frame of Knowledge: Explorations in the Interrelations of Scientific and Theological Enterprise* (Belfast: Christian Journals, 1984), pp. 36ff.

both Greek and Hebrew wondered about the justice of the universe, albeit in very different ways,[12] while many cultures have depicted human life on earth as sharing in a battle between good and evil, light and darkness. So it may be with the metaphor of sacrifice. Perhaps we cannot claim absolute universality for the language and practice of sacrifice, for it may be that some early societies did exist without such a practice. Still, the notion appears to derive from something deep in human nature and the human response to the world – something one plausibly supposes to be a universal or near universal feature of our life on earth.

In the second place, the quest for transcendentals cannot be for universal or abstract predicates. We seek something at once more concrete and more elusive. 'Goodness', 'being', and the like, have the air of timeless abstractions. 'Sacrifice' introduces us to more concretely relational matters. It has something to do, certainly in its 'primitive' form, with the way in which the human race comes to terms with the world: with life, death, pollution, and cleansing. At a religious level, sacrifice is a function of the human relation to the power that makes life what it is: sacrifice has to do with creation, fall, and redemption, that is, with relations to God.

To be sure, one must concede that the argument is by no means straightforward. There is no suggestion that the word 'sacrifice' and the phenomenon it purports to denote take the same form in every case. There are, after all, large differences among cultures (as well as between, say, a biblical usage and the decadent forms the word often takes today). Some Greeks, for instance, thought that the gods could be bought off by a timely sacrifice, while many of the prophets clearly believed that the true sacrifice was a life in accordance with the covenant law. And yet, within so vast a spectrum of usage, can some common or at least overlapping features be found? Negatively, it can be suggested that sacrifice emerges from human experience of pollution and uncleanness, and a corresponding need to be

---

[12] See Colin Gunton, 'The Justice of God', *Free Church Chronicle* 40 (1985), pp. 13–19; H. Lloyd Jones, *The Justice of Zeus* (London: University of California Press, 1971). The latter book and the importance of the topic in general were brought to my attention by Alasdair MacIntyre, *After Virtue: A Study in Moral Theory* (London: Duckworth, 1981), p. 126.

purified if life on earth is to take due form.[13] Positively, it may be suggested that we are in the realm of the gift, that feature of our existence in which we realize our dependence on and relation to the other as the most fundamental feature of our existence in the image of the Trinity. But those most general characterizations take us to the beginning of our theological enquiry proper. In it we shall attempt to find the transcendental in the concrete: to examine some features of the Christian tradition in order to ask whether there can be found in them the kind of universality that may support the suggestion that here there is something that cannot be ignored.

In Search of the Concrete Transcendental

The Christian theological case for the centrality of the concept of sacrifice offers two places where our hypothetical transcendental takes concrete form: what we may call the linguistic and the practical. It takes concrete form linguistically because the biblical metaphor of sacrifice has given rise, in the context of the life and, particularly, the worship of the Church, to a tradition of theology in which the reality of God savingly present in Jesus Christ has been articulated. That is to say, by expressing the significance of the life, death, and resurrection of Jesus in terms of the language of sacrifice, a certain way of expressing the reality of salvation – authentic human life under God – has taken shape. Let us review briefly some features of the linguistic tradition.[14]

[13] See G. B. Caird, *The Language and Imagery of the Bible* (London: Duckworth, 1980), p. 17: 'Deep in the heart of mankind there is an instinctive aversion to dirt, disease, and death; and in almost every language the words which convey this abhorrence are used metaphorically to express and evoke a similar loathing for sin, and especially for sins of fraud, sensuality, and violence.' See also note 19 below.

[14] Material in the next three paragraphs is taken from my article 'Christ the Sacrifice: Aspects of the Language and Imagery of the Bible', in *The Glory of Christ in the New Testament: Studies in Christology in Memory of George Bradford Caird*, eds L. D. Hurst and N. T. Wright (Oxford: Oxford University Press, 1987), pp. 229–38. Parts of this chapter also draw freely on Colin Gunton, *The Actuality of Atonement* (Edinburgh: T&T Clark, 1988; Grand Rapids: Eerdmans, 1989).

In the Old Testament we find the concept of sacrifice already being transformed by means of metaphorical transfer. In the Psalms, for example, we hear that the sacrifice which God requires is the humble heart (Ps. 51.17), the response to God's covenant goodness consisting in a particular way of living before him. This is a metaphor because the chief – and so literal – meaning of the term was, and continued to be, the animal slaughtered before the Lord. Indeed, the two usages continued to exist side by side, as so many uses of metaphor continue to live beside the parent. Despite the fulminations of the prophets, literal (animal) sacrifice continued into the time of Jesus, and he is recorded as acquiescing in the cult (Mark 1.44). And yet the psalmist and those who were like him prepared the way for the greatest metaphorical transformation of all.

For the most part, the Old Testament institution of sacrifice was concerned, through all its variations, with the response of Israel to the covenant love of God. The sacrifices were indeed of divine institution, but they were primarily human gifts by which Israel ordered and reordered her relationship to her God. In the New Testament, because the metaphor now takes shape through what happens with Jesus, the element of divine initiative is heightened: 'God will provide the lamb' (Gen. 2.28). It is surely right to see in some of the words Paul uses to describe God's gift of himself in Christ the language of sacrifice: God 'did not spare' but 'gave up' his only Son for us (Rom. 8.32). The metaphor of sacrifice is used as a way of expressing the meaning of all that happened with and to Jesus. The whole of the life and its outcome are understood, at one level, as the gift of God to the world. The one who, according to the old dispensation, received the sacrifice, now becomes the giver.

Yet there is also another level at which the matter must be understood, for, particularly in the theology of the writer to the Hebrews, the one who is God's gift of himself to the world is also seen as humankind's response to God, the one offering of a true human life to the Father. Before we proceed to examine the theological significance of such a claim, we must pause to examine what has happened linguistically. To call the death of Jesus a sacrifice is obviously a metaphor: although there is a death, it is not on an altar, and we are assured that it was voluntary. Only some of the features of the old order – specifically the fact of the death – are retained. With the change in language, however, goes a change in meaning: 'sacrifice' does not now mean the death of a dumb creature, but the kind of thing that Jesus did in both life and death. With the new meaning come implications for life, as when Paul enjoins his readers to give their bodies as a living sacrifice (Rom. 12.1). We can believe those ancient Christian writers who claimed that the death of Jesus had led to the abolition of animal sacrifice. New metaphors mean new realities, new ways of looking at and being in the world. To put it provisionally, we can focus on the notion of gift: in response to the gift by God of his Son and to God by his Son, the human heart is 'cleansed from dead works' (Heb. 9.14) and enabled to come before God with the sacrifice that is true worship and life.

But what kind of sacrifice is it, and what does it achieve? We now come to face the problems and develop the possibilities bequeathed to us by the tradition. The problems, as we have seen, are twofold: the protest of the Enlightenment (and that of commonsense human moralism in general) at the morality and appropriateness of the matter, and the danger of rhetoric – that we shall proclaim a past act in such a way that it will appear mere abstract assertion. We shall approach both aspects of the problem in the light of the treatment of the atonement by that much neglected nineteenth-century Calvinist divine, Edward Irving.

The concern underlying Irving's interesting and orthodox dogmatic treatment of both Trinity and Christology was in large part to present an adequate Christian soteriology particularly in face of recent Calvinism's shortcomings. There were two: the doctrine of limited atonement and a mathematical conception of the work of Christ. This latter, what Irving called 'Stock-Exchange Divinity', is the teaching of a form of substitutionary atonement wherein Jesus, by bearing an equivalent quantity of sins, released from penalty those for whom he died.

Two comments are here in order. The first is that Irving rightly discerns the empty rhetoric behind the teaching that, because Jesus has borne a certain number of sins, even if that number be infinite, others are able to be remitted. Such teaching runs the danger of becoming non-relational and abstractly mathematical because it speaks not of a renewed relationship

between God and the sinner, but of an external transaction.[15]
Irving's concern was with some of the cruder theories of a
debased Calvinism. He observes that, given these theories, the
sinner can continue to say, 'That example of the sinfulness of
sin . . . is not applicable to me, who have but my own sin to
bear.'[16]

Second, we can recognize that the object of Irving's protest is
a theology of atonement that is largely or wholly dependent
upon a legal conception of the relation between God and the
sinner. Legal imagery, as a central theme of the New Testament,
must be taken with due seriousness and has its place in the
theology of atonement. But it is worth noting that Paul himself
interprets that imagery with metaphors taken from the altar of
sacrifice – in Romans 3.24ff. explicitly, but elsewhere in his use
of language. That is also the path taken by Irving. There are two
focuses to Irving's work, corresponding to the inadequacies of
that of some of his predecessors. In place of the limited atonement, Irving bases his theology in the Trinity, and in the eternal
gracious purposes of God for his creation. The atonement is
accordingly not the outworking of the gratuitous will of God to
damn all but pluck a few from the burning, but rather the
expression of the gracious will to self-giving. To use the daring
metaphor of St John the Divine, the (sacrificial!) lamb slain
from the foundation of the world is the revelation of the inner
being of God. That is to say, Jesus as the eternal Son made flesh
is the self-giving of the Father in expression and realization of
his eternal will for covenant.

[15] The tendency to think of the atonement in almost aesthetic, mathematical
terms, probably dates from Origen's speculations about the fall of the rational
spirits and the need to fill up the complement of heaven. It explains the otherwise puzzling amount of attention that Anselm gives to the question of whether
the number of the saved is to equal the number of fallen angels, and probably
underlies some doctrines of limited atonement and penal substitution. See
Anselm, *Cur Deus Homo* I.16–18. ET; *Anselm of Canterbury*, eds J. Hopkins and
H. Richardson (London: SCM Press; New York: Mellen, 1974). However, such
points should not be taken to belittle Anselm's massive contribution to the
development of the doctrine of the atonement. I have tried to say something of
this in chapter 5 of *The Actuality of Atonement*.
[16] Edward Irving, *The Collected Writings of Edward Irving in Five Volumes*, ed.
G. Carlyle, vol. 5, *The Doctrine of the Incarnation Opened* (London: Alexander
Strahan, 1865), p. 218. Subsequent references to this work will be made
parenthetically in the body of the text.

In this way Irving treats the atonement as a saving act of God. But (and here we come to the second focus) it is in his treatment of the humanity of the saviour that Irving is at his most interesting and original. What does Jesus achieve as man? On one theory, he bears as our substitute the penalty for our sin. There are, I believe, elements of truth in the old substitutionary theory, but that is not the point to be pursued here. What is rather worth pursuing is that Irving, drawing on an old Calvinist tradition, and particularly, it can be supposed, on insights contained in such writings as Calvin's commentary on the Letter to the Hebrews, developed a view of the humanity of Christ in continuity with the use of the sacrifice metaphor in the New Testament. On such an understanding, Jesus as our representative offers to the Father a human life – the very sacrifice which the psalmist described as 'a broken and contrite heart' and which, because of our sin, we refuse to give. Calvin sees in the life and death of Christ a human self-giving which is effective in giving life to others.[17]

Irving deserves to be celebrated today primarily for developing this insight into the doctrine for which he was convicted of heresy: that at the incarnation the eternal Son took to himself the fallen flesh that all human beings share. Irving's concern is not, of course, to teach the sinfulness of Christ, but to give an adequate account of the representative nature of his humanity. If salvation is really to be communicated to us, then our flesh must be healed. And it must be healed as it is, that is, as infected by 'the simple, single, common power of sin diffused throughout, and present in, the substance of flesh of fallen human nature' (p. 217). Our sinfulness, then, is not conceived *mathematically* as the accumulation of wrong acts, but *relationally* as that which universally qualifies human existence in the flesh. If so, then, as the anti-Apollinarian theologians had argued, precisely *that* fallen flesh must be assumed by the saviour.

The first step to be taken in such a process of salvation is that the Son should assume flesh taken, so to speak, randomly from the fallen world (the word 'random' is Irving's, p. 154). And to that end, argues Irving, the Holy Spirit formed for the Son a

[17] John Calvin, *Commentaries on the Epistle of Paul the Apostle to the Hebrews*, tr. J. Owen (Edinburgh: Calvin Translation Society, 1853), ad. Heb. 7.26, 8.2, 9.14.

body from the fallen flesh of Mary. The salvation of this representative piece of flesh becomes the basis for the salvation of the rest. How? Irving's second and crucial step is to re-establish the place of the Holy Spirit in the theology of the incarnation.

If the representative offering of worship to the Father is to be true worship, it must be the offering of a spotless life before the throne of grace; if, on the other hand, it is to be truly representative, it must be not only authentically human worship, but also an offering which enables in turn the response of the rest of us. And so Irving holds that through the leading of the Holy Spirit the incarnate Son is able to bear fallen flesh through all the trials of his human life without himself falling. The human life of the Son is not, so to speak, pre-programmed from the start – as much nearly docetic Christology sometimes suggests – but is maintained in holiness by virtue of Jesus' free response to the guidance of the Spirit. According to Irving, after the resurrection that same Spirit enables believers to offer, in turn, a true human response to the Father.

In this way Irving prepares the ground for the development of the concrete link between past sacrifice and present sacrifices. But it must be recalled that at this stage we are attempting to make conceptual sense of the metaphor of sacrifice. What conception of sacrifice is here being developed? I have already suggested that the notion of gift is somewhere in the atmosphere. But that is a relatively banal conclusion, and gives no indication of the kind of gift that is involved or of the universality that is being sought. What is the character of the representative gift of worship and life that the incarnate Son offers to the Father?

Daniel Hardy has suggested to me that the clue to the meaning of sacrifice is the idea of concentration. At the heart of what Jesus does is not simply the offering of a human life, but of the concentrated summation of humanity: it is the kind of offering that, so to speak, longs to offer not only itself, but all flesh. That one offering can stand in for the others because, in anticipation of the eschatological presenting of all God's people spotless before the throne, it takes the representative and random sample of fallen flesh and offers it, through the Spirit, perfect to the Father. It is noteworthy that earlier this century P. T. Forsyth used a similar notion in speaking of the atoning death of Christ as 'the condensed action of His whole personality – His whole holy personality'.[18]

What dogmatic conclusions can then be drawn from the exposition of the atonement as a sacrifice? First, the incarnation and its outcome are sacrificial in that they are the concentrated self-giving of the eternal Son of God, rooted in the eternal trinitarian relations. The Son's giving of himself in and for the world is the outworking, realized through the Holy Spirit, of the Father's giving up of the Son in pursuit of his eternal will for communion with the creature. In that dimension, the atonement must be understood as the eternal love of God, 'contracted to a span' in the historical incarnation of the Son. This gives us our first answer to the question about the universality of sacrifice: sacrifice, in this concrete realization of the transcendental, is the expression and outworking of the inner-trinitarian relations of giving and receiving. The inner being of God is a taxis, a dynamic orderedness, of love construed in terms of mutual and reciprocal gift and reception. If the sacrifice that is Jesus' human life and death is a realization in time of the eternal taxis, then it is indeed universal.

Second, the Son's taking of fallen flesh and offering it, through the Spirit to the Father, both in the ministry and on the cross which was its outcome, is the concentrated offering of human worship which, because of our sin, we are otherwise unable to achieve. That, too, says something about the universal significance of Jesus, with important implications for what it is for the rest of us to be human. In the light of Jesus' sacrifice we are able to understand that to realize our humanity is to realize, at our creaturely level, first the response of praise and, second, the reciprocity of creaturely giving and receiving that are together the living out of our being in the image of God. The manner of Jesus' offering to his Father of a life and death is indicative at once of the inadequacy of the 'blood of bulls and goats' (Heb. 9.13) to cleanse the conscience from dead works and of the rightness of the psalmists' and prophets' insistence that the true sacrifice is a mode of life before God and with others. This is a universal claim about human being: it is truly

---

[18] P. T. Forsyth, *The Church, the Gospel, and Society* (London: Independent Press, 1962), p. 10.

human only when it gives to God the free sacrifice that is its 'logical service.' (A literal translation of Romans 12.1, rendered 'spiritual act of worship' by the RSV, makes the point that 'the living sacrifice, holy and acceptable to God' is the true *logic* of our humanity.)

A third conclusion takes us into the next phase of the discussion – the practical. It concerns Jesus as the mediator of reconciliation. Sacrifice, like the other metaphors of atonement, concerns the restoration and perfection of relations: it is about reconciliation. It brings to expression one (again, universal) dimension of the divine – human relationship. As legal imagery sees sin as offence against law, and military imagery conceives it as bondage to uncontrollable evil, here we are in the realm of the moral and religious pollution that bars the sinner from the presence of the holy God. Because Jesus is at once priest and victim, the otherwise unreconciled creature and creator are by him restored to fellowship. It is scarcely surprising that the Letter to the Hebrews makes so much of the function of the priest–sacrifice to bring the otherwise disbarred believer into the presence of the holy God whose eyes are too pure to look upon corruption.

But our nagging question returns. Even if the universality of sacrifice is given concrete expression by reference to the life and death of Jesus, what is it about this past historical act that brings us, now, into the presence of God? What makes the eternal sacrifice of the the Letter to the Hebrews into one that, abstract platonizing apart, enables us to say that the sacrifice is the means and vehicle of the sacrifices that are the human means of approach to the presence of God?

The Metaphor: the Sacrifices

We have seen that a distinctive element of Edward Irving's Christology is the part it ascribes to the Holy Spirit as the one who maintains Jesus in truth. The strength of the emphasis is twofold: it allows due importance to be given to the humanity of Christ; and it provides the basis of a link between Jesus' humanity and ours. What the Spirit was to Jesus, he may be for us, because by virtue of his resurrection Jesus now becomes the one who gives the Spirit to those who believe. That is where we find the link between the sacrifice and the sacrifices – between the once for all divine-human sacrifice and the response of believers in the various sacrifices (e.g., sacrifices of worship and Christian living) that are realized through this sacrifice. On such an understanding the Spirit is to be understood as the 'second' hand of God who enables believers to realize, through the once for all atonement of Christ, the form of life that the atonement made and makes possible.

The traditional way of conceiving the matter is to speak of the Spirit as applying the benefits of Christ to the believer. Without denying that insight, it must be said that it is deficient in a number of ways. In the first place, it reproduces the traditional inability of pneumatological thought to attribute to the Spirit a distinctive mode of action; that is, it fails to make pneumatology any more than an appendage of Christology. Second, it tends to create an individualist apprehension of the work of the Spirit: the work of Christ is mediated to the believer, rather than to believers. The missing dimensions are the eschatological and ecclesiological. In realizing the former, we attribute to the Holy Spirit the distinctive action of not so much a general 'applying' of the benefits of Christ as a 'particularizing' in the present of the blessings, mediated through Christ, of the world to come. In developing the latter, the work of Christ is realized through the creation of community. Third, the conventional account tends to restrict the work of the Spirit to the personal realm. But if we are to take seriously the promise of God's will to reconcile all things to himself in Jesus, should we not look beyond the merely personal to the wider created world? Only so shall we be able to realize something of what it means to make claims for the transcendentality of our metaphor, because only so shall we be able to show something of how it reveals one of the marks of all being.

To approach a pneumatology of sacrifice, we return to the trinitarian considerations of the previous section. We saw that the notion of sacrifice, as realized in the life, death, and resurrection of Jesus, took us to the heart of the being of God. The life of the Trinity is nothing but what the persons give to and receive from each other: it is pure (concentrated) community or communion. The work of Christ, considered negatively, is to wipe away the pollution – both personal and worldly – which bars the way to communion, both 'vertically,' with God, and 'horizontally' with the neighbour who is embodied in the created world.[19] Considered positively, it is to realize the communion that is the will of the Father from eternity. Final realization is eschatological: it is to be achieved only at the end. But the promise of the Spirit is that – amidst the particularities of our worldliness – we shall be given anticipations of what is to come. That is to say, the Spirit's gift is at once communion with God and community among his people not merely personalistically but in the context of their inhabiting a particular environment *as creation*.

The notion of sacrifice as realized in the context of life in the creation could be developed in a number of ways, but perhaps primarily through worship. The New Testament clearly connects the metaphors of sacrifice and the worship of the Church. One particularly clear example is found in its teaching about the Lord's Supper. Paul, Mark, and Matthew alike link the cup with the covenant and with death, deliberately relating Jesus' death with an earlier covenantal sacrifice (1 Cor. 11.25f., Mark 14.24, Matt. 26.28, cf. Exod. 24.8); while Luke and, almost certainly, John make a direct link with the Passover (Luke 22.15, John 19.14). Such differences as there are between the usages are important as indicating both the metaphorical character of what is said and the freedom of the authors in adapting their language to fit the altered context. The language is developed in order to draw out in different ways the redemptive significance of the event. Thus Paul, linking the metaphor of sacrifice with that of the law court, associates communion with judgement (1 Cor. 11.32: 'when we are judged by the Lord we are chastened'), while Luke's use of Passover rather than covenantal language links the Supper with liberation (the obverse of his concern to show that the encounter with the demonic, begun at the temptation, comes to a head in the passion of Jesus, Luke 22.40).

[19] Mary Douglas has pointed out the connection between the notion of the clean and the unclean – the converse of the notion of sacrifice – and that of the order of creation. Pollution, and that which removes it, are a function of our relatedness to the created order, and we cannot therefore understand sacrifice merely in terms of social custom or 'inner' needs. The notions are a function of the way in which we live in the world. See Mary Douglas, *Purity and Danger: An Analysis of the Concepts of Pollution and Taboo* (London: Ark Books, 1984).

It is a surprising feature of the Church's understanding of the Lord's Supper that the link between communion and community has rarely been emphasized. Yet for Paul it is clearly paramount. Much of his horror in the first letter to Corinth is reserved for breaches of community in the celebration of the Lord's Supper, the heart of the Church's anticipation of the eschatological banquet (1 Cor. 11.26).[20] Underlying such a concern is an ecclesiology in which the work of Christ and the Spirit is to create, in time and space, a living echo of the communion that God is in eternity. That is the true sacrifice: the offering to God in praise of the life of his people. Historically there has been much dispute about whether and in what sense the Lord's Supper is a sacrifice. The dispute can be seen to derive largely from taking the metaphor too literally. The Reformers were right to oppose any suggestion that the sacrifice of Jesus is in any way made or repeated by a churchly celebration. But the corresponding danger is that the metaphor should be deprived of its content in so far as it refers to the human response deriving from and made possible by the once and for all death of the saviour. The sacrifice is the basis and enabler of sacrifices: yet what is offered is not Christ, but that which he came to realize, the gift to God in worship and life of the perfected creation.

Here both Catholic and Reformed have fallen short in stressing too strongly the notions of sin and forgiveness conceived legally, and the corresponding legal-institutional aspects of ecclesiology. In both traditions there has been a loss of the dimensions of community and the wider aspects of life in the world. It is noteworthy that Irving was aware of the cosmic dimensions of the sacrifice. Because the sacrifice is made from the foundation of the world, he says, its historic and concrete realization in Jesus is likewise universal and cosmic:

> Whether you regard the life of any individual, or the life of the race of men, or the life of animals, or the vegetable life of the world, it is all a fruit, a common fruit of redemption, a benefit of the death of Christ, from all eternity purposed, and so far as God is concerned accomplished also. (pp. 295f.)

The World Council of Churches' 'Lima Document' expresses

---

[20] There is an extended treatment of this topic in Chapter 13 below.

something of the wider implications of the theology of sacrifice: 'The eucharist is the great sacrifice of praise by which the Church speaks on behalf of the whole creation . . . [It] opens up the vision of the divine rule which has been promised as the final renewal of creation.'[21] We might develop all this by saying that just as the humanity of Christ is the concentrated – and so representative – offering through the Spirit of true humanity to the Father, so the bread and wine become through the same Spirit the concentrated offering of all of the life of the creation. The work of the Spirit is to enable the created order to realize its perfection by making it a sacrifice of praise to its creator.

Again, we must remember that such a conception of sacrifice is more than merely personal and ecclesial. As the giver of the first fruits (another metaphor of sacrifice) the Spirit is the agent of that which is celebrated in Romans 8: 'because the creation itself is to be set free from its bondage to decay and obtain the glorious liberty of the children of God' (Rom. 8.21). Sacrifice means the offering of the perfected creation back in praise to God. In his play *Amadeus* Peter Shaffer puts into the mouth of Mozart something of what this means:

> I tell you I want to write a finale lasting half an hour! A quartet becoming a quintet becoming a sextet. On and on, wider and wider – all sounds multiplying and rising together – and together making a sound entirely new! . . . I bet you that's how God hears the world. Millions of sounds ascending at

[21] World Council of Churches, *Baptism, Eucharist, Ministry: Faith and Order Paper No. III* (Geneva: World Council of Churches, 1982), 'Eucharist', 4, 22 (pp. 10, 14). 1 should like to make it clear that I am here using the Lima text as one example of the way in which worship may be understood as sacrifice. More generally, I would want to take the already-cited Romans 12.1 as the primary expression of the sacrifice that is the response to the sacrifice. This view of the Eucharist is consistent with the traditional Lutheran and Reformed insistence that the Lord's Supper is primarily God's gift to his people rather than their gift to God: the argument of the essay is that any sacrifice we make is determined by (1) the sacrifice that is the Father's gift of the Son to the world and the Son's responding gift of himself for us and on our behalf to the Father; and (2) the Father's gift to us through the Son of the Spirit who is the sole enabler of such sacrifices as we make in response. Just as the Old Testament sacrificial system was the divine covenantal dispensation whereby Israel was enabled to maintain her relationship with God, so the worship of the Church, sacraments included, is the universal covenantal dispensation in continuity with Israel's worship. I intend, therefore, to share the Reformers' insistence.

once and mixing in His ear to become an unending music, unimaginable to us![22]

If such a statement is not to appear to evade the reality of evil, it must be construed christologically. God hears the world as praise in Christ, by virtue of his sacrifice. The Church's calling is to represent and realize, in the Spirit, the world's praise of God. Such a realization is not, of course, the exclusive prerogative of the Church, for the Spirit cannot be so restricted. Yet the Church is called to realize, by its worship and life, that which is the destiny of all things. That is what is meant by 'reconciliation': the liberation of all things to praise their maker.

By such a route, we return to the matter of the transcendental. Can we understand sacrifice as one of the essential marks of being? According to the theology here attempted, to be the created world is to be that whose perfection is to be expressed in the offering back to the creator, through Christ and in the Spirit, of his perfected work. To repeat, that is what it means to be the world: to give and to be given in the perfection of praise to the creator. Thus the notion of sacrifice takes us not only to the heart of the being of God, but also to the heart of creaturely being.[23] The latter becomes truly itself under two conditions: when in itself it echoes at its creaturely level the giving and receiving that God is eternally; and when through a redeemed giving and receiving it is enabled to give itself in praise to its maker. That, surely, is something of what Barth was saying when he said that Mozart had a place in eschatology, for he 'causes us to hear that . . . in its totality, creation praises its Master and is therefore perfect'.[24] As it is, for various reasons, including 'pollution' and human sin, creation does not praise its Master. But that it will, and may now, by the Spirit, praise its creator along with the people of God, is one of the implications of the doctrine of the atonement which we must learn to realize.

---

[22] Peter Shaffer, *Amadeus* (Harmondsworth: Penguin Books, 1981), p. 70.

[23] We might even call this a kind of analogy of being.

[24] Karl Barth, *Church Dogmatics*, eds G. W. Bromiley and T. F. Torrance (Edinburgh: T&T Clark, 1957–1975), 3/3, p. 299.

12

Baptism: Baptism and the Christian Community[1]

The Problem in its Context

What is now the United Reformed Church in Great Britain was formed in 1972 as a union of Congregationalists and Presbyterians from England and Wales. It has since been re-formed with the addition to it of a number of congregations of the Churches of Christ, and it is there that is to be found what may be a unique contribution to an ecumenical theology of baptism. For the union represents the coming together in one Church of *communities* holding different positions on the administration of baptism: the one paedobaptist, the other practising only the baptism of believers. In the new Church all congregations are expected to offer both forms of baptism; no minister, however, is compelled to administer baptism in a form that conscience forbids.

Essential to such an arrangement is the commitment to respect the form of baptism administered by those whose convictions are different. The Church's constitution is insistent that entry to the Church is by baptism, which may be administered once only to any person, so that all baptisms in both forms administered in the new Church and formerly administered in its constituent parts are recognized as real baptisms. The commitment to recognize what was once rejected may be supposed

---

[1] First published in *Incarnational Ministry. The Presence of Christ in Church, Society, and Family. Essays in Honor of Ray S. Anderson*, eds Christian D. Kettler and Todd H. Speidell (Colorado Springs: Helmers & Howard, 1990), pp. 98–109.

to be most difficult for those whose convictions have been that baptism is to be administered only to those able to confess belief. But it is respect that is required, not abandonment of convictions. Thus the United Reformed Church is a testing ground for the acceptance of differences within *community* that will be required of all who hope to grow together with formerly separated branches of the Church.

For the most part the respect for different forms of baptism has been given, and in ways which, it is to be hoped, will form a model for ecumenical relationships in the future. However, as often happens in such matters, the expected strains and stresses have appeared at other places than might have been expected. Into the picture have come the forces of what has come to be called restorationism,[2] with its strong stress on both the failure of the mainline Churches and a call to individual renewal, a call which often denies the validity of the baptism that converts may have received as infants. Inevitably, the pressures make themselves felt in the traditional denominations, particularly in calls for what is sometimes called 'rebaptism'.[3] Many churches are feeling the pressures; but they bear with particular force on a Church which affirms the necessity to respect the reality of both forms of baptism in the one community.

The pastoral problem arising from requests for 'second' baptism forms the immediate context for this chapter. But, like all movements which renew or trouble the Church – and sometimes both – restorationism does not come out of the blue. Along with its cousin, Pentecostalism, its genesis can be seen to be in part a reaction to widely acknowledged weaknesses in the shape traditional Christianity has taken. A frequent object of its criticism is institutionalism, against which so many movements of protest have been directed (only to fall into it themselves in due time). But institutionalism is, it seems to me, the obverse of an equal failure, which is only too evident in both restorationism and so many of the political fashions of recent decades. It is, of course, individualism. In that respect, it is easy to recognize the pedigree of so many recent revivalist movements, for

---

[2] Andrew Walker, *Restoring the Kingdom* (London: Hodder & Stoughton, 1985).

[3] Cited by Alan Sell, *Theology in Turmoil* (Grand Rapids: Baker, 1986), p. 140.

example in a statement cited by Alan Sell from Robert Mackintosh's nineteenth-century *The Insufficiency of Revivalism*.

> Evangelicalism does not wish to be distracted by any wider moral outlook than the desire to save one's own soul in the first place and, secondly, to promote the salvation of the souls of other individuals ... Infant baptism is the great rock of offence to the triumphant revival (because it places the infant individual within a covenanted fellowship).[4]

It is the heirs of the evangelical revival who succumb most easily to temptations of individualism, for reasons which this quotation makes only too clear. And yet those of us who are suspicious of evangelicalism should beware of casting too many stones in that direction. We too live in a glass house of our own making, and it can be argued that our current disorder derives at once from sloppy pastoral practice and an inadequate theology of baptism that is itself deeply stained by individualism. I shall begin by sketching in broad strokes some of the historical roots of the problem.

The enthusiasts for rebaptism, like those for some recent political movements of a strongly individualist stamp, are alike the spiritual descendants of the Age of Reason. Karl Barth pointed out long ago that rationalist and pietist are but two sides of the same coin because both place the human individual in the centre: the reason or experience of the individual are what is decisive, over against and if necessary in opposition to the traditions and life of the *community* as a whole.[5] This is very important for a theology of baptism, because, as I shall hope to show, while baptism is in part the concern of the particular person, it is not primarily a matter for the person as *individual* but for the person in relation to other people in the community of salvation, the covenant people of God. Baptism cannot, and should not,

---

[4] Karl Barth, *Protestant Theology in the Nineteenth Century. Its Background and History*, tr. Brian Cozens *et al.* (London: SCM Press, 1972), pp. 84f.

[5] It is here that individualism and institutionalism are two aspects of the same ecclesiastical phenomenon. Baptism on such an account is something performed for and upon an individual by an institution. One symptom of the coincidence of the two is the English practice, now coming increasingly into question, of performing private baptisms, with only family and friends present, outside the context of the life of the worshipping community.

be treated in isolation from the life of the community of faith.

And yet the root cause of recent difficulties over baptism is that we live at the end of a long history, beginning well before the Enlightenment, in which it has been treated individualistically and in abstraction from the life and worship of the covenant community. The present outbreak of enthusiasm for rebaptism does not appear out of thin air, but is a response to the particular way in which the sacrament has been used in the life of the Church for many centuries. Dominating the history is the phenomenon of Christendom, that now almost completely departed era when to be a Christian could often mean little more than being born in Europe. In the centuries after the conversion of Emperor Constantine early in the fourth century there developed a society in which Christianity became the official ideology. To be baptized under such arrangement came to involve little more than undergoing a social rite of passage. Against such practice, traces of which still remain, it is scarcely surprising that protests have arisen.

In parallel with the social development, and in a complicated relation to it, there arose an equally inadequate theology of baptism. It was based on a pessimistic view of the human condition, owing more to a form of Platonic philosophy than to the gospel. It taught that to be a human being was to inherit, by virtue of the process of human descent from Adam, a stain – 'original sin' – which meant that without the baptism which was supposed to remove that stain one was destined for hell. The points about this which we should note in particular are three. The first is that there developed from it an essentially negative conception of baptism, which was conceived more as a means of avoiding an unpleasant fate than as entry into a rich inheritance. Of course, such teaching was never in practice unmixed with more positive, gospel, contents, but it went very deep into the consciousness of Western society, as is revealed by the fact that fear of the consequences of a lack of baptism still operates as a motive in parents seeking baptism for their children. Baptism came to be as much a prophylactic handed out to individuals by an institution as the means of entry into the community of salvation.

The second point to note is that underlying the development I have sketched is an inadequate conception of a sacrament.

The popular and grossly misleading definition of a sacrament as 'an outward and visible sign of an inward and spiritual grace' falsely divides the world into two, the inner and outer, and supposes that a sacrament is something that, although it makes no visible difference to the outside of a person, causes something to happen 'inside'. Thus, baptism comes to be conceived as an inner cleansing from the stain of original sin, performed 'efficaciously' by an official representative of the Church.[6] The third point follows directly, and it is that we have inherited a very individualistic conception of baptism as rather that which is performed on the individual to save him or her from an inherited stain or a hellish fate than that by which a person is brought into a new relation with God through the medium of the covenant community. It must, of course, be remembered that the two latter points are caricatures, and that the Reformers and others protested against the abuse of both baptism and the Lord's Supper; but they are caricatures which have continued to affect our thinking and practice. Because they have been present, they have prevented an adequate theology from emerging, and so contributed to the present disorder.

Before I move to what I hope will be a somewhat more adequate theology, two more items of ground clearing are in order. First, in the light of the misuse of baptism by the tradition, it is understandable that some have come to argue that only 'believers' ought to be baptized or, more radically, that the official baptism dispensed by the Churches is not 'real' because it is merely a social rite of passage. The protest is a proper one against the secularizing of baptism, its being turned into more of a social rite of passage than a truly churchly ordinance. Despite this, I would wish to argue that the protest takes the wrong form, for it perpetuates the individualism of the tradition. It is not the baptism of infants that is the problem, but the indiscriminate baptism of those whose parents have no living relation to the covenant community, or, more strictly, of those for whom there is no likelihood that baptism is truly initiation into the life of that community.

---

[6] I have tried to spell out something of what this might mean in *Yesterday and Today. A Study of Continuities in Christology.* (London: Darton, Longman & Todd, 1983; 2nd edn, London: SPCK, 1997), pp. 125–35.

Second, there is nothing to be gained by arguments about whether the primitive Church did or did not practise the baptism of infants. The arguments are inconclusive, and likely to remain so. In any case, that is not the point, which is whether the logic of the gospel justifies the practice of the baptism of those who have little or no choice in the matter. By the 'logic' of the gospel I mean not something deduced from, for example, the words of Scripture, but the way in which the content of the gospel can be seen, perhaps after years of reflection, to invite or require a certain response or course of action.[7] As an example, we could take one discovery of what the logic of the gospel involves that took far too long to make. The primitive Church appears to have condoned the practice of slavery.[8] Yet, later generations came to believe that the logic of the gospel prohibits the institution. The question for us is similar: what does the logic of the gospel have to say to us about the nature and practice of baptism?

The Nature of Baptism

Baptism takes its reality from the death of Jesus on the cross. We baptize because Christ died on the cross for the sins of the world. That is the element which we may not ignore or play down, because it is the place of our redemption. It is said that when Luther experienced his trials of faith, he would pace the room exclaiming: 'I have been baptized!' His baptism had not been an 'experience' for him as we so often want to make it.

---

[7] For a major, early and important exception, see Trevor Dennis, 'Man Beyond Price: Gregory of Nyssa on Slavery' in *Heaven and Earth. Essex Essays in Theology and Ethics*, eds Andrew Linzey and Peter J. Wexler (Worthing: Churchman Publishing, 1986), pp. 129–45. It is an account of 'a root and branch attack' on slavery by Gregory of Nyssa.

[8] The statement about means should not be taken undialectically, as has been pointed out to me by several readers of the chapter. Baptism should not be conceived as taking the place of the divine action, but has the character it has 'because God uses the human practice ... in order to establish the relationship that includes us into the community of his covenant people' (Christoph Schwoebel). Similarly, as a *symbol* baptism both is and is not what it represents: it therefore both makes and does not make us members of the Church.

Rather, it determined his experience, because it was grounded
in the historic event that provided the framework for his existence. The cross was something that happened apart from his
knowledge or wishes. Indeed, it happened when, to use Paul's
expression, we were helpless. That is its significance: that
before we can possibly be in a position to know or appropriate
its meaning, something has been done for us and for all the
world.

It is in the light of that absolute givenness of the cross that we
must interpret other features of biblical talk of baptism. There
are two of particular note. The first is the commission recorded
at the end of Matthew's Gospel. It is now widely believed that
the dominical command to baptize in the name of the Father,
Son and Holy Spirit is not a report of actual words of the risen
Jesus, but the invention of the early Church. While it seems to
me that that is a matter of opinion because the truth cannot be
known either way, what is not in question is the fact that the
practice of baptism is justified because Christ died and rose.
Such 'invention' as there was must be seen as the obedient
response to what the Church believed to be the logic of the
gospel. The rightness of baptizing is not dependent upon the
outcome of a historical investigation into the origin of a particular text. We rather accept it as a command from God because it
is the means whereby we enter into relation to the saving death
of Christ.

Second is the baptism of Jesus by John in the Jordan. Here I
would want to argue that although the baptism of Jesus is relevant to our understanding and practice of baptism, we should
not move directly from that to our own experience and practice. Jesus' baptism by John gains its significance from the fact
that it was the baptism of this particular person in his relation
to the people from which he came. The significance of this
baptism is – among other things – that it signified Jesus' identification of himself with Israel under the judgement of God
represented and proclaimed by John, and that it points forward to his acceptance by death of the judgement of God on
human sin. It is therefore an anticipation of his death on the
cross, as the words of Jesus recorded by Luke (12.50) make
clear. Jesus dies as the representative of humankind under
judgement, as the passion stories, perhaps Mark's especially,
show us. His death accordingly, is the death of all (2 Cor.

5.14).[9] Thus while the baptism of Jesus is an essential element of the theology of baptism, we do not baptize because Jesus baptized, but because he went to the cross, which was foreshadowed in his baptism.

What, then, are we to make of the baptism of Jesus and its completion on the cross? Two aspects are especially significant: the public nature of what happened and its communal or corporate dimensions. The baptism and crucifixion of Jesus are not interesting by virtue of some experiences he may be supposed to have undergone, but for what they mean in the context of his life and ministry, and that means also in the context of the history of Israel and all humankind. They are *public* events, signalling the way by which God takes his place among us to achieve our redemption, that is to say, our reconciliation with God and restoration to the path of true life. It is in this man that all the nations of the earth are to be blessed in fulfilment of God's promise to Abraham. The baptism and death are also of *communal* significance. As we have seen, the baptism of Jesus takes place in relation to the sin and judgement of Israel. Jesus is what he is by virtue of his relation to the people from which he comes and to which he is called. His death and resurrection universalize the relationship, that is to say, reveal its significance for all humankind. After that, it is around him, the crucified and risen, that the covenant people of God is reconstituted by the action of the Holy Spirit. To be brought into relation with him is to be made a member of the people of God.

And the means whereby we are brought into relation with him is baptism. Just as Jesus' baptism bound him up with Israel, and his death with the whole human race under judgement, so our baptism binds us to Christ and the covenant people of God reconstituted in him. That, I want to suggest, is the primary significance of baptism. It is not first of all the expression of the faith of an individual or some invisible inner cleansing but is public and communal: it is the means by which a person is brought into relation with Christ through the medium of his

[9] Whether that 'all' encompasses the death of all men and women, as Karl Barth takes it in *Church Dogmatics* 4/1 or simply the 'all' addressed by Paul in that particular letter ('all of us') is irrelevant in this context, though it is theologically important. Karl Barth, *Church Dogmatics*, eds G. W. Bromiley and T. F. Torrance (Edinburgh: T&T Clark, 1957–1975)

body, the Church. The crucial link is between the once for all death of Christ on the cross and the baptism which appropriates that death for the member of his body. The logic is that as Christ died once, so can there be only one baptism into his death. Almost universally, the Church has accepted that logic. Even those of baptist persuasion who believe that it is right to baptize as adults those who have been baptized as infants recognize the logic by claiming that the baptism of an infant is not a real baptism.[10]

The practice of rebaptism, as it has taken place in recent years, therefore raises the question of 'validity'. Here I want to make two points. The first is to repeat that the basis of the rite, and so of its validity, is the death of Jesus on the cross. There is nothing automatically valid about the saying of particular words over, and the application of, water, in whatever way, to a person. But, second, given that the words have been said and the water used in a public ceremony, we deny the reality of that baptism at our peril, because by doing so we risk unbelief in the promise of God which underlies the use of the words. If the baptism was performed in the light of the promise, then we are bound to say that those who are baptized have been brought into relation to Christ. What right have we to deny it? We may like neither the pastoral practice of indiscriminate baptism nor the fact that many baptisms are performed out of the context of the regular worship of the local community. But that does not license us to decide that the baptism was not a 'real' baptism. Baptism is a churchly and public rite before it is an individual or experiential one. It is therefore not just for the 'saved', and certainly not for those alone who have been through a certain kind of experience, but for all who are called to share the life of those who are on the way to salvation. Once we lose the criterion of the public and churchly character of the sacrament, we are on the slippery slope of a merely subjective or experiential judgement. We must confess that so many baptisms have not, in practice, expressed the churchly dimension adequately. But is that enough to deny that they were baptisms?

[10] Those who would use sleight of hand in the matter sometimes speak of the infant rite as a 'christening' in order to justify a later repetition of something like the same thing.

The Baptism of Infants and the Doctrine of the Church

Up to this point, I have argued that baptism brings us into relation with God through the medium of his community, the body of Christ. It follows that any other supposed or second baptism is not a baptism, because one cannot be brought into the body of Christ when one is already there. Baptism, of whatever kind, can be performed only once because by it we are incorporate into Christ. On this basis, Churches whose practice is to baptize only believers, and those who baptize infants also, can share one element of unity at least. Both build upon the same bedrock: that as Christ died, once for all, for the forgiveness of sins, so there is but one way into his Church: by the once for all baptism by which we are incorporate in him.

That said, however, I wish in the rest of this chapter to argue very strongly for the rightness, indeed necessity, of the baptism of the infant children of those who are active worshipping members of the community of faith. I agree that there are arguments on the other side, and that some doubt must always remain, particularly as we come to terms with past abuse of the sacrament, as to whether the decision to baptize infants was the correct one. But the reaction against past abuse seems to me to result in an impoverished conception of the Church, so that it is important to present those who hold that only believers should be baptized with the strongest possible defence of the opposing position. The question is: whom should we expect to enter the life of the community by baptism? In other words, who are those who are called to share the life of those who are on the way to salvation?

As I have already suggested, such a question cannot be answered simply by proofs of whether or not children were baptized in the early Church, partly because all such debate is inconclusive. But there are a number of general considerations which can be brought to bear. The first concerns the Church's continuity with Israel. It is, of course, a continuity which contains differences. The basis of the Church is not nationhood, but relation to Christ, its head. And yet in so far as the Church is, like Israel, a people, is there any reason why children should be excluded? J. S. Whale, in a brief discussion of this very matter, quotes a sentence of J. V. Bartlet: 'The idea that a parent, especially the *paterfamilias*, should stand in a religious relation to God, merely as an individual, and distinct from his own flesh and blood, would never occur to the ancients, least of all to a Jew'. He goes an to cite the evidence which is crucial for this discussion. In 1 Cor. 7.14 Paul affirms that in a 'mixed' marriage the Christian partner makes the other partner and the children 'holy'. The logic of such a conception of the solidarity of the family for our doctrine of Church membership is spelled out in passages like those of Ephesians 6, where children are instructed to obey their parents 'in the Lord'. As Whale observes, this clearly means that they are regarded as being members of the household of faiths. And if they are, does not that at least suggest that they are baptized?[11]

Such arguments from New Testament theology are not, it seems to me, in themselves enough to establish the case, particularly in view of my own argument above that it is the logic of the gospel, not simple appeals to Scripture, which must guide us. The weight of the case hangs rather on the kind of entity that we believe the Church to be. Is the Church to be conceived simply as a *community* of converted adults? Are we going to deny that the children of Christian people are members of the covenant community? And what of the mentally handicapped and those who will never reach an 'age of reason' that enables them to make the prior decision upon which baptism is supposedly to depend? The logic of the gospel here presses very hard. If children are called to be part of the covenant people, how may they enter it except by baptism, which is, according to universal Church confession, the way of entry into the Church? But if they are not, we are in danger of a seriously impoverished view of the Church, that it is only for those who are of the 'age of reason': adult or near adult believers who have qualified themselves for membership by virtue of a particular experience or decision.

So far, the basis of the things that have been said has been heavily christological. Baptism is incorporation into the body of Christ, which is the Church. To follow up the question of who may be in the Church, let us turn to matters pneumatological. Here, the dogmatic basis of what is to be said is that the Holy Spirit is the agent of our incorporation into Christ through the

[11] J. S. Whale, *Victor, and Victim* (Cambridge: Cambridge University Press, 1960), pp. 130f.

medium of the community of faith. Who, then, is brought into the body by the Spirit, and how? There are two answers that I wish to avoid. The first is that *anyone* may be brought into the Church by baptism: that is to say, that baptism may be administered to anyone, because the saying of particular words and the administration of water achieves an automatic pouring out of the Spirit.[12] That seems to me to be a dangerously 'magical' view of the matter, making the gifts of the Spirit at the disposal of the Church or her representatives. Equally important, it is to evade the character of baptism as incorporation into a living community of belief.

The second answer I wish to avoid is the equal and opposite view, that baptism may be administered only to those who have been through a certain experience. Do we have the right to say that a sharing in the Spirit's gifts and graces that is membership of the community is granted only to adult believers? Again, the question can be put ecclesiologically. In so far as the Church is the community of those who give to and receive from each other in the Spirit the riches of the gifts and graces they have received, it must be asked whether we have nothing to receive, within the body of Christ, from children and those without the full capacity for reason and decision. Do only adults have the gifts and graces of the Spirit? Unless we can deny this, do we not have a dangerously impoverished view of the Church? Are not our children 'in the Lord' so that unless we are prepared to receive from as well as to give to them we deny ourselves some of the gifts of the Spirit? (See Matt. 21.16: 'From the mouth of children and infants you have ordained praise.')

In saying all this I do not wish to deny that in a culture that has in large measure taken leave of its Christian heritage the Church will increasingly expect to gain new members by conversion. In what it is now fashionable to call a 'missionary situation' a major, if not the chief, means of entry into the body of Christ will be by the baptism of believers. Indeed, advocates of the legitimacy of infant baptism should be prepared to affirm gladly that the prior form of baptism is that of adult believers, and that of infants is derivative from it. Yet none of that seems to

---

[12] To be sure, in one sense anyone ('all the peoples', Matt. 28) may be baptized; but not on any terms or under any conditions.

me to entail that the *sole* way of receiving the Spirit's gifts and sharing his call should be through adult confession. Baptism is the appropriate sacrament to administer to those who are converted out of our pagan society, but there seems to me no compelling reason why we should so limit the capacity of the Spirit to bring sheep into the fold. Who is to say that the Spirit may work in only one way? If children are brought by their parents to share in the life of worship, work and play that is the calling of the Christian community, are we to deny that that is the working of the Spirit, too?

Here we return to the matter of individualism. It is easy, though wrong, to conceive the Spirit as primarily the possession of individuals. It need not be denied that particular persons are given distinctive gifts, and indeed it is the glory of the Church that in it all are called to exercise some form of ministry. Nor can it be denied that faith is the greatest of the Spirit's gifts. But it is not the only gift, and it should not be forgotten that there is a strong stress in the New Testament that the Spirit works in the Church: his is a churchly rather than an individual sphere of activity, in the sense that particular gifts are given for the building up of the life of the people of God. The *charismata* are for the building up of the community (1 Cor. 12–14). This means that to baptize is not so much to confer a gift upon an individual, as to bring a person into the sphere of the Spirit's working, into the place where his or her gifts may be exercised for the glory of God. The Spirit is the Spirit who creates the community of the Last Days, that worshipping body which is brought into the presence of the Father in the Son and by the Spirit.

Baptism, therefore, brings a person into relation with that community, so that he or she is now by means of a sacramental action brought within a new pattern of relationships: relationships which are what they are by virtue of their derivation from and orientation to the triune God. This is surely the point of Paul's 'if anyone is in Christ, there is a new creation' (2 Cor. 5.17). I do not believe that this refers to some invisible inner change or (as in some forms of pietism) an instant or other transformation in the individual brought about by conversion. Indeed, it is not meant individualistically at all. By 'in Christ' Paul means at least chiefly in membership of the body of Christ, the Church. There is, indeed, a new creation because of the addition to the community of 'someone': some unique and particular person.

But that means something for the Church, as well. By virtue of the addition of a new member, the Church is by each baptism reconstituted. That is the new creation of which Paul speaks. By virtue of its relationship to Abraham, it is the same Church: the one historical people of God called and elected to praise him on earth. But it is also a different Church, for the addition of a unique person to its membership means that new patterns of relationships and therefore a new reality has come to be. If that reality does not include our children and young people, then our notion of community and of the way God works toward and through it is indeed an impoverished one. It is finally on the necessity that the Church be a complete – catholic – community that I would rest the case for the membership, and therefore baptism, of all called by the Spirit, in all the many and various ways in which he does it, to share in the life of the people of God.

Pastoral Practice

The kind of pastoral practice that would follow from the above argument can be set out briefly. The first implication is that if we believe what we say about baptism being the way of entry into the body of Christ, we should treat all who are baptized as members with us of the covenant community. It does not, of course, follow that we should treat all, regardless of age, exactly the same, any more than we have the same expectations of every member of a family. Baptism is about membership of a community of worship, not about function within it. The second implication is that we should not baptize any child whom we do not expect to enter into a living relation with the community of worship. Many requests for rebaptism would lose in credibility if as a matter of pastoral practice some such criterion had operated in the Churches of Christendom, and the baptized had truly been brought to share in the life of the community. Another way of making the same point would be to say that the promises made in services of baptism should be taken on all sides with complete seriousness, and not asked of those who are unlikely to be able or willing to keep them.

The third implication is that if we believe what we say about the inclusion of infants in the life of the covenant community we should actively encourage the baptism of the infants of active Christian people. If we do not, we are depriving our children of the status they have under the gospel, and are impoverishing both the life of the Church and our conception of what it is to be the Church. Recent controversy has sometimes led advocates of infant baptism to be apologetic and defensive about the practice. Yet if it is an implication of the logic of the gospel and obedience to the promises of God, we should be glad to welcome our children into the community. Infant baptism may be derivative of the primary form, but that is not to say that it is second best. There is one baptism for the forgiveness of sins, in whichever form it is administered.

It is the neglect of the seriousness of baptism as a churchly action, the treating of it in an individualist and institutionalized way, that has led to the pastoral scandals of Christendom. Baptism has been treated as a rite dispensed to the individual by an institution rather than as the means by which the person enters a new sphere of relationships which, by virtue of the new member, are themselves changed. And that has implications beyond the life of the Church: it means much for the ministry of the Church to those outside the life of the worshipping community. One of the ways in which we may enable our own society to emerge from the stranglehold of individualism is in developing, under the gospel, forms of life in which each person is accorded that uniqueness which is the gift of existence in true community. In that way the Church may be, as Calvin taught that it should, the sacrament of society: a living reminder to society of its true nature. Treating baptism with due seriousness is at the very beginning of such a process: it is the first of the ways by which the Church may learn to be the Church of God on earth and so a reflection of Jesus, the light of the world.

13

The Church and the Lord's Supper: 'Until He Comes'. Towards an Eschatology of Church Membership[1]

Eschatology and the Church

It is often said that our era is one in which eschatology has been rediscovered, although there is neither clarity nor agreement as to how that eschatology might be understood. If we merely review some of the responses to the rediscovery there will be enough evidence of the disarray. Some late nineteenth- and early twentieth-century biblical scholars and Church historians took the discovery of Jesus' essentially eschatological message as Christianity's death-warrant. Jesus saw himself, they held, as the prophet of the end; but the end did not come, and so he was mistaken. The genius of Barth is that he took the very same discoveries to be a life-warrant: 'If Christianity is not thoroughgoing eschatology, it is nothing.'[2] Yet the eschatology of the second edition of his *Epistle to the Romans*, like that of Bultmann's (in the end not so dissimilar) proposals, owes, it is often enough claimed, more to Kantian dualism than to the peculiarly elusive biblical representations of eschatology. The later Barth replaced his early eschatology with what was

---

[1] The Drew Lecture on Immortality, Spurgeon's College, London, 11 November 1999. It might be subtitled: 'A conversation with Robert Jenson, with particular respect to the First Letter to the Corinthians'. It was previously published in *Called to One Hope. Perspective on the Life to Come. Drew Lectures on Immortality*, ed. John Colwell (Carlisle: Paternoster Press, 2001), pp. 252–66; and in *International Journal of Systematic Theology* 3 (2001), pp. 187–200.

[2] Karl Barth, *Epistle to the Romans*, tr. E. C. Hoskyns (Oxford: Oxford University Press, 1933), p. 314.

216

effectively a realized eschatology of revelation. In Jesus Christ, who is the *eschatos*, the end has already come, because in him God's covenant purpose, to reconcile all people in him, was realized. In their response to the later Barth, however, Moltmann and Pannenberg discerned a similar flaw to that of the early work, this time in a tendency to reduce eschatology, effectively disarming it by the orientation of Barth's theology to the beginning; or at least, in the more subtle criticisms of Robert Jenson, weakening its impact.[3] But are Pannenberg and Moltmann any more successful in maintaining the right relation of beginning, middle and end, for that is surely the key to the matter? Not in every way, it must be said. Pannenberg's employment of Plotinus' concept of time in his recent work does not inspire confidence that he has solved the problem,[4] while the emanationist aspects of Moltmann's recent writing on the Spirit work against eschatology rather than for it.[5]

Here we must beware of supposing that it is primarily the calling of the theologian to solve problems. Part of the point of eschatology is that it warns us that certain central questions are not patient of solution this side of the end. We are part of a culture that seeks to bring in the Kingdom, or some kind of kingdom, by human activity, and it is a recurring feature of the over-realized secular eschatology of the day that we are so prone to seek to solve that which is beyond immediate solution. That is one clue indeed to our frantic modern restlessness and to the ineffective attempts of modern governments of all stamps to bring in the Kingdom by legislation. In all life, and especially in the life of the Church, eschatological reserve should be the hallmark of thought and action: a recollection of the limits of our possibilities, given at once both human finitude and the sin that continues to hold back even, sometimes especially, those who are on the way to final redemption.

---

[3] Robert W. Jenson, *God After God. The God of the Past and the God of the Future, Seen in the Work of Karl Barth* (Indianapolis and New York: Bobbs Merrill, 1969).

[4] Wolfhart Pannenberg, *Metaphysics and the Idea of God,* tr. Philip Clayton (Edinburgh: T&T Clark, 1990), pp. 75ff.

[5] Jürgen Moltmann, *The Spirit of Life,* tr. Margaret Kohl (London: SCM Press, 1992).

In this chapter, I want to look at something of the limits we should place on what we might expect of the Church. I accept that in many ways we expect too little, but it is equally the case that expecting too much often derives from an over-realized eschatology, which distorts the community's life and witness. Let me instance three symptoms of an over-realized eschatology in matters ecclesial. The first is historical, and well described in Moltmann's recent study of eschatology.[6] Making excessive claims for the Church's capacity to represent, even to be, the Kingdom, has led to some of the political excesses which have disfigured Church history, and are still a major feature of secularist attacks on Christianity. The story is too well rehearsed to require further comment. The second danger characterizes the thought of that recent ethical thinking often labelled Anabaptist and represented by John Howard Yoder and Stanley Hauerwas. These are two seminal and important thinkers, and one might cautiously apply to them the much overused adjective, prophetic. Yet in their tendency to reject or minimize the importance of the doctrine of justification by grace alone they risk placing upon the faithful a burden greater than they can bear. Let me be cautious, for once. Their call to the Church to be a distinctive and holy community, *for* the world by being self-consciously *other* than it, is salutary and, indeed, right – especially in view of the perceptive recent observation that the mainline denominations have generally succeeded in being of the world but not in it. And the charges against them of sectarianism are mostly merely silly. Yet the function of the law or of ethical teaching in eschatological perspective does require clearer exposition than it is sometimes given if we are not to impose ethical overload by a failure to recognize limits.

The third example comes from the other end of the ecclesial spectrum, and concerns Christology, specifically the over-weighting of the theology of the body of Christ. It is often enough observed that the difference between Luther and Calvin on the Lord's Supper derives from a difference in Christology; indeed, at a time when the Chalcedonian Definition of

---

[6] Jürgen Moltmann, *The Coming of God. Christian Eschatology*, tr. Margaret Kohl (London: SCM Press, 1996).

the person of Christ remained for the most part unquestioned, Reformation christological dispute was centred on that topic. Luther's Christology, tending as it does to the monophysite, and holding the communication of attributes – roughly, in this context, that anything you can say of divinity of Christ you must also be able to say of his humanity – led to the conclusion that because God could be everywhere, so could Christ's human body, and hence it could be present in with and under the elements of bread and wine. Calvin has often enough been accused of separating the divine and the human, though that has been shown by Bruce McCormack to be mistaken.[7] His Christology was essentially Cyrillian, while his teaching of the union of the faithful with Christ also militated against a mere transcendence of the ascended saviour. Yet the ascension did imply for him that Christ's body is located at the right hand of God, and could not therefore be ubiquitous. To be bodily is to be particular and to be located in space, and this ruled out the claim that Christ's body could be everywhere at once. This gives greater space for the Spirit's distinctive work in relation to the Church rather than to the bread and wine. The Spirit is primarily seen as one who lifts worshippers into the presence of God rather than achieving a transformation of the elements. But it is in conversation with a representative of the Lutheran tradition that our theme can best be developed.

In our day, with the continued fading of the Constantinian settlement, the problem of the nature of the Church and of her relation to the social order in which she is set – the question of what kind of political entity the Church is – is receiving renewed attention. And it is here that a recent ecclesiology is of great interest to us. Let me say briefly first what I cannot, and then what I can, take from Robert Jenson's account of the Church in his recent *Systematic Theology*. In so far as Christ is risen, he is for this writer risen into, almost as, the Church: 'The church, according to Paul, is the risen body of Christ. She is this because the bread and cup in the congregation's midst is the very same

---

[7] Bruce McCormack, *For Us and Our Salvation. Incarnation and Atonement in the Reformed Tradition* (Princeton: Princeton Theological Seminary, 1993), pp. 7–8.

body of Christ.'[8] The monophysite undertones of this are
apparent in other formulations:

> For the proposition that the church is a human body of the
> risen Christ to be ontically and straightforwardly true, all that
> is required is that Jesus indeed be the Logos of God . . .
> He needs no other body to be a risen man, body and soul.
> There is and needs to be no other place than the church for
> him to be embodied, nor in that other place any other entity
> to be the 'real' body of Christ.[9]

The church is repeatedly described in this work as Christ's
availability for the world, just as our bodies are our availability
for others. 'That the church is the body of Christ . . . means that
she is the object in the world as which the risen Christ is an
object for the world.'[10] Despite a brief obeisance to transcendence – to the Church as the bride, and therefore other, of Christ
– it is immanence that dominates: 'that the church is ontologically the risen Christ's human body . . .'.[11] Here the 'Lutheran'
Christology is fully at work, apparently denying that the risen
and ascended Christ is 'at the right hand of the Father' in anything other than an immanent sense.[12] The Church, it would

---

[8] Robert W. Jenson, *Systematic Theology*, vol. 1, *The Triune God*; vol. 2, *The Works of God* (New York and Oxford: Oxford University Press, 1997, 1999), vol. 1, p. 205. For Jenson Christ is risen 'almost' as the Church, because the position is more nuanced than some citations I shall use suggest. In a paper on the roots of Jenson's ecclesiology in the thought of his teacher Peter Brunner, David Yeago argues that Jenson tends to conflate two things that Brunner more care-fully keeps apart. 'Brunner . . . continues to distinguish . . . *two* modes in which the risen body of the Lord exists. Jenson on the other hand regards a *distinct* mode of existence before God's throne as unnecessary, simply identifying "heaven" with the eucharistic assembly.' David Yeago, '. . .' in *Trinity, Time and Church. A Response to the Theology of Robert W. Jenson*, ed. Colin E. Gunton (Grand Rapids: Eerdmans, 2000).
[9] Jenson, *Systematic Theology*, 1, p. 206.
[10] Jenson, *Systematic Theology*, 2, p. 213.
[11] Jenson, *Systematic Theology*, 2, p. 213. The distinction appears merely to be this, 'just in that the church gathers around objects distinct from herself, the bread and the cup, which are the availability *to her* of the same Christ'.
[12] Jenson, *Systematic Theology* 1, p. 204: 'Although Paul clearly thinks of the Lord as in some sense visibly located in a heaven spatially related to the rest of the creation, the only body of Christ to which Paul actually refers is not an entity in this heaven but the Eucharist's loaf and cup and the church assembled around them.'

seem, not just represents but actually *is* the presence on earth of the eschatological kingdom. This, for reasons that we shall come to, simply will not do.

On the other hand, there is something I would like to appropriate from Robert Jenson, and this is his teaching that the Church, as Church, is a social-political reality in its own right. It has, or more accurately is, a polity, a way of being politically and socially in the world. In this respect, Jenson points out, first, 'that when the New Testament does refer to the church as God's people, this is in every case but one done at least in part to identify her with Israel'.[13] It follows that if the Church is identical or continuous with Israel, then, like Israel, she is a polity, an organized way of being in the world. Second, the discontinuity with Israel that is also involved centres on the rite of baptism, in which one becomes, in Aquinas' words, 'a member of Christ', and receives the gifts of the Spirit which 'are all in fact "rights and privileges" of the *community* into which the rite initiates'.[14] 'A *people* united in a common *spirit*, that is, a people who have become a community, is a *polity* . . .'. And the polity is for Jenson an anticipated eschatology. 'The church anticipates [the] eschatological peace [of the Kingdom] in the imperfect but real concord of her members, situated in mutual and complementary modes of leading and obeying.'[15] Third, the distinctive polity entails a distinctive ethic, which Jenson elaborates in terms of the Decalogue. With all these features I am in agreement, though not with the all details of their articulation.

Aspects of 1 Corinthians

I shall in this second section concentrate not, as might be expected in the light of the chapter title, on the Lord's Supper, but on the prior question of the nature of the Church, and in particular on the sense in which we can say that the end is

[13] Jenson, *Systematic Theology* 2, p. 191.

[14] Jenson, *Systematic Theology* 2, p. 196.

[15] Jenson, *Systematic Theology* 2, p. 204. I leave on one side here, for the sake of brevity, the important additional point that polities require government, and this polity one which 'forswears all coercion', p. 205.

realized in her life. Is the Church an eschatological reality, and in what sense? Let us, at least for the sake of discussion, begin by treating the Supper as a subspecies of the meal in general. Jenson again:

> All meals are intrinsically religious occasions, indeed sacrifices, and were so understood especially in Israel. For all life belongs intimately to God, so that the killing involved in eating – which we do not at all avoid by eating vegetables – is an intrusion into his domain. . . . Sharing a meal is therefore always a communal act of worship and establishes fellowship precisely before the Lord.[16]

In this regard, the interest of the words 'until he comes' derives at least as much from the sharing of meals in general as from what we think, because of the tradition, of its specifically eucharistic significance.

Three aspects of the broader context will enable the case to be made. It is evident, first, that much of the argument of Paul's letter concerns the domain within which the members of the infant Church have their being and to which they give their allegiance. Sharing meals is at the heart of it. Speaking purely theologically, so to say, to share the meals of the pagan temples is harmless, because their gods do not exist. Paul has, however, a number of reasons for discouraging his flock from so indulging. The first is moral: it is a sin against love to offend the Christian neighbour unnecessarily. But a second goes further. There are, he writes, gods many and lords many (8.5), and, even though in one sense they are non-existent, they yet exercise authority over those who enter their realm. To eat with the non-existent idols is to enter a social and political sphere in competition with that of the God of Israel. It is the same with those who have recourse to pagan law courts to settle inner-churchly disputes. In this instance the eschatological dimensions of the matter come into view. Those who are to judge angels place themselves under the authority of the demonic. The Church is a social and political reality that does things differently from other institutions, because it is eschatologically different, which means that the basis of its being and authority are also radically different. Here

---

[16] Jenson, *Systematic Theology* 2, p. 185.

Hauerwas and Yoder are right. It follows that in so far as all meals are of religious significance, to share table fellowship with idols is, to use the fashionable expression, to sleep with the enemy. I use that metaphor because it opens up another related aspect of the Corinthian church's situation. For Paul, transgressing sexual boundaries is another way of entering the realm of that which is demonic because it is opposed to the rule of God; that is, it is a way of entering into relations that are constitutive of our human being contrary to those of the eschatological kingdom. In all these realms of action, the Corinthians' errors are of a piece in that they place themselves outside the authority of the ascended Christ.

That takes me to the second piece of context. For Paul we are at once – and here we meet the eschatological tension that characterizes the whole of this work – what we do in the body and what our bodies are eschatologically. We are what we do and yet we are what we shall be. The human body, that which is nourished by the meals of which we have spoken, is the way we are in the world, and by this is meant not the world distinct from the Church but the world that is God's creation. This is especially the case in the way we are related to our fellow human beings, those made in the image of God. What we do with and in the body anticipates – or, I suppose we should say, *may* anticipate – what we shall be. Let us here simply listen to part of the outcome of Paul's discussion of sexual morality and pagan eating alongside one another:

> 'Food is for the stomach, and the stomach for food' [presumably Paul is here quoting his opponents] – but God will destroy them both. The body is not meant for sexual immorality, but for the Lord, and the Lord for the body. By his power God raised the Lord from the dead, and he will raise us also. Do you not know that your bodies are members of Christ himself? Shall I then take the members of Christ himself, and unite them with a prostitute? (1 Cor. 6.13–15).

Paul then proceeds, citing Genesis, to say that sexual union is literally a form of union, which in the wrong context displaces union with Christ. Then follow some points whose trinitarian logic should be noted:

> But he who unites himself with the Lord is one with him in

spirit. . . . Do you not know that your body is a temple of the
Holy Spirit . . .? You are not your own; you were bought at a
price. Therefore honour God with your body. (1 Cor. 6. 17,
19, 20)

To be at once a member of Christ and the place of the Spirit's
activity; that is the high status of the body in Paul's theology.
And the reasons are twofold: atonement and eschatology. 'You
were bought with a price'; 'God will raise us also.'

The third contextual consideration follows naturally from
this. The verses we have just heard from chapter 6 anticipate
chapter 15, that eschatological climax which, like all eschatology, throws its light back on what has gone before. That later
chapter also introduces the trinitarian considerations on which
depend the way in which we shall understand the relation
between past reconciliation and eschatological fulfilment, and
therefore life in the Church. There, too, is to be found the basis
for the differences between what for the sake of simplicity we
can call Lutheran and Reformed Christology and ecclesiology.
1 Corinthians 15 describes Jesus Christ as a particular human
being rather than the apparently social or corporate person we
have met in Jenson and possibly in earlier chapters of this letter.
Jesus is the first and only one to have been raised, and indeed,
part of the heresy Paul appears to be combating is the denial of
this unique resurrection in favour of ascribing some such realized status to all the members of the Church. So, he insists,
there is a distinction to be made between the time of Christ's
resurrection and that of ours: 'Christ, the first fruits; then, when
he comes, those who belong to him' (v. 23). Here, Christ is
patently distinguished from the Church. He is, to use Irenaean
language, one of God the Father's two hands whose *present*
reign, as the risen and ascended Lord, will be completed only
when every enemy – 'all dominion, authority and power' and,
ultimately, death; that is to say, those 'gods many and lords
many' into whose hands the erring Corinthians were placing
themselves – has been defeated. Only when those bodies which
are the location of human being and activity have been raised
and transformed, will Christ's incarnate work be done.

Alongside, therefore, the close identification of Christ with
the Church, which Jenson has rightly observed, is the polar pull
in another direction: he is one with the Church only as also its

transcendent Lord. Transcendence is not swallowed up in immanence, any more than death is yet finally swallowed up in victory. That is why we must attempt to hear the passage from chapter 11 with ears freed as much as possible from traditional debate about the presence of Christ in the bread and the wine. 'In memory of him . . . until he comes' presupposes, according to Richard Hays, that he is in fact absent.[17] *In that respect*, Paul is speaking of real absence, not real presence. The passage, furthermore, is devoted to the Church's polity, its social and political constitution, as much as to its eucharistic worship, indeed, more than that, at least if the latter is narrowly conceived. Let us follow the logic of Paul's argument. Chapter 11 begins with the much discussed passage about the covering of women's heads, which I shall take as concerned essentially not with who takes part in the leading of worship, but with the due and dignified order in which that takes place; that is to say, with proper ecclesial polity. There then follows a second discussion of the Church's political order: of the scandal of the carrying over of worldly social divisions into the meals that they share. Only at this stage do we hear what are called the words of institution, which are a simple recollection of what Jesus once did.

After that comes Paul's lapidary comment: 'For whenever you eat this bread and drink this cup, you proclaim the Lord's death until he comes.' Notice that in parallel with the bread is not 'wine' but 'cup'. As Caird writes, 'In Paul's account, as in the others, the parallel to "bread" is not "wine" but "cup". Elsewhere in the recorded words of Jesus the cup is a symbol of his crucifixion (Mark 10: 38, 14: 36).'[18] It is the narrated passion and resurrection that determine the Church and its worship. Therefore I believe that the notion, much touted in ecumenical conversations, that the eucharist makes the Church should be rejected. The Church is the creature of the Word, as the broad context of this epistle – the main support of Jenson's sacramen-

---

[17] '[T]he meal acknowledges the *absence* of the Lord and mingles memory and hope, recalling his death and awaiting his coming again.' Richard B. Hays, *First Corinthians* (Louisville: John Knox, 1997), p. 199.

[18] G. B. Caird, *New Testament Theology*, ed. L. D. Hurst (Oxford: Clarendon Press, 1994), p. 229.

tology – makes absolutely clear.[19] Must we not therefore qualify the immediacy of talk of the Church as Christ's availability to the world? Is not the priority rather to be given to the word, first of Scripture and then of proclamation, to which the visible word of the Supper is appended, and on which it is dependent for both its being and its intelligibility? '[A] sacrament is never without a preceding promise but is joined to it as a sort of appendix, with the purpose of confirming and sealing the promise itself . . .'[20] Sacraments are appendices to the Word, and that means secondary to the atoning work of Christ which is, for eschatological reasons, first a heard and proclaimed word by virtue of the fact that we are the Church between that which we remember and that to which we move.

But let us continue our review of 1 Corinthians 11. After the words I have discussed, Paul returns to – ethics and judgement. Talk of eating and drinking unworthily returns us to the problem of the church's polity. Here we meet what may be an insoluble problem of interpretation. The almost universal translation of v. 29, 'anyone who eats and drinks without recognizing [or discerning] the body eats and drinks judgement on himself' is at best a guess. According to Caird, 'nowhere else in Greek literature does diakrinô mean "to recognise", and this sense hardly fits the second occurrence of the word at v. 31 ("we shall not be *judged*")'.[21] Listen to the repeated allusions to judgement:

> Anyone who eats and drinks [offending in whatever way is intended] eats and drinks judgement (*krima*) on himself. That is why many of you are weak and sick, and a number of you have fallen asleep. But if we judged (*diekrinomen*) our-

[19] Christoph Schwöebel, 'The Creature of the Word. Recovering the Ecclesiology of the Reformers', in *On Being the Church. Essays on the Christian Community*, eds Colin E. Gunton and Daniel W. Hardy (Edinburgh: T&T Clark, 1989), pp. 110–55.

[20] John Calvin, *Institutes of the Christian Religion*, ed. J. T. McNeill, tr. and index F. L. Battles, Library of Christian Classics vols 20 and 21 (Philadelphia: Westminster Press, 1960), IV. xiv. 3. Where I would differ from Calvin is in taking exception to his view that all of this is 'for our ignorance and dullness, then for our weakness'. Does it not indicate a suspicion that the materiality of the thing is somehow secondary?

[21] Caird, *New Testament Theology*, p. 228.

selves, we would not come under judgement (*ekrinometha*). When we are judged (*krinomenoi*) by the Lord, we are being disciplined (*paideuometha*), so that we will not be condemned (*katakrithômen*) with the world. (vv. 29–31).

Whatever else is the case, the one thing 'the body' that is not discerned – or whatever – cannot refer to is the eucharistic elements. If a body is being unrecognized, that body is the community whose social structure is being torn apart by bad behaviour rather than inadequate sacramentology. It would seem that Paul is deploying a series of puns on the theme of judgement, to the effect that to share the cup is to undergo judgement (meaning godly discipline) and so avoid judgement (meaning eschatological rejection), the latter of which is the unintended outcome revealed in some of the symptoms of the Church's disordered life.

It is in this light that we should refer back to the previous chapter, 1 Corinthians 10, which begins with the theme of judgement: with the death in the wilderness of thousands of Israelites. 'Therefore . . . flee from idolatry'; that is to say, flee from the worship of anything that is not God, from entering any sphere of influence than that of the God of Israel. *That is to say*: join yourselves to this community of worship and not to any other solidarity of sacrifice. If all meals are of religious significance, then it makes all the difference with whom you eat. (What does it imply that the Archbishop of Canterbury recently sat to eat with the President of China, for example?[22]) That is the religious, moral and political context of the Corinthians' meal, and that is the primary connotation of participation in the blood and body of Christ. The blood is a reference to the cross, to the atonement, which is, according to Paul, the only thing he wishes to proclaim (1 Cor. 1.18–2.5); and 'the body' refers to the community that is what it is because it eats and drinks together. It is a matter of polity: 'You cannot drink the cup of the Lord and the cup of demons too . . .' (1 Cor. 10.21).

Here a question needs to be asked. Am I seeking to moralize this passage, to turn this into a matter of mere ethics? The answer is a qualified denial. It is a denial because the calling of

[22] See a discussion of its significance by Paul Johnson in *The Spectator*, 30 October 1999.

the Church is to worship God simply in and for himself before it is a call to act morally and politically. Yet that denial must be qualified because of the character of the being and action of the God who is worshipped. The triune God is one whose triune *koinônia* has overflowed into the creation and redemption of a world he loves, and particularly of those creatures he has made in his image and remade in the image of his Son Jesus. It is for that reason – because God is himself communion – that the worship of the Church cannot be disentangled from its social and political matrix and outcome. That is the message Paul and Jenson share. How are we to bring together in due relation to one another these two interrelated realms of worship and life? In two ways, it seems to me, and here I can only be exploratory.

First, much depends on the meaning of the words from moral and political philosophy that are being so freely used in this interpretation of 1 Corinthians. It can never be forgotten that this is a book whose roots are in the Old Testament rather than in Aristotle, and we employ the latter's pagan heritage at our peril. In chapter after chapter of this letter, Paul is concerned with what can only be called Torah, which means not merely law but the whole gracious divine dispensation for human living on earth and in the body. It is consistently a matter of the sphere of authority within which one places oneself: of whom or what one worships (hence the concern with the idolatry which is to be shunned) and of the source of one's authority for the shape of one's life on earth. In both realms, there is an absolute choice to be made. For members of the body of Christ to enter the sphere of pagan worship or to have recourse to pagan law courts is, as we have seen, to enter the sphere of the demonic. Rather, as chapter 6 continues, one must give one's allegiance to the Torah, and here the Decalogue is summarized and repeated as the canon by which membership of the community of salvation is measured. And the reason? The fact of that past atonement which has achieved through trinitarian agency a transfer of allegiance: 'But you were washed, you were sanctified, you were justified in the name of the Lord Jesus Christ and by the Spirit of our God' (1 Cor. 6.11).

The second way of understanding the relation of worship and polity is with the notion of sacrifice. Let us again recall Jenson's point: 'All meals are intrinsically religious occasions, indeed sacrifices . . .' We therefore need to pause to consider some of the things that sacrifice is according to the Scriptures. Here, it seems to me, there is a definite hierarchy. First, although there is no one satisfactory 'explanation' of the meaning of sacrifice, worship and thanksgiving come high up the list of meanings. For Scripture, giving thanks and praise to God is a large part of what sacrifice means. We cannot moralize this passage if it means taking it out of its prior context of worship, which is praise and thanks to God for the price Christ has paid – another sacrificial term, used, as we have seen, in this letter. And yet, second, as prophet and psalmist point out repeatedly, indeed, relentlessly, right worship is inseparable from right conduct. For both Old and New Testament, sacrifice is inseparable from obedience. If Jacob Milgrom is right, the priestly writer achieved what is in effect a moralization of sacrifice by taking it out of paganism's merely cultic and religious realm. For Leviticus, whose influence penetrates deeply into the letter we are examining, sacrifice is largely a matter of Israel's social and political reality, in ways directly analogous to the situation of the Corinthian church. The priestly writer achieved a demytho-logization of sacrifice, which was concerned not now with the exorcism of the demonic, as in the pagan peoples around, but with holiness conceived in mostly ethical terms.[23] Life or death – precisely as in 1 Corinthians – is the issue, not ritual impurity. Similarly, for Paul, if we may cross-refer to another of his letters, the primary sacrifice under the new dispensation, is that of the body: 'offer your bodies as *a* living sacrifice . . .' (Rom. 12.1). In that parallel passage in Romans, where too the relationship of the body and its members is at issue, we find again the social-political concern that the diverse offerings of the distinct mem-bers of the body *together* make a single sacrifice of praise. How we are to hold the two dimensions of worship and ethics in right relation is surely in part a matter of eschatology, and to that we now turn.

---

[23] 'The purification offering taught the ecology of morality, that the sins of the individual adversely affect society even when committed inadvertently . . . The ethical thrust of these two expiatory sacrifices can be shown to be evident in other respects as well.' Jacob Milgrom, *Leviticus 1–16* (London: Doubleday, 1991), p. 51. Milgrom evinces also the book's concern for the poor, and that 'the blood prohibition is an index of P's concern for the welfare of humanity', p. 47.

Towards an Eschatology of Church Membership

'Until He Comes': Christ's rule is exercised through the
Church, but it is the very Church whose members from time to
time go to pagan temples and law courts, and generally behave
in ways which would frustrate that rule. Therefore any too close
identification of the Church with Christ after the manner of
Jenson risks two offences against eschatology. The first is the
empirical self-deception or special pleading that presumes
upon the judgement of God – which, after all, begins with the
people of God. To suggest that the Church is *literally* Christ's
body raises expectations beyond that attributable, in eschatological perspective, to the body with which we are actually concerned. Second, it also claims for the Church an immediacy that
is simply unjustifiable because it derives from an over-realized
eschatology. This serves as a recipe for the clericalism and
sacerdotalism which has historically militated, and still does
militate, against the participation of the whole people of God in
koinônia and mission. Against this, Paul's position, it seems to
me, implies that while it may be necessary in particular cases to
exclude from fellowship those who commit serious offences and
remain unrepentant, the body of Christ remains those very
people who are doing the things he deplores – so long, that is,
as they submit to the godly discipline consequent upon membership of the body, accepting the need to become what they
eschatologically are in promise.

The key to ecclesiology as to eschatology is pneumatology,
and in this connection, that means the role of the Spirit in
enabling the Church to be the Church at once in worship and
in the obedience that is definitive of its being. If, as Calvin held,
the Christian life is that which takes place between the resurrection and return of Christ, then the Father's Spirit is the one who
determines the ascended Christ's relation to the world during
that period. Crucial here is an important distinction: that the
presence of Christ is not *as* but *through* the Spirit, who is the
mediator of both Christ's presence and his (eschatological)
otherness. Here we must engage with Calvin's teaching that the
body of Christ is in some sense spatially 'in the heavens' with the
Father. Jenson is perhaps right that this becomes impossible on
a Copernican world view, although how far we should allow our
Christology to be determined by a natural theology must be

doubtful.[24] The weakness in Calvin, as Douglas Farrow has recently argued, is that he 'handled the dialectic of presence and absence almost exclusively in spatial terms, and to that extent in a *non*-eschatological fashion'.[25] The aspect of his Christology that must not be lost, however, is his maintaining of Christ's otherness in the relation mediated by the Spirit. While being other than the Church even when that is understood as his body, he is present to and in it in so far as the Spirit enables it from time to time to be that which it is elected to be.

What does this imply, first, for ethics? Let me return to the place where I began, with the recovery in the last hundred years or so of the eschatological moment of New Testament faith. One of the most celebrated of the rediscoverers, Albert Schweitzer, spoke of the moral teaching of Jesus as an interim ethic: the unworldly behaviour recommended for those for whom the return of the Lord was an immediate expectation.[26] He thought that it was designed only for a Church that expected to be around for a very short time. Here, in this letter that is among the earliest of New Testament writings, we see a rather different picture, whatever is to be made of some of the recommendations about marriage in chapter 7. Paul's ethic is highly concrete, and concerns obedience and love rather than an emergency dispensation. If we alter the eschatology, we shall be able to extend the meaning and content of this 'interim ethic'. The 'unworldly' behaviour enabled from time to time by the Spirit is the worldly obedience and love that all too rarely characterize the kingdoms this world – including, we must confess, the realm of the Church, as 1 and 2 Corinthians make all too clear. Here we must say: in so far as the Church's mode of life does from time to time anticipate that of the age to come, it is enabled to do so by the Spirit who both makes present the

[24] Jenson, *Systematic Theology* 1, pp. 202, 205.
[25] Douglas Farrow, 'In Support of (something like) a Reformed View of Ascension and Eucharist' (unpublished, p. 15 of typescript).
[26] By the end of his life, Schweitzer's account of Jesus' ethic had been completely spiritualized: 'The ethics of Jesus are concerned only with the attainment of inner perfection. They renounce moral works. They have nothing to do with the achievement of anything in the world.' Albert Schweitzer, *The Kingdom of God and Primitive Christianity*, tr. L. A. Garrard (London: A&C Black, 1968), p. 98.

life-giving death of Christ and will complete its eschatological perfecting on the last day. That is why worship, and especially what we call sacramental worship, cannot but be the focus of the Church's life, for in both baptism – which is in part concerned with anticipation of eschatological judgement – and the Lord's Supper we are, so to speak, positioned in the realm of the eschatological kingdom while we live in created time and space.

The Kingdom that Christ will hand over to the Father is his rule over the created world as that is entrusted, for the time – the interim? – of the covenants, to those made in his image. For Paul, our engagement with that world is centred on two things: what we do most intimately with our bodies in eating and drinking and in relations between man and woman. There also is to be found the heart of our social being. Our being in relation to God is inextricable from our closest relations with the world – ingesting it – and our most intimate relations with one another. It is from these that flow all those things that we have come to call justice, often in abstraction from that justice of God which justifies the godless: our economic, political, legal and other institutional forms of relation with the kingdoms of the world which are not yet the kingdoms of our God. The greatest disservice that the Church can do to the world is to believe that it can concern itself with the latter in abstraction from *both* of the former. The relation between eucharist and economic justice has been much treated, and in various ways, but not, I think in the broader terms of the Torah as Paul republishes it.[27] The space which God the Father opens up by the death and resurrection of his Son is given shape by this ethic, which is now ordered to him, the embodiment of God's dispensation for the world. It is the shape to be taken by the life of those who live between the atonement and the end. It is thus an eschatological 'interim' ethic.

What does this development imply, second, for sacramental worship? Much Protestant theology has been uncomfortable

---

[27] William T. Cavanaugh, *Torture and Eucharist. Theology, Politics and the Body of Christ* (Oxford: Blackwell, 1998). Robert Jenson is on surer ground in remarking on the relation between sexual disorder and criminality: 'the simultaneity of the lack of sexual regulation in young males of American cities' *Lumpenproletariat* and their criminality is regularly taken as coincidence. It is nothing of the sort; the first causes the second.' Jenson, *Systematic Theology* 2, p. 91 n. 81.

with the apparently 'material' implications of Patristic talk of the Lord's Supper as the medicine of immortality. But we should recall the disturbing verse we have met, so far without comment. 'That is why many of you are weak and sick, and a number of you have fallen asleep' (1 Cor. 11.30). The tenor of our argument suggests that in the things that shape our human being in the present we encounter a choice between life and death, eschatologically construed. To be related to God the Father through Christ and in the Spirit – to be in the Church – is to be elect for the former, for eternal life. That is made especially the case in the gospel sacraments, those things so intimately bound up with our membership of Christ. On the one hand, water is a natural substance, that which at once maintains life, cleanses it and can destroy it by drowning, so that Jesus' baptism in the Jordan, and consequently the new life of the Christian, constitutes the end of the old world, the world in which life is swallowed up by death, by the acceptance of eschatological judgement on that world. On the other hand, in the Lord's Supper we encounter nature manufactured, substances which are at once nature and culture, the creator's gifts handled and changed – killed – by human hand. The outcome of Jesus' life, especially as that is expounded by 1 Corinthians 15, carries the promise that what human beings do with and in their world will in some way be taken up into the reign of God, so that man and nature may alike praise the one who is their maker.

'Until He Comes': in this context, we are primarily concerned with personal immortality, with the promised resurrection of those made in the image of God and being remade in the image of the risen Jesus. Even, especially, in an age of non-discrimination and of ecological anxiety, we must reaffirm with Isaac Watts that the saints are God's supreme delight, and so reiterate that law, even – especially – when considered in eschatological framework, is a function of gospel, and secondary to that worship through the eternal Word, incarnate, heard and seen which is the Church's primary calling. It is the incarnation which provides the key. The sacrifice of praise that is the worship and ethic of the Church is eschatological in that it is bracketed by two other sacrifices: the remembered one that is at once the Father's gift of his Son and the Son's gift of his life for the life of the world; and the anticipated one which is his handing over of all rule and authority to the Father. In the interim, Christ's presence in all its manifold forms is realized only through anticipation, and that means through the mediation of the eschatological Spirit, as anticipated eschatology. Our eschatological membership of the body and bride of Christ belongs in that period of fulfilment and promise, in sure hope of the resurrection of the dead.[28]

[28] Parts of this chapter are marked by interaction with at least four of my former and present students: John Colwell, Steve Holmes, Douglas Knight and Douglas Farrow, the first two listed being members of Spurgeon's College. See Douglas Farrow, *Ascension and Ecclesia. On the Significance of the Doctrine of the Ascension for Ecclesiology and Christian Cosmology* (Edinburgh: T&T Clark, 1999).

Index